Civil Rights Legacy of Harry S. Truman

D1337898

The Civil Rights Legacy of Harry S. Truman
Truman Legacy Series, Volume 2

Based in part on the Second Truman Legacy Symposium
Harry Truman and Civil Rights
14–15 May 2004
Key West, Florida

Edited by
Raymond H. Geselbracht

THE CIVIL RIGHTS
LEGACY of
HARRY S. TRUMAN

Edited By

Raymond H. Geselbracht

Volume 2

Truman State University Press

Cover Photo: President Truman meeting with African American leaders who want more African Americans in important positions in agencies involved in the administration's defense program, 28 February 1951. The President's prominent visitors include Mary McLeod Bethune, president emeritus of the National Council of Negro Women, Lester Granger, executive secretary of the National Urban League, Tobias Channing, director of the Phelps-Stokes Foundation, and Walter White, executive secretary of the NAACP.

Cover design: Shaun Hoffeditz
Type: Garamond Light, ITC Garamond is a registered trademark of International Typeface Corporation; Bauer Text Initials, copyright Phil's Fonts.
Printed by: Edwards Brothers, Inc., Ann Arbor, Michigan USA

Library of Congress Cataloging-in-Publication Data
The civil rights legacy of Harry S. Truman / edited by Raymond H. Geselbracht.
    p. cm. — (Truman legacy series; v. 2)
"Based on the Second Truman Legacy Symposium, Harry Truman and civil rights, May 14–15, 2004, Key West, Florida."
Includes bibliographical references and index.
ISBN 978-1-931112-67-3 (pbk. : alk. paper)
1. Truman, Harry S., 1884–1972—Political and social views. 2. Civil rights—United States—History—20th century. 3. African Americans—Civil rights—History—20th century. 4. United States—Race relations—Political aspects—History—20th century. 5. United States—Politics and government—1945–1953. I. Geselbracht, Raymond H. II. Truman Legacy Symposium (2nd : 2004 : Key West, Fla.)
    E813.C58 2007
    973.918092—dc22

                                                                2007013223

CONTENTS

CONSIDERING TRUMAN'S CIVIL RIGHTS ACHIEVEMENTS

HONORING TRUMAN'S CIVIL RIGHTS LEGACY

ILLUSTRATIONS

TL................. Truman Presidential Museum and Library

Preface

Eight of the eleven essays in this volume originated as presentations at a conference titled "Harry S. Truman and Civil Rights," held at Key West, Florida, in May 2004. The conference held its opening session at the Little White House, now a Florida state historic site but once the residence of the commandant of the U.S. naval base at Key West. Truman loved going to the base to escape the pressures of the presidency. He made eleven visits between 1946 and 1952, for a total of 175 days, bringing White House staff along with him for these working vacations. Historians may never know exactly how much work was done during these getaways to the warm and friendly island of Key West, but there is no doubt that the president found them restorative.

The remaining three essays originated elsewhere. Colin Powell's essay is based on a presentation sponsored by the Truman Library on the occasion of the fiftieth anniversary of Executive Order 9981. This order, issued by President Truman on 26 July 1948, ordered the desegregation of the armed forces. The content of General Powell's talk makes clear why he believed the event being commemorated justified his interrupting his vacation and flying five thousand miles to the Truman Library to be part of the program.

Carol Anderson's essay was first presented at a July 2003 teachers institute held at the Truman Library and titled "Harry's Farewell." In his 1953 farewell address, Truman listed the accomplishments of his presidency; the participants in the institute examined all these claims. The editor wishes to thank the University of Missouri Press for granting permission to publish this essay, which is taken from the book *Harry's Farewell: Interpreting and Teaching the Truman Presidency* (2004), edited by Richard S. Kirkendall.

Ken Hechler's essay was specially written for this book. Hechler participated in the 2004 Key West conference and also in a symposium held in Kansas City in July 2006 to mark the fifty-eighth anniversary of the issuance of Executive Order 9981, but on neither occasion did he prepare a paper. One of the last living members of

Truman's White House staff, Hechler feels a responsibility to record what the Truman presidency was really like for the people who participated in it. At least some of what historians have written about Truman over the years has probably seemed strange to a man who saw the president often and who experienced day-to-day life in the White House during the years of the Truman presidency.

The efforts of many people and several institutions are reflected in this book. The Key West conference on Truman's civil rights legacy was convened by Robert P. Watson, professor of political science at Florida Atlantic University; Michael J. Devine, director of the Truman Presidential Museum and Library; and Robert J. Wolz, director of the Harry S. Truman Little White House. Florida Keys Community College provided a venue for most of the conference's sessions. The sponsors included Historic Tours of America, the Monroe County Tourist Development Council, the Harry S. Truman Little White House, the Harry S. Truman Library Institute for National and International Affairs, the Lifelong Learning Society at Florida Atlantic University, the John D. Evans Foundation, the Florida Atlantic University Foundation, and the Larkin Charitable Trust. Gratitude is due to many people associated with all the organizations mentioned above, and especially to Ed Swift and Chris Belland, president and CEO, respectively, of Historic Tours of America; Piper Smith and Monica Muoz of Historic Tours of America; William Seeker, president of Florida Keys Community College; Kathy Knotts, vice president for development of the Harry S. Truman Library Foundation for National and International Affairs; Frank T. Brogan, president of Florida Atlantic University; Richard Yon of Florida Atlantic University; and Liz Safly and Scott Roley of the Truman Library.

INTRODUCTION
Interpreting the Civil Rights Legacy
of Harry S. Truman

Raymond H. Geselbracht

On 13 April 1966, about twenty historians, political scientists, and archivists came together at the Truman Library to talk about the Truman administration and the work being undertaken by scholars to understand it. This was the fourth biennial conference sponsored by the Truman Library's nonprofit partner, the Harry S. Truman Library Institute for National and International Affairs. It was designed to be different from the first three conferences in that, for the first time, formal papers were presented and discussed; these papers were published the following year under the title *The Truman Period as a Research Field*. The book was edited by Richard S. Kirkendall, a young historian at the University of Missouri whose involvement with Truman scholarship and the Truman Library would extend well into the twenty-first century. Besides this planned formal difference in the 1966 conference, something else was very different too. The scholars and archivists witnessed the presentation of some jarring content, the like of which had not been heard at the Truman Library before. President Truman was still alive and well and he came to the library virtually every day; he was on the Truman Library Institute's board, as were several former members of his administration. There was an unspoken understanding that the institute-sponsored conferences of scholars would be constructive and benevolent. But now, at this 1966 conference, participants heard some troubling things from some of the scholars. Perhaps the Cold War had been brought on by President Truman's unnecessarily belligerent attitude toward the Soviet Union; perhaps his administration acquiesced in the domination of the economy by big business; perhaps he pursued his civil rights program sporadically, without deep commitment, and largely for political reasons. The President Truman put forward by some of the scholars at the 1966 conference was not a heroic figure, not a great idealist, not a partisan of all the people who did what was right because it was right. He was something smaller, a president who was complicit with existing elites, crafty if not cynical, reckless and sometimes simpleminded in his management of world affairs. Revisionist history had made its way to the Truman Library and been sponsored by the Truman Library Institute. Not everyone associated with the library and the institute liked this brand of history, and the institute in time decided to sponsor a different kind of conference, not focused on scholars and scholarship, but rather on capturing the memories of surviving members of Truman's administration and recording their typically laudatory assessments of Truman's leadership. Revisionists were too unpleasant to invite into one's own space.

It was in this environment of historiographical division that the first substantial literature relating to the Truman administration's civil rights program was created. When the Truman Library Institute brought sixteen scholars together in 1968 to discuss the Truman administration's civil rights achievements, the conversation seemed probing and largely formless. It was almost as if there were no experts among these scholars. Some were better informed and better able to generalize about Truman and civil rights than others, but as a group they did not seem to share a basic sense of the narrative of the Truman administration's involvement with civil rights.[1] The literature did not exist that would have given them a basic sense of what had happened and what it might mean.

Within five years, such a literature did exist. Between 1969 and 1973, three books and two articles established the narrative of Harry S. Truman and civil rights. The first book to appear, in 1969, was Richard M. Dalfiume's *Desegregation of the U.S. Armed Forces: Fighting on Two Fronts, 1939–1953*. Then, in 1970, came William Berman's *The Politics of Civil Rights in the Truman Administration,* and, in the same year, Barton Bernstein's article "The Ambiguous Legacy: The Truman Administration and Civil Rights," which appeared in Bernstein's edited volume of revisionist essays, *Politics and Policies of the Truman Administration.* Harvard Sitkoff's article, "Harry Truman and the Election of 1948:

The Coming of Age of Civil Rights in American Politics" appeared in 1971, and two years later, Donald McCoy and Richard Ruetten's *Quest and Response: Minority Rights and the Truman Administration* was published. In five short years, an accomplished body of literature about Truman's civil rights program had been created. It was sophisticated and thoroughly researched, making use of manuscript collections that were being opened, including the papers of Harry S. Truman and members of his administration. The different pieces of this literature can almost be read as a single work, telling the same story, or important elements of it, from different perspectives, and fractured along the same divide as was apparent during the Truman Library's 1966 conference.

On one side of the divide were Dalfuime, McCoy, and Reutten, the "liberal" historians, according to one prominent historian who observed the unfolding of this historiography. On the other side of the divide were Berman, Bernstein, and Sitkoff, who were the "radicals" or "revisionists." The liberals, judging Truman from the perspective of his own time, concluded that his civil rights accomplishments were substantial and important, and were motivated largely by sincerely held principle. The revisionists, while often very appreciative of what Truman did to advance civil rights, were inclined to regard his achievement as meager, hesitantly undertaken, polluted by political motives, and, when viewed from the perspective of the troubled late 1960s and early 1970s, terribly inadequate in view of what the race problem had become.[2] Berman's use of "politics" as his book title's opening word suggests his view that Truman was not always a principled advocate of civil rights; Bernstein labels the result of Truman's efforts on behalf of civil rights an "ambiguous legacy," and Sitkoff describes Truman as a "reluctant champion" of civil rights.

Despite their somewhat discordant interpretative framework, these books and articles established a compelling narrative of the Truman administration's encounter with civil rights. The narrative remains compelling today, and it is found in more or less complete form in several of the essays in this book. The old dialogue between liberal and revisionist interpretations is considerably altered in these essays as a result both of the opening of new materials relating to Truman's personal views on race and civil rights, and of the development of new perspectives on Truman's civil rights program in response to the events of the last thirty-five years.

Some of Harry Truman's personal writings, which were not available at the time the books and articles described above were being written, depict a president and a person who had a deep commitment to civil rights for all Americans. It is harder now than it was in 1970 to argue that Truman approached civil rights solely or primarily as a crafty politician, trying to keep the South in the Democratic Party and to win the African American vote. He did want to do these things, but his personal writings strongly suggest that he also genuinely wanted all Americans to have the rights he believed were promised them by the Declaration of Independence and the Constitution. Truman's personal writings also reveal a man who had all the racial prejudices of his region and his time; some of the essays in this book express the surprise many historians feel when telling the story of what one called "The Conversion of Harry S. Truman" from racist to champion of civil rights.[3]

The liberal versus revisionist dialogue has also been altered by new perspectives on Truman's civil rights program that have grown out of the events of the last few decades. Both sides of the historiography relating to Truman and civil rights have been affected by these events. The liberal side has become largely detatched from a faded liberalism and is now associated with a depiction of President Truman as a partly mythic person and leader, almost an Abraham Lincoln of the twentieth century. The timing of the emergence of this mythic Truman, and the surprising popularity of some of the literature that has helped create the myth, suggests that the nation, beginning at about the time Truman died, longed for such a mythic figure to help it recover from the Vietnam War and the Watergate scandals. Margaret Truman's adoring biography of her father, *Harry S. Truman* (1972), appeared at about the time he died. Merle Miller's immensely popular *Plain Speaking*, which was based partly on the author's extensive interviews with a very folksy old Harry Truman and was full of appealing common sense without a hint of pretense or disingenuousness, was published in 1974. Sam Gallu's play, *Give'em Hell, Harry* (1975), continued the process of converting the real Harry S. Truman into a figure of folk culture. At the play's end, Gallu's Truman comes upon a little boy during one of his walks, and says to the young fellow, "What my job is is just to try to keep this country in some sort of working order so that when it comes time to turn it over to you young folks, it'll be in good shape." Members of the audience during the play's early performances—including President Gerald Ford, who attended the play's gala premier at Ford's Theater—probably doubted Presidents Johnson and Nixon had measured up to this simple job description. Two collections of Truman's very artful and artless (both at the same time) personal writings, *Off the Record* (1980) and *Dear Bess* (1983), demonstrated that the real Truman was perhaps as appealing as his admirers contended. David McCullough's *Truman* (1992) brought this highly favorable view of its subject to millions of readers. The Harry S. Truman presented in this literature is not quite the flesh and blood man who was president of the United States from 1945 to 1953, but he is the Truman most Americans who think about Truman believe in, because they want to believe in their country and in the best selves of all their countrymen. This Truman was capable of undertaking the noble mission of providing civil rights to all Americans, and that is how those sharing this very favorable, partly mythic, view of Truman see his civil rights program.

The other side in the new historiographical dialogue, the successor to the old revisionist side, has also developed a new perspective in response to events. Where the old revisionist interpretation emphasized political calculation, its new successor emphasizes geopolitical calculation. The old revisionists believed Truman was moved by domestic political concerns to limit his civil rights program within narrow bounds; the new revisionists believe geopolitical aspirations caused Truman to limit his civil rights program. The new perspective views Truman's civil rights program as a function of American foreign policy, and consequently tends strongly to view it globally, in the context of the Cold War. This perspective emerges from such books as Mary Dudziak's *Cold War Civil Rights: Race and the Image of American Democracy* (2000), Thomas Borstelmann's *The Cold War and the Color Line: American Race Relations in the Global Arena* (2001), and Carol Anderson's *Eyes Off the Prize: The United Nations and the African American Struggle for Human Rights, 1944–1955* (2003). From this foreign policy and globalist perspective, Truman's commitment to so-called civil rights—a concept derived from American history and American social and economic beliefs and practices, and including rights of legal equality and the right to a broadened, if not necessarily equal, opportunity to advance oneself socially and economically—was inadequate to the needs of disadvantaged people of color all over the world, including African Americans. These people of color often lacked what the United Nations called their "human rights," a concept which included a broad entitlement to social and economic rights as well as the right to the legal equality included in "civil rights." Although Truman sometimes in his speeches advocated broad human rights for African Americans, he did not include these broad rights in the civil rights legislation he proposed.

When Truman's civil rights program is viewed within a global perspective, it is possible to see an element of hypocrisy in it. Truman said many times that the Cold War confrontation with the Soviet Union was a battle for the minds and hearts of the people of the world in which the United States must live up to its great ideals. But in actual practice it seemed impossible for the United States to live up to its ideals, both because of its treatment of its own people of color, and because of the treatment of people of color in different areas of the world by some of the United States' closest allies, imperial powers, sometimes seeking to retain or regain colonies with American assistance. Since the Truman administration was not willing to force the kind of change that would have accorded full human rights to its own people of color or to force its allies to accord full human rights to the people of color under their control, it could be satisfied with doing only what was required to create for the United States a reasonably good international image. With the assistance of some skillful propaganda and a certain amount of strong arm diplomacy within the United Nations, both of which the American government provided, a civil rights program—even a partly unsuccessful one—could be sufficient for purposes of image, and nothing more need be attempted.

From the global perspective then—essentially the perspective of outside people looking in on the predominantly white American polity that Truman headed for eight years—the Truman administration's civil rights program can very easily appear inadequte in design and execution and underlain by tainted motivation, in this interpretation more geopolitical than political, which enforced limits on acceptable social and economic change. Within such a perspective, the actual conditions in which people of color live are more important than the sometimes interesting and dramatic stories of what a president did and the odds against which he fought to achieve very limited results. If his actions in the end didn't amount to much, if people of color were still suffering poverty and injustice, then the president can be judged harshly.

The essays that comprise *The Civil Rights Legacy of Harry S. Truman* demonstrate the ways in which the basic components that an interpretation of Truman's civil rights program must consider—

fundamental commitment, politics, geopolitics—are being reinter-
preted and reorganized more than three decades after the first important body of literature on Harry S. Truman and civil rights was
written.

The Civil Rights Legacy of Harry S. Truman is organized in
four sections. The first, titled "Viewpoint From the Descendants
of Slaves," includes essays by former congresswoman Carrie
Meek and current congressman John Lewis. Both essays are moving evocations of what the civil rights achievements of President
Truman and those presidents and civil rights activists who came
after him have meant to the people who suffered from Jim Crow
laws and practices. Meek says Truman's civil rights legacy shows
that "there is a goodness to be had when people are treated fairly
and treated right." She is the daughter of a sharecropper and the
granddaughter of a slave; she is an African American and a
woman. No one, she says, thought she would achieve anything
of importance. But she got a good chance in life because of Truman's legacy, and she made the most of it. John Lewis's father
was also a sharecropper, but he got a chance too because, as he
puts it, "as president of the United States of America, Harry S.
Truman got in trouble. It was good trouble, it was necessary trouble. He got in the way. It was necessary for him to get in the way
on the question of civil rights." Both Lewis and Meek have filled
their essays with colorful anecdotes and with the vitality that
enabled them to endure and finally transcend the Jim Crow
America in which they grew up, and to devote their lives to continuing President Truman's work of ensuring that all Americans
are treated fairly and treated right.

The three essays in the second section comprise a symposium in which the authors assess Truman's civil rights legacy from
different perspectives. The first two essays are strongly contrast-
ing. Michael Gardner presents a twenty-first-century version of
the old liberal view of Truman and civil rights. This essay—like
his book, *Harry Truman and Civil Rights*—provides an admiring
view of its subject. Truman, Gardner writes, knew in his heart that
African Americans must be accorded equal civil rights, and he did
all in his power to make it so, even at the risk of great political
cost to himself and his party. "Harry Truman knew in his heart
and soul," Gardner writes, "that civil rights equality was a moral
imperative that had to be pursued regardless of the political consequences." One interesting part of Gardner's assessment is his
attempt to give Truman credit for the decisions in favor of civil

rights handed down by the Supreme Court during his presidency and by extension, for the *Brown v. Board of Education* decision of 1954. Gardner believes that Truman appointed men to the court who thought as he did about civil rights, in effect anticipating the decisions they later rendered. By this reasoning, the decisions become an extension of Truman's actions as president.[4]

Carol Anderson's essay presents a much different, much more critical view. She titles her essay "Clutching at Civil Rights Straws" because that, in her view, was what African Americans who wanted to believe in President Truman's leadership had to do during his eight years in office. She admits that Truman did more for civil rights than the presidents immediately before and after him, Franklin D. Roosevelt and Dwight D. Eisenhower. But those presidents accomplished very little in the area of civil rights, and if one judges Truman by a higher standard than they provide, she argues, he appears very wanting indeed. His Justice Department was so poorly led that it was largely incapable of protecting the constitutional rights of African Americans; it could not secure their right to vote, nor could it protect them from lynching and other brutal acts of violence. In addition, the Truman administration's housing program effectively mandated segregation. The Federal Housing Administration, in order to minimize loan risk, employed redlining and restrictive covenants to prevent black incursions into white neighborhoods. Anderson maintains that Truman could be a forceful and effective leader when he was fighting the Cold War on the international stage, but when he and his hapless assistants in the White House and the Justice Department turned their attention to civil rights, "helplessness, hopelessness, and mediocrity reigned." Anderson ends by identifying "an anomaly in American society in the area of civil rights...where the mere act of trying—and not necessarily succeeding—becomes more than enough. At some point, as a democracy, we must realize it is not."

Ken Hechler, who served on President Truman's White House staff from 1949 to 1953, presents in his essay a very different portrayal of President Truman from that drawn by Carol Anderson. Hechler views Truman as an effective and energetic advocate African Americans. Truman spoke eloquently and forcefully for civil rights on many occasions; created a President's Committee on Civil Rights with members who believed in what they were doing and would make serious, guiding recommendations; used his executive powers in unprecedented ways to desegregate the armed forces and achieve other civil rights goals; did his best to get Congress to pass the civil rights legislation he wanted; and caused his Justice Department, which was not ineffective and hapless, to send briefs to the Supreme Court in favor of plaintiffs who were fighting for their civil rights. He did all these things, Hechler contends, in the absence of any well-organized civil rights movement such as emerged in the 1950s. Truman acted because it was the right thing to do. Hechler concludes with a strongly stated contention that Truman did "everything within his constitutional power to ensure that it was public policy to guarantee civil and human rights to all Americans...."

Hechler specifically counters the argument that Truman issued Executive Order 9981 because A. Philip Randolph (leader of the Brotherhood of Sleeping Car Porters) threatened to incite African Americans not to serve in a segregated military when the draft was reinstated in August 1948. Hechler, in the course of writing his essay, raised the question with former White House assistant George Elsey, who helped Truman develop his civil rights policy. Elsey responded that Truman never mentioned Randolph to the staff who worked with him on civil rights matters, and asserted that "Randolph's 'pressure' is simply not discernable."

The third section includes three essays that focus on discrete areas of the Truman administration's civil rights record. Raymond Frey focuses on Truman's speech to the National Association for the Advancement of Colored People, delivered at the Lincoln Memorial on 29 June 1947. This essay demonstrates the influence that Truman's personal writings have had on the interpretation of his civil rights record. Thirty-five years ago, the revisionists sometimes argued that Truman's actions on behalf of civil rights failed to match the promise of his rhetoric, and that he probably did not completely mean what he said in speeches such as the one he made to the NAACP. Frey thinks he did mean what he said in the NAACP speech, partly because the day before the speech he wrote a letter to his sister, who he knew was prejudiced against African Americans, in which he says this: "Mama won't like what I say because I wind up by quoting old Abe. But I believe what I say and I'm hopeful we may implement it." Frey also makes an assertion echoed by some other authors in this book: that Truman was certainly interested in the black vote, but by courting it he risked losing the white South and thus committing political suicide. The old revisionist argument about the crafty politician using civil rights rhetoric for political advantage is thus turned on its head. Truman is seen as a reckless politician who does not seem to care much for his own future, who is principled and does what is right regardless of political consequences.

The essay by Richard Yon and Tom Lansford, like Frey's, focuses on one part of Truman's civil rights record—in this instance, the desegregation of the armed forces, which they believe was the most important civil rights achievement of the Truman administration. Truman was constitutionally empowered to take action to desegregate the military without congressional approval or assistance. As the authors show, he not only took executive action to this end—by issuing Executive Order 9981—he continued to manage the process of desegregation over a period of years until, by the end of his administration, integration had been almost fully achieved throughout the military. The authors depict a president who combined a concern for military efficiency with a belief that African Americans deserved the same civil rights as white Americans, and who was at the same time fully aware of the political benefits and costs of integrating the military. In this instance, political pragmatism blended well with idealistic motives and with the commander in chief's responsibility toward the military. The armed forces were integrated and became an inspiration to those who wished all of American society to be integrated as well. Yon and Lansford also give attention to the Cold War context within which the desegregation of the military occurred. Racial injustice greatly harmed the image of America abroad and made a mockery of the high moral pretensions the United States presented to the rest of the world in order to gain allies in its confrontation with the Soviet Union. This factor was always on Truman's mind, and he often mentioned it in his civil rights speeches.

The next essay in this section is an extraordinary account of the great importance that desegregation of the armed forces has had for African Americans. General Colin Powell presents the familiar narrative about Truman and civil rights right up to the point where Executive Order 9981 was issued, and then begins telling his moving personal story about "an eleven-year-old kid who had been born in Harlem and was growing up in the South Bronx." He was a kid who knew he was different and knew there were many dreams he could not dream. He recited the Pledge of Allegiance every day at school, but he knew the words "with liberty and justice for all" did not apply to him or the black kids around him. What he did not know was that President Truman had recently signed an order that would very soon desegregate the armed forces. He went to college, joined the ROTC (Reserve Officers Training Corps), and rose in rank to lead the army that Truman's order had made—an army open, fair, and just to people of every race. Powell recognizes, though, that despite the great importance desegregation of the armed forces has had for him personally, Truman's civil rights agenda was modest in its ambition. It was no more than a start in the right direction; the struggle for racial justice had much further to go than Truman was able or willing to lead it. "The second reconstruction period is not yet over," Powell writes, "and we must not quit too early this time. Too much is at stake."

The essay by Michael Dukakis, the Democratic Party's nominee for president in 1988, is a departure from the others in this section. It is primarily about Truman's national health insurance proposal, which the Congress would not approve. Dukakis argues that health security is a civil right, something President Truman also argued, notably in his civil rights message to Congress on 2 February 1948: "We cannot be satisfied until all our people have equal opportunities for jobs, for homes, for education, for health, and for political expression, and until all our people have equal protection under the law." Truman typically used the term "civil rights" in a more limiting sense than appears to be the case here. Usually, civil rights were for him the rights necessary to assure equality under the law. These rights did not include, as Truman made clear on a number of occasions, social equality—Truman was very selective in picking desegretation fights—and while "civil rights" might occasionally be expanded to include the rights to health care, a good education, and decent housing, these latter rights were usually regarded as being due all Americans, and Truman pursued their realization through his Fair Deal measures. Dukakis, who clearly prefers the broader civil rights concept, describes in his essay Truman's glorious failure to provide all Americans with a national health care system.

The last section has only a single essay, by the editor of this volume. It is about the Truman Library's commemoration of Truman's civil rights legacy in its museum exhibits, research services, programs for students and teachers, conferences, and lectures. A legacy should not be confused with a monument. Truman's civil rights legacy is living, dynamic, and developing. It is more an indicated direction and a degree of momentum than an established fact, and it derives its vitality from the engagement of the American people with it. The Truman Library's programs are designed to initiate or advance such an engagement, as seen through an examination of the design of the library's permanent exhibition on Truman's presidency, its provision of online access to some of its holdings, its opening of new materials relating to civil rights, and its presentation of educational programs that require active involvement and public programs that advance challenging perspectives. As the essay says, "All those who come in contact with Truman's legacy through whatever means...are the true and inevitable interpreters of that legacy, and they are the people who will determine what influence the legacy will have on the future."

The certainly applies to readers of this book.

Raymond H. Geselbracht
Truman Presidential Library

Notes

[1] McCoy, Reutten, and Fuchs, *Conference of Scholars*.

[2] Hamby, "The Clash of Perspectives," 137–39.

[3] Leuchtenburg, "Conversion of Harry Truman." The quotation comes from the blurb for the article on the magazine's cover.

[4] Michael J. Klarman *(From Jim Crow to Civil Rights*, 193–95) asserts that Truman was indifferent to the racial views of Supreme Court nominees, choosing justices based primarily on his judgment that they would be likely to sustain the constitutionality of the New Deal and Fair Deal. Truman's four appointees, who included two men from the border South, were supportive of civil rights, according to Klarman, apparently because of their wish to support the government's view that advances in civil rights were required by what he calls "the Cold War imperative for racial change."

VIEWPOINT FROM THE DESCENDANTS OF SLAVES

A Legacy Beyond Books, A Legacy That Gets into You

Carrie Meek

As I was thinking about what I wanted to write about Harry Truman and civil rights, and as I read and learned about what he accomplished during his presidency, I changed my mind about him. I've changed my entire idea of what Mr. Truman was all about. I'm sort of a semi-historian and a person who has dedicated my life to civil rights and to human rights—to equal rights for everyone. I've read books about Mr. Truman, I've heard lectures about him. The more I've learned about him, the more I've changed my mind.

Truman's presidency was not really about all the paperwork, all the bureaucracy, and it was not really about what the historians have said, even though that was important. In thinking about what Harry Truman was all about, what I have gleaned is that in his heart he was man of deep attunement with God. He had that attunement with God that makes a person do the right thing and that made him know what doing the right thing was all about. It made him know that there was a great need to do the right thing and to be humane, even though he was a politician. I just left Congress—I just left twenty-four years of being a politician—so I know what that is all about.

To me, part of Harry Truman's legacy has been to teach politicians and other elected officials to keep their word once they give it. Many of us have not yet learned to do that—to keep our word—but that is what I see in him. The people who represent

Truman today are very proud of him. At the Little White House in Key West, Florida, which was Truman's favorite vacation spot during his presidency, they told me that the people who worked for him still worship him even though he's long dead. There is a goodness to be had when people are treated fairly and treated right, and Truman did that in his presidency. He played a significant role in the lives of plenty of people; he played a significant role in the lives of people who caused me to be where I am today. I'm the child of a sharecropper, the granddaughter of a slave. People did not think I would ever go anyplace because women could not go anyplace, and I had the extra handicap of being black. A woman and a black woman. But there was this legacy of Mr. Truman's that insisted everyone be given a chance. That was another part of the Truman legacy—to be fair and to give people what was right.

I was brought up in the shadow of the capitol building in Tallahassee, yet my family and I were not able to go into that capitol. The same was true at Florida State College for Women, now Florida State University. My mother and I used to walk down there and look at it, but we could not go inside. When I graduated from Florida A & M University, it was the only black college in the state. I could not attend Florida State University, I could not attend the University of Florida because the laws of Florida said I couldn't. It was codified in the Florida statutes that no black person could go to college at a white university. That is why it is so important that the Truman legacy be passed down, because one person in the executive branch or the judicial branch or the legislative branch— one single person who does not follow the Truman legacy of doing what is right for people—can break the whole chain of fairness and equality.

If there is one person in the crowd who sees something in another person, sees that individual's ability and doesn't keep him or her back because of race, then that second person just might go far. The result will be more John Lewises, more Carrie Meeks, more Martin Luther Kings. There will be more and more of them because of the legacy Truman left more than fifty years ago. That legacy is sometimes insidious once it gets into a person. I know this not only from reading about Truman, but from listening to other people and seeing what his legacy has begotten.

In my public service role, in Congress and in the state legislature, Truman's legacy is evident. When you are a public servant, you are there to serve the people. You are not there always to repeat what you hear others say, but you're there to listen to the people and learn something from them, and you are there to make public policy after listening to what the people are saying. Public policy is made in a lot of different ways. It's like bologna or sausage: if you knew how it was made, you'd never want to eat it again, because, like public policy, it's made in a very funny way. But despite this, public servants learn that if they choose to do the right thing, then their constituents will know someone is there who will speak up for them as Mr. Truman did. Truman did not want public servants ever to forget that they are often the only ones who can represent the underrepresented.

A legacy is much more than what is contained in books. A legacy is a kind of reciprocal innervation that one gets from listening to someone, that one gets from talking to someone, that one gets from learning about the example that someone like Mr. Truman left behind.

When Truman became president in 1945, the whole climate of civil rights was undergoing major changes. He stepped right into this changing climate, and began to take action. There were many so-called liberals at that time who did not want to do the right thing. They expressed a lot of liberal and radical views, but they were not the ones to stand up and say, "Let's desegregate the military, let's be sure that is done." Mr. Truman was the one who did that.

Truman was not afraid of things. If you are afraid of racism, if you are afraid of sexism, if you are afraid of these kinds of isms in this country, things will overwhelm you. But Truman was not afraid, and he could see ahead like the great explorer Christopher Columbus. He felt the winds of change and he knew changes had to come. So he caused the country to change. He started by talking about equality, and talking about giving people the rights they should have under the Constitution.

What I've learned from the historical point of view is that the Truman legacy needs to be replicated. I wish you could clone some of the scholars who know about Truman and civil rights so they could take the message of Truman's legacy much, much further. That reciprocal innervation that comes from Truman's legacy is what is still needed and people need to know about what he did. The scholars who know about Truman and civil rights can become agents of change who cause people to want to serve their country and cause people to understand what it means not to be a victim. It is easy to become a victim in this country.

I'll never forget Medgar Evars, I'll never forget Malcolm X, I'll never forget Dr. Martin Luther King, I'll never forget the models of public service who started the civil rights movement. I'll never forget Harry T. Moore, who was killed in the Florida orange groves. I'll never forget the struggle of the NAACP or the Southern Christian Leadership Conference. I grew up in that time, and I'll never forget the indignities I have seen or had thrown against me. I'll never forget those times. But what I have felt as I learned about Truman's legacy—and I felt this also when I was in the Florida legislature and in Congress—is that there's unfinished business. That unfinished business includes the unfair immigration laws we have in this country—they must be changed.

The spirit of Harry S. Truman requires that we look at what we have and try to change it. I know that many of our people are being disenfranchised because of the Voting Rights Act; this is more unfinished business. Many people were denied the right to vote in Florida in the election of 2000, and the same thing happened in other states, too. Truman would say, "That's not fair. Let's change this." Minorities have been underrepresented in the census and in the redistricting that follows. That's not right, we have to keep fighting that. This is part of the unfinished agenda Mr. Truman was thinking about fifty years and more ago when he was trying to level the playing field here in the United States.

We must also continue to work to ensure that our students' progress is fairly and accurately measured as they go through their education. We want all of our children to be well educated, and we want all of our youngsters in high school to give public service, because public service is the price you pay for the space that God has let you occupy. Mr. Truman knew this too, and he was right in this as in so many other things.

A President Who Got in Trouble— Good Trouble, Necessary Trouble

John Lewis

I did not grow up in a big city like Chicago or New York or Miami, or like Atlanta or Washington or Boston. I grew up on a farm. My father was a sharecropper, a tenant farmer, but back in 1944 when I was four years old, my father had three hundred dollars saved, and with that three hundred dollars he bought 110 acres of land. On this farm we raised a lot of cotton, corn, peanuts, hogs, cows, and chickens.

If you come to Washington and visit my congressional office, the first thing the staff will offer you will be a Coca-Cola, because Atlanta is the home of the Coca-Cola Company, and the company provides all members of the Georgia congressional delegation with an adequate supply of Coca-Cola products to give to our visitors. The next thing my staff will offer you will be some peanuts because in Georgia we raise a lot of peanuts, and the Georgia Peanut Commission provides us with peanuts to give to our visitors. I don't eat many of those peanuts. I ate so many peanuts when I was growing up in rural Alabama, I just do not want to see any more peanuts. Years ago, I would get on a flight from Atlanta to Washington, or Washington back to Atlanta, and when the flight attendant tried to push some peanuts on me, I said, "I don't care for any peanuts. No thank you."

I said that on our farm we raised a lot of chickens. When I was growing up in rural Alabama in the 1940s and 1950s, it was my responsibility to care for the chickens. I fell in love with raising chickens like no one else ever fell in love with raising chickens. I'm guessing that few if any of the people reading this essay know anything about raising chickens, so I'll just school all of you, if that's all right. Here is what I had to do as a young black boy growing up in rural Alabama during the 1940s and 1950s: I had to take the fresh eggs, mark them with a pencil, place them under a setting hen, and wait for three long weeks for the little chicks to hatch. I know some smart reader is now about to ask me the question, "John Lewis, why do you mark those fresh eggs with a pencil before you place them under the setting hen?" Well, from time to time, another hen would get on this same nest, and there would be some more eggs, so you had to be able to tell the fresh eggs from the eggs that were already under the setting hen. When these little chicks would hatch, I would fool these setting hens, I would cheat on these setting hens. I would take these little chicks and put them in a box with a lantern and raise them on their own, without the setting hen. Then I would get some more fresh eggs, mark them with a pencil, place them under the setting hen, and encourage the setting hen to sit on the nest for another three weeks. I kept on fooling these setting hens and cheating on these setting hens, and when I look back on it, it was not the right thing to do. It was not the moral thing to do. It was not the most loving thing to do. It was not the most nonviolent thing to do. But I was never quite able to save eighteen dollars and ninety-eight cents to buy the most inexpensive incubator from the Sears and Roebuck store in Atlanta. So I just kept on cheating on these setting hens and fooling these setting hens.

As a little child, seven and a half or eight years old, I wanted to be a minister, so one of my uncles asked Santa Claus to bring me a Bible. I wanted to read the Bible. Then I started speaking, preaching from time to time. With the help of my brothers and sisters and our first cousins, I would gather all of our chickens together in the chicken yard or in the chicken house and we would have a church meeting. My chickens and my brothers and sisters and first cousins would make up the congregation, and I would start speaking or preaching. I noticed some of these chickens would bow their heads and shake their heads. They never quite said "Amen," but I am convinced that some of those chickens I preached to in the 1940s and 1950s listened to me much better than some of my colleagues listen to me today in the Congress. As a matter of fact, some of these chickens were a little more productive. At least they produced eggs.

When I was growing up in rural Alabama during the 1940s and 1950s, I would visit the little town of Troy, visit Montgomery, visit Birmingham, visit Tuskegee. I saw those signs that said "White Men," "Colored Men"; I saw those signs that said "White Women," "Colored Women"; I saw those signs that said "White Waiting," "Colored Waiting." As a young child, I tasted the bitter fruits of segregation and racial discrimination, and I didn't like it. I asked my mother, my father, my grandparents, my great-grandparents, "Why segregation? Why racial discrimination?" They would say, "That's the way it is. Don't get in trouble. Don't get in the way." But as a student I got in the way, I got in trouble. It was good trouble, it was necessary trouble. As president of the United States of America, Harry S. Truman got in trouble. It was good trouble, it was necessary trouble. He got in the way. It was necessary for him to get in the way on the question of civil rights. As Michael Gardner says in his essay in this book, Harry S. Truman was the first president since Lincoln to say that the question of civil rights, the question of race, is a moral issue.

When I finished high school in 1957, I wanted to attend college. But even before that time, I had been deeply inspired by the actions of hundreds of thousands of people fighting for civil rights. I made my first trip to Tuskegee University when I was maybe six or seven years old. I was just starting school and I went with the other students on a field trip. It was 1946 or 1947. I was deeply inspired by visiting the campus and seeing the work of George Washington Carver and Booker T. Washington and others.

President Truman, long before others were talking about civil rights or doing anything about civil rights, issued executive orders establishing the President's Committee on Civil Rights, calling for the desegregation of the armed forces, and promoting equal opportunity in federal employment. When we talk about affirmative action and equal opportunity today, we think it all happened just a short time ago. Maybe two or three years ago at the most. But in fact President Truman was on the case many, many years ago. And never in my estimation did he put his finger in the air to see which way the wind was blowing. He did what he thought was right. He spoke from his gut, from his heart.

In 1955 when I was fifteen years old and in the tenth grade, I heard of Rosa Parks and heard of Martin Luther King Jr., and I was so deeply inspired. I followed the drummer of Montgomery, and I was so moved. With some of my brothers and sisters and first cousins, I went down to the public library in the little town of Troy, Alabama, and tried to check some books out, tried to get library cards. We were told by the librarian that the library was for whites only and not for coloreds. But on 5 July 1998, I went back to that library for a signing of my book, *Walking with the Wind,* and hundreds of black and white citizens showed up, and the library gave me a library card. That says something about the distance we have come and the progress we have made in laying down the burden of race.

When I finished high school in May 1957, I wanted to attend a little school called Troy State College now known as Troy University. I submitted my application, my high school transcript, but I never heard a word from the college. So I wrote a letter to Martin Luther King Jr. I didn't tell my mother, my father, any of my sisters or brothers; I didn't tell my teachers. I told Dr. King I wanted to attend Troy State. Martin Luther King Jr. wrote me back, sent me a round-trip Greyhound bus ticket, and invited me to come to Montgomery. In the meantime, I had been accepted to a college in Nashville, Tennessee. One Saturday morning, an uncle of mine gave me a hundred dollar bill, more money than I ever had before, and he gave me a footlocker. I put everything I owned in that footlocker (except those chickens) and went off to school in Nashville. After being there for two or three weeks, I told one of my teachers that I had been in contact with Martin Luther King Jr. This particular teacher was a friend of Dr. King's, one of his classmates at Morehouse College in Atlanta. He informed Dr. King that I was in Nashville. Dr. King suggested that when I was home for spring break, I come and see him. On a Saturday morning in March of 1958—by this time I was eighteen years old—my father drove me to the Greyhound bus station where I boarded the bus for fifty mile trip from Troy to Montgomery. When I arrived at downtown Montgomery, a lawyer—I had never seen a lawyer before, black or white—a young lawyer by the name of Fred Gray, met me at the Greyhound bus station. He was one of the civil rights lawyers, the lawyer for Rosa Parks, for Dr. King and the Montgomery movement and he drove me to the First Baptist Church, where the Reverend Ralph Abernathy, a colleague of Dr. King's, was pastor. He ushered me into the office of the church. I saw Martin Luther King Jr. and Reverend Abernathy standing behind a desk. I was so scared, I didn't know what I was going to say. Dr. King said, "Are you the boy from Troy? Are you John Lewis?" And I said, "Dr. King, I am John Robert Lewis." I gave my whole name. I guess I didn't want there to be any mistake about my being the right person. That was the beginning of my involvement in the civil rights movement and of my relationship with Martin Luther King Jr.

During the 1940s, during the 1950s, during the presidency of Harry S. Truman, all across the American South, segregation was the order of the day. People in the heart of the American South, in Alabama, in Georgia, in Mississippi, and in so many other parts of the South, could not register to vote, could not participate in the democratic process, could not use public accommodations at lunch counters, in restaurants, could not stay in hotels. In a city in Alabama, blacks and whites could not ride in the same taxicab.

The country had to change. It is my belief that the actions of President Truman created the climate, created the environment, laid the foundation for the modern American civil rights movement. You had hundreds of thousands of men who had served in the military returning home. Two of my uncles fought in Europe in World War II. They did not like the idea of coming back to a segregated South, and so they left, they went to Buffalo, New York. My first trip out of the American South, out of the state of Alabama was in the summer of 1951 when I traveled by car all the way to Buffalo with my uncle, aunt, and first cousin. I remember my mother frying chicken and cooking pies and cakes and wrapping this food in wax paper, putting this food in brown bags and shoe boxes, because we could not stop along the way to get something to eat. I saw Buffalo as being different from Troy in rural Alabama. I was only eleven years old and I had an unbelievable imagination. Some of my cousins and I wanted to get out of Alabama; we had this idea that we were going to saw down a very large pine tree and somehow we were going to take this pine tree, and make a bus. It would have wheels, and we were just going to roll in this pine tree bus out of Alabama and make it to Buffalo, New York. That was what we did in our imagination, when we were children. We did not like segregation, we did not like racial discrimination, and we wanted to do something about it.

Forty years ago, in Alabama, in Georgia, in Mississippi, you had to pass a so-called literacy test to vote. On one occasion in 1963, a black man who had a PhD flunked the literacy test. He was told he could not read or write well enough. On another occasion, a man was asked to give the number of bubbles in a bar of soap. During the 1960s, people stood in unmoving lines just to become participants in the democratic process. I will never forget that just over forty years ago, my old organization, the Student Nonviolent Coordinating Committee, organized something called the Mississippi Summer Project, through which more than a thousand students, young people, lawyers, teachers, doctors, ministers, priests, rabbis, and nuns came to Mississippi to work in the Freedom Schools and prepare people to pass the so-called literacy test. Mississippi had a black voting-age population of more than four hundred and fifty thousand, but only about sixteen thousand blacks were registered to vote. We were preaching one man, one vote. On the summer night of 21 June 1964, three young men that I knew—Andy Goodman and Mickey Schwerner, both white, and James Chaney, an African American—went out to investigate the burning of a black church. They were stopped by the sheriff and taken to jail. Later that same Sunday night, the three men were taken from the jail by the sheriff and his deputy and turned over to the Klan, who beat them and shot and killed them. These three young men didn't die in Eastern Europe, they didn't die in the Middle East, they didn't die in Africa or Central or South America. They died right here in our own country, trying to encourage all of our people to become participants in the democratic process. Today some are saying we should forget about what happened during the 2000 election in Florida and other parts of the country, but I say we cannot forget about what happened. People died for the right of all to participate in the democratic process.

If Harry Truman could speak to us today, he would tell each and every one of us that when it comes to the issue of civil rights, we should find a way to get in the way. If he could speak to us today, he would say to us again, "Stand up for what is right, for what is fair, and for what is just. It is the right thing to do." We have an obligation, a mission, to uphold the legacy of this president who made a lasting contribution to the cause of civil rights.

When I was growing up outside Troy, Alabama, fifty miles from Montgomery, I had an aunt by the name of Seneva. My aunt lived in what we call a shotgun house. A shotgun house is an old house, maybe with a tin roof, with one way in and one way out. In a nonviolent sense, you can bounce a basketball through the front door and it would go straight out the back door. Some people would say you can fire a shotgun through the front door and the bullet would go straight out the back door. My aunt Seneva lived in one of these shotgun houses. She did not have a green, manicured lawn. She had a simple, plain, dirt yard. Sometimes at night you could look up through the holes in the ceiling, through the holes in the tin roof, and count the stars. When it would rain, she would get a pail, a bucket, a tub, and catch the rain water. From time to time she would walk out in the woods and take branches from a dogwood tree and make a broom. She would keep that yard very clean. She would sweep that yard sometimes two and three times a week, especially on Friday and Saturday, becuase she wanted that dirt yard to look good during the weekend.

One Saturday afternoon, a group of my brothers and sisters, and a few of my first cousins, about twelve or fifteen of us young chilldren, were out playing in my aunt Seneva's yard, when an unbelievable storm came up. The wind started blowing. The thunder started rolling. The lightning started flashing and the rain started beating down on the tin roof of this old shotgun house. My aunt became terrified. She started crying. And we all started crying. She thought this old house was going to blow away. She gathered all of us little children together and told us to hold hands, and we did as we were told. The wind continued to beat on the tin roof of this old shotgun house. And we cried and we cried, and we kept crying.

And when one corner of this old house appeared to be lifting from its foundation, my aunt had us walk to that corner of the house to try to hold it down with our little bodies. When the other side appeared to be lifting, she had us walk to that side to hold down the house with our little bodies. We were children, walking with the wind, but we never, ever left the house.

That is what the civil rights movement was all about, trying to hold the Amecan house together, trying to hold the American house down. That's what President Truman was trying to do, to hold the American house together. Storms may come, winds may blow, the thunder may roll, the lightning may flash, and the rain may beat down on the house. Call it the house of equal justice. Call it the house of civil rights. Call it the American house. Call it the world house. We must never, ever leave the house. Maybe our foremothers and forefathers all came to this great land in different ships, but we're all in the same boat now. We are one people. We are one family. We are one house. You must not give in. You must not give up. You must not give out.

If somebody had told me back in 1946, if somebody had told me while I was preaching to those chickens, if somebody had told me while I was sitting-in, getting arrested, going to jail, if somebody had told me back then that one day I would be a member of the House of Representatives—you know how I would have felt. I would never have believed it.

Harry Truman never gave in or gave up. He kept the faith. As citizens of America, and as citizens of the world, we must not give in either, we must not give up. We must keep the faith and not get lost in a sea of despair. I say today walk with the wind and let the spirit of Harry S. Truman be our guide.

ASSESSING
TRUMAN'S
CIVIL RIGHTS
LEGACY

A President Who Regarded Civil Rights as a Moral Imperative

Michael R. Gardner

Most people, including most historians, think of President Harry S. Truman in the context of his global contributions. He was the architect of the Truman Doctrine, the Marshall Plan, the North Atlantic Treaty Organization, the recognition of Israel, of numerous policies that had a profound and lasting impact during the Cold War. But President Truman's most important continuing legacy may well be none of these things, but rather his crusade to make civil rights equality a reality in America. It is in Truman's actions on behalf of civil rights that one sees most clearly into his soul and understands the moral imperative that made him America's pioneering civil rights president in the twentieth century.

To get into Truman's soul, however, one must consider two things: Truman's family background and the condition of the country with respect to civil rights when he became president.

In 1860, before the start of the Civil War, Missouri had 114,931 slaves in a total population of about 1.2 million. Approximately 10 percent of the population of Missouri consisted of slaves. Harry Truman was born only nineteen years after the end of the Civil War, into a family of farmers who shared the segregationist values that were pervasive throughout the state. Both sets of grandparents had owned slaves throughout the pre–Civil War era, and Truman's mother, née Martha Ellen Young, is on record as detesting anything Yankee, and especially Abraham Lincoln. When she was eleven years old, Martha Ellen, together with her mother and five of her siblings, was forced by Union soldiers to load family belongings into an oxcart and move from their farm to a holding camp in Kansas City. The family farm had already been ransacked by Union troops.[1] Martha Ellen never forgot these experiences.

Besides coming from a segregationist family, Truman lived in a largely segregated state. He attended segregated schools. When he enlisted to serve in the army at the beginning of World War I, he entered a totally segregated military and became captain of Battery D, an outfit of 194 young men who were mostly Irish Catholics from Kansas City. When he ran for elective office for the first time in 1922, the tough race was made particularly hard because the Ku Klux Klan opposed him. The Klan was very powerful in Missouri at this time, with one out of twenty people in Jackson County—Truman's county—donning white sheets on Saturday nights to go to Klan meetings.[2]

Harry Truman, given his family background, his Missouri roots, his experiences as a boy and young man, should have been a racist. As an insight to the condition of the country with respect to race when Truman became president, consider what Washington DC was like. Not unlike Cape Town, South Africa, thirty years later, it was defined by a system of apartheid. Schools, public pools, playgrounds, even the only theater in Washington, the National Theatre, were open only to white people.[3] As a result of actions taken by President Woodrow Wilson in 1913, the entire federal government was segregated. Even in the Executive Office Building across the street from the White House, whites and blacks used separate bathrooms and separate cafeterias, and drank at separate water fountains. A striking passage from the 1948 report of the National Committee on Segregation in the Nation's Capital demonstrates what Washington was like when Truman became president:

> Often an alien Negro will be allowed to eat sitting down at a lunch counter if he has a diplomatic pass or some other means of proving that he is not an American Negro. Four Negro students from the British West Indies sat at a downtown lunch counter. The waitress informed them that they would have to stand to be served. But when they produced their British diplomatic passes she apologized, remarking that she didn't realize that they were "not niggers."[4]

Racism such as this was not confined to the nation's capital or to the South. When Truman became president in 1945, thirty of the forty-eight states had public segregation rules in some form, either by constitution or through other laws. Throughout much of the northern and western parts of the country, cities were blanketed with restrictive covenants, which ghettoized African Americans to impoverished parts of the cities. Eighty percent of Chicago in 1946 was subject to such covenants, as was 75 percent of Westchester County, north of New York City.[5]

Unlike the 1960s, the years of Truman's presidency were not marked by national riots, sit-ins, or protests led by such figures as Martin Luther King Jr., nor was there significant demand in the media for action on civil rights. What was happening during the Truman years, however—and this was very important to President Truman—was a tidal wave of veterans coming home from war. Twelve million veterans came back home; 880,000 of these were black Americans who had served with distinction in a segregated military, often in color-blind parts of the world.[6] Many of these black veterans came home with a sense of liberation, but they quickly encountered a re-energized Ku Klux Klan, which felt threatened by these "uppity blacks" and advocated racial violence. This violence initially did not evoke much attention from the nation; only a few incidents were widely publicized.

A seminal meeting on 19 September 1946 in the Oval Office shaped the country's civil rights future. Walter White, then the executive director of the National Association for the Advancement of Colored People (NAACP), went with other members of the National Emergency Committee Against Mob Violence to brief President Truman about the violence being suffered by African Americans. White and Truman had become trusted friends by this time; they had first met only twenty-three days after Truman became president. After that earlier meeting, Truman did something his predecessor, Franklin D. Rosevelt, had been unwilling to do—he sent a message to Congress asking for a permanent Fair Employment Practices Committee.

During the 19 September 1946 meeting, White told President Truman a story that forever changed the course of civil rights in America. It involved Sergeant Isaac Woodard, a twenty-seven-year-old black veteran, who, just hours after being honorably discharged from Camp Gordon in Augusta, Georgia, the prior February, had gotten on a bus to return to his home in Winnsboro, South Carolina. He was still in uniform. Several hours later the bus pulled into Batesburg, South Carolina. Woodard was removed from the bus by the Batesburg police chief Lynwood Lanier Shull and arrested for disorderly conduct. The record of the arrest and Shull's own subsequent testimony confirm that Woodard did not resist arrest, he was not violent, he did not threaten anyone. Still, he was incarcerated and, during the night, was beaten so badly that one eye was gouged out and the other was blinded.[7]

When President Truman heard this story from Walter White during the September 19 meeting, he was repulsed and he was angry. He knew the valor demonstrated by servicemen, black and white, during the war, and he had known of the Klan and their tactics at least since the early 1920s. He told White and the others in the meeting that he was going to do something about the violence. The next day he wrote to Attorney General Tom Clark. He recounted the story of Isaac Woodard, and then he wrote this: "I have been very much alarmed at the increased feeling all over the country and I am wondering if it wouldn't be well to appoint a commission to analyze the situation and have a remedy to present to the next Congress." The government, he went on, needed a policy to prevent such violent attacks.[8]

Six days later, Attorney General Clark indicted Lynwood Shull. This was a rare and spectacular action in the America of the 1940s. A federal investigation and a trial followed. Three days after the trial began in Columbia, South Carolina, an all-white jury took just thirty minutes to return a not guilty verdict, despite hearing evidence that Woodard had not provoked the violent treatment he suffered as well as Shull's admission that he had used deadly force.[9] Such an outcome was typical in the South at this time.

On 5 December 1946, President Truman did what he had told his attorney general needed to be done—he created the President's Committee on Civil Rights by Executive Order. This was not a committee set up to take political heat but accomplish nothing—this committee was designed for decisive action. It had subpoena power and had some of the toughest people in the country on it: Sadie Alexander, a black lawyer from Philadelphia; Charles Wilson, president of General Electric; and Franklin D. Roosevelt Jr. President Truman met with the committee early in January 1947. "I want our Bill of Rights implemented in fact," he told the committee. "We have been trying to do this for 150 years. We are making progress, but we are not making progress fast enough." He said something tangible had to be done to prevent the rise of racial violence.[10]

While the President's Committee on Civil Rights was involved in its work, President Truman agreed to speak to the NAACP and its supporters, who gathered in huge numbers in front of the Lincoln Memorial in Washington DC on 29 June 1947. Truman was the first president ever to speak to the NAACP. The night before he spoke, Truman wrote a letter to his sister, Mary Jane Truman. It was a long, chatty letter about all sorts of things going on in Washington. At the letter's end, he said, "I've got to make a speech to the Society [sic] for the Advancement of Colored People tomorrow, and I wish I didn't have to make it. Mamma won't like what I say because I wind up by quoting Old Abe. But I believe what I say and I'm hopeful we may implement it." Truman was sixty-three years old; his beloved mother was ninety-four. Truman knew how his mother felt about Abraham Lincoln. When she visited the White House in 1945, he had offered to let her spend the night in the Lincoln Bedroom. Martha Ellen Truman immediately turned to Truman's wife and said, "Bess, if you'll get my bags packed, I'll be going home this evening." Truman knew that what he would say in his speech to the NAACP would upset his mother, and perhaps quite a few other people as well.[11]

The next day, with millions of people listening on radio, with Chief Justice Fred Vinson, Eleanor Roosevelt, and about ten thousand African Americans gathered in front of him, President Truman made some groundbreaking statements. He asserted that civil rights was a national imperative. "It is my deep conviction that we have reached a turning point...in our country's efforts to guarantee freedom and equality to all our citizens," he said. "Recent events in the United States and abroad have made us realize that it is more important today than ever before to insure that all Americans enjoy these rights. When I say all Americans I mean all Americans." He insisted that action must be quick and that it must be undertaken by the federal government. "We can no longer afford the luxury of a leisurely attack upon prejudice and discrimination.... We cannot, any longer, await the growth of a will to action in the slowest State or the most backward community. Our National Government must show the way."[12] This was heresy to most members of Congress, Republicans and Democrats alike. For Democrat congressmen from the South, segregation was a sacred way of life; for states-rights-fixated GOP members of Congress, it was anathema for the president to recommend that the federal government force a national policy of racial equality on state governments.

Sixteen years later, when the March on Washington occurred on 28 August 1963, President John F. Kennedy was not willing to climb the steps of the Lincoln Memorial and say things like this; he felt it was too risky politically to do so. But President Truman went up those steps in 1947, when there were no riots, when there was no nationwide pressure for civil rights reform. He did it because he believed it was the morally right thing to do. He was the first president of the United States to take action on civil rights because of moral imperative.

A few months later, on 29 October 1947, the President's Committee on Civil Rights presented a radical report to Truman. *To Secure These Rights* was 178 pages long and contained thirty-five specific recommendations. President Truman embraced the report and its recommendations entirely, unequivocally, and publicly. The *Washington Post* reported that when he accepted the report, "President Truman said he hoped the Committee had given the nation a document as broad as the Declaration of Independence—'An American Charter of Human Freedom in our time.'"[13]

Two months after this, on 7 January 1948, Truman went to Congress to deliver his State of the Union address. Typically in a presidential election year, this is the speech in which the president begins the political campaign. What did Truman say to the Republican 80th Congress, which he would savagely attack as the "do-nothing" Congress later in the year? He presented them with five broad goals for the country, including equitably shared prosperity and world peace based on freedom, justice, and the equality of all nations. But the first goal that President Truman put forward was "to secure fully the essential human rights of our citizens." The United States, he said, has always believed in human rights. "Today, however, some of our citizens are still denied equal opportunity for education, for jobs and economic advancement, and for the expression of their views at the polls. Most serious of all, some are denied equal protection under laws. Whether discrimination is based on race, or creed, or color, or land of origin, it is utterly contrary to American ideals of democracy."[14]

Less than a month later, on 2 February 1948, Truman sent the first presidential special message on civil rights to the Congress. It contained ten detailed legislative proposals to make civil rights a reality. A Gallup poll conducted one month later showed that 82 percent of Americans opposed the president's civil rights proposals; only 9 percent approved them.[15]

It is very difficult to imagine a modern politician at any level going against an 82 percent majority of the American people in a presidential election year. But Truman did go against this poll. One can understand why by reading some undated notes, probably written by Truman after he left office. "I wonder how far Moses would have gone if he'd taken a poll in Egypt?" he wrote. "What would Jesus Christ have preached if he'd taken a poll in Israel? Where would the Reformation have gone if Martin Luther had taken a poll? It isn't polls or public opinion of the moment that counts. It is right and wrong and leadership—men with fortitude, honesty and a belief in the right that makes epochs in the history of the world."[16]

Congress refused to pass Truman's civil rights proposals. Most members of Congress, Republican and Democratic, wanted civil rights to go away. Then, out of the blue on 3 May 1948, the Supreme Court issued an important decision, *Shelley v. Kraemer*. By their unanimous decision, the court, headed by Truman's good friend, Chief Justice Fred Vinson, eliminated the restrictive housing covenants that blanketed the country. This was not an accidental decision. Truman knew what Vinson was like when he appointed him to the Supreme Court in 1946; in fact, he thought enough of him to hope Vinson would succeed him as president. Furthermore, the court included another Truman appointee, Justice Harold Burton. Truman had also tried to influence the decision through amicus curiae briefs filed by the Justice Department, attacking the *Plessy v. Ferguson* doctrine of "separate but equal."[17]

Civil rights became a contentious issue at the 1948 Democratic National Convention in Philadelphia. The Truman forces proposed a plank for the party platform that described civil rights reform in general language reflecting a concept of racial equality based on the U.S. Constitution. The supporters of states' rights reacted by putting forward a regressive plank that argued for "the reserved powers of the state...to control and regulate local affairs and act in the exercise of police powers." This in turn prompted Hubert Humphrey (then mayor of Minneapolis) and other liberals to come up with a very controversial plank that went beyond generalities to specify "basic and fundamental principles" with respect to civil rights that the Democratic Party would stand for. This proposed plank eventually won the support of the convention by a tiny margin. Although this plank was not the choice of the Truman forces, it codified what Truman had said to the Congress in his special message on civil rights.[18]

Truman accepted the convention's nomination for president early in the morning of 15 July. In his rousing speech, he castigated the "do-nothing" Republican-controlled Congress, blasting the Republican leadership and holding them responsible for every problem in the country, including the sad state of civil rights for African Americans. "Everybody knows that I recommended to the Congress the civil rights program," Truman said to the delegates in a voice full of indignation. "I did that because I believed it to be my duty under the Constitution. Some of the members of my own party disagree with me violently on this matter. But they stand up and do it openly! People can tell where they stand. But the Republicans all professed to be for these measures. But Congress failed to act." Truman announced with great flourish that he would summon Congress back into session in just eleven days. "On the 26th day of July, which out in Missouri we call 'Turnip Day,' I am going to call Congress back.... Now, my friends, if there is any reality behind the Republican platform, we ought to get some action from a short session of the 80th Congress."[19] In other words, he would give the hypocritical Republicans another chance to pass the civil rights legislation their party platform claimed to support.

Truman won the nomination of his party, but not unanimously; the tally was 947 for and 263 against. He got only thirteen of the 276 votes from Southern delegates. When revisionist historians say Truman proposed his civil rights program as a cynical attempt to win the African American vote, they should be reminded that, of the 1,234 delegates at the Democratic National Convention, only seventeen—1.3 percent—were African American.[20] It is difficult to argue that Truman took such risks to pander to a segment of the vote that was embryonic and not yet well defined demographically. The African American vote did indeed become very important, but President Truman was clearly not pandering to this future reality when he articulated his revolutionary civil rights crusade from 1946 to 1948. The main political result of Truman's civil rights proposals was that the Democratic Party fractured. The states' rights "Dixiecrats" broke from the party and nominated Governor J. Strom Thurmond of South Carolina as their presidential candidate; shortly thereafter, the Progressive Party nominated Henry A. Wallace. Two of the three mainstays of the Democratic coalition—the Southern Democrats and the western Progressives—now supported presidential candidates other than the official choice of the Democratic Party.

Truman did call Congress back to Washington for his special "Turnip Day" session on July 26. It was hot and steamy, and most of the grouchy members of Congress wanted to be back home campaigning. Truman hit them with a political blow they didn't see coming, issuing two executive orders on the very day the special session began. Executive Orders 9980 and 9981 made it government policy to end discrimination in the federal work force and to desegregate the armed forces, respectively. For its part, Congress did almost nothing during the special session, just as Truman had predicted.

Shortly after the end of the special session, Truman received a letter from Ernie Roberts, an old friend from Kansas City. Roberts reminded Truman that they were both Southerners and advised him to forget about his equal rights bill. "Harry, let us let the South take care of the Niggers...," he wrote, "and if the Niggers do not like the Southern treatment, let them come to Mrs. Roosevelt." Truman's response, not released until after his death, is extremely instructive as to the soul of the man. In his letter to his lifelong friend, Truman wrote that he was sending Roberts a copy of *To Secure These Rights,* telling him that after he reads the report, "If you still have that ant[e]bellum proslavery outlook, I'll be thoroughly disappointed in you." He continues,

> The main difficulty with the South is that they are living eighty years behind the times and the sooner they come out of it the better it will be for the country and themselves.... When a Mayor and a City Marshal can take a negro [*sic*] Sergeant off a bus in South Carolina, beat him up and put out one of his eyes, and nothing is done about it by the State authorities, something is radically wrong.... I can't approve of such goings on and I shall never approve it, as long as I am here, as I told you before. I am going to try to remedy it and if that ends up in my failure to be reelected that failure will be in a good cause.[21]

This was a private letter written less than three months before the election. Truman was telling his well-intentioned but thoroughly racist friend to read his civil rights report, because he had to do what he was doing with regard to civil rights. If after reading the report, Roberts still disagreed with what Truman was doing, then so be it. Truman was not backing off, even if it cost him the White House.

On 6 September 1948, Truman got on the train to begin his Whistle Stop campaign. He was probably the only person on the campaign train who thought he could win. On 11 October, *Newsweek* magazine published a poll of fifty prominent journalists who had been asked the simple question, who was going to win the election? All fifty predicted that Governor Thomas E. Dewey of New York would be the next president. Truman was unmoved by his failure to garner even a single vote—he remained optimistic.[22]

On 29 October, only four days before the election, Truman went to Harlem in New York City. The first president to make a speech in Harlem, he reiterated his determination to pursue his civil rights program. "Our determination to attain the goal of equal rights and equal opportunity must be resolute and unwavering," he said.[23] Once again he was going down the path that had ruptured the Democratic Party.

To everyone's surprise except for his, Harry Truman won on 2 November. His popular-vote margin over Dewey was over two million; the electoral vote tally was 303 delegates for Truman, 189 for Dewey, 39 for Thurmond, and 0 for Wallace. Truman also helped bring both houses of Congress back to Democratic control. The House of Representatives swung strongly to the Democrats, who would outnumber Republicans in the first session of the 81st Congress 263 to 171.

Despite Truman's spectacular upset victory, one should not overlook the threat the Dixiecrats had posed in the election. If Thurmond had won only 38 more electoral votes, or if 38 more votes had gone to Dewey or Wallace, the election would have had to be resolved by the House of Representatives, and civil rights reform would have been derailed.

From the very start of his second term, Truman fought for civil rights in every way he could. He insisted that his be the first fully integrated inaugural in American history. Soon thereafter, he renewed his effort to persuade the Congress to pass civil rights legislation. He also continued his attempt to create a Supreme Court that would be supportive of civil rights. When, in 1949, he was able to appoint two new justices to the Supreme Court, he chose competent men he knew were committed to civil rights: Tom Clark, his attorney general, and Sherman Minton, with whom he had served in the Senate. Four of the justices on the Supreme Court, including the chief justice, were now Truman's appointees. He also continued to use the Justice Department to hammer at the court by submitting amicus briefs calling for federally enforced racial equality.

Before 1949 ended, Truman did something else that was enormously significant both symbolically and substantively. He named William Hastie to the Third Circuit Court of Appeals based in Philadelphia. This was the first time an African American had been named to the federal courts in the continental United States. At a time when juries in many parts of the country were still all white, there was an African American judge in the Third District.

In his State of the Union address in January 1950, Truman again asked Congress for civil rights legislation. Not surprisingly, Congress still would not act.

On 5 June 1950, the Supreme Court gave Truman something to be very pleased about: three decisions, all unanimous, that substantially invalidated the "separate but equal" doctrine. The first decision was in a case called *Henderson v. United States,* involving train travel. In the 1940s, an African American who had a first-class train ticket was restricted to one table in every ten in the dining car. If those few seats were occupied, a black person could not be seated, even if the rest of the dining car was empty. The table designated for blacks was enclosed with a curtain to isolate it from the white tables. Justice Burton, a Truman appointee, wrote the opinion that ended this discrimination.[24]

The two other opinions—*Sweatt v. Painter* and *McLaurin v. Oklahoma State Regents*—were even more important than *Henderson.* Both written by Chief Justice Vinson and both concerning education, they established important precedents for later cases such as the celebrated *Brown v. Board of Education.*

The facts in the *Sweatt* and *McLaurin* cases were simple. Herman M. Sweatt was a black man who wanted to go to the University of Texas law school. The state of Texas responded by setting up an alternative law school; though arguably a good one, it was still "separate but equal." Vinson, in his decision, wrote that *separate* could not be *equal*; something intangible was missing if you separated African Americans from everyone else. This was a revolutionary new argument not previously articulated in American jurisprudence, and Vinson used it again in the *McLaurin* case. George W. McLaurin, a sixty-three-year-old black man, was earning a doctorate at the University of Oklahoma. When he went to the university cafeteria or to the library, he had to sit at a separate table, apart from the white students. A photograph shows McLaurin sitting outside his classroom, listening to the same lecture as the white students inside the room. In his decision, Chief Justice Vinson again argued that such a separate education could not be equal, because of that very important intangible element. After these two decisions were issued, Thurgood Marshall, legal counsel with the NAACP and later a Supreme Court justice himself, said, "The complete destruction of all enforced segregation is now in sight."[25]

Seven weeks before the end of his term, Truman's Justice Department filed a very compelling amicus brief in the *Brown* case. This case took almost five years to reach a decision. Its origins are in the words of the Truman administration and the Vinson court, and it took its general shape before Truman left office. When it was finally decided in 1954, Chief Justice Earl Warren in his opinion cited only two cases—*Sweatt v. Painter* and *McLaurin v. Oklahoma State Regents,* both written by Truman's very good friend Fred Vinson. Warren wrote

> In *Sweatt v. Painter*...in finding that a segregated law school for Negroes could not provide them equal educational opportunities, this Court relied in large part on "those qualities which are incapable of objective measurement but which make for greatness in a law school." In *McLaurin v. Oklahoma State Regents,* ...the Court, in requiring that a Negro admitted to a white graduate school be treated like all other students, again resorted to intangible considerations: "...his ability to study, to engage in discussions and exchange views with other students, and, in general, to learn his profession." Such considerations apply with added force to children in grade and high schools. To separate them from others of similar age and qualifications solely because of their race generates a feeling of inferiority as to their status in the community and may affect their hearts and in a way unlikely to ever be undone.[26]

Although Truman still had a Democratic Congress to work with during his last two years in office, he was unable to get any substantial civil rights legislation passed. Nonetheless, he continued to do what he could through executive action, and he used his presidential pulpit to argue again and again that equality for the races must become a reality in America. When he left office on 20 January 1953, his popularity rating was only 31 percent. That did not bother him, however, at least partly because he knew his civil rights program had taken root, and there was no turning back for Americans, regardless of their race.

Truman's civil rights achievements did not end with his presidency. They have continued to accumulate in the achievements of Martin Luther King Jr., John Lewis, Dorothy Height, and many others who experienced, because of President Truman's work on behalf of civil rights, a new level of expectation as to what their rights are under the Constitution. All this started because high-school-educated Harry Truman knew in his heart and soul that civil rights equality was a moral imperative that had to be pursued regardless of the political consequences.

Notes

[1] McCullough, *Truman,* 31–32, 385; and Miller, *Plain Speaking,* 78.

[2] "Klan at Convention Hall," *Jackson* (MO) *Examiner,* 13 July 1922; and "Klan Puts Out Ticket," *Independence* (MO) *Examiner,* 6 November 1922.

[3] President's Committee on Civil Rights, *To Secure These Rights,* 87–95.

[4] National Committee on Segregation in the Nation's Capital, *Segregation in Washington,* 6.

[5] President's Committee on Civil Rights, *To Secure These Rights,* 68–69.

[6] President's Committee on Civil Rights, *To Secure These Rights,* 44–45.

[7] Frederickson, 54–56.

[8] White, *A Man Called White,* 331; and Truman to Tom Clark, 20 September 1946, Niles Papers, Truman Library.

[9] "Police Chief Freed in Negro Beating," *New York Times,* 6 November 1946.

[10] Truman, Remarks to the President's Committee on Civil Rights, 15 January 1947, in *Public Papers of the Presidents, Truman, 1947,* 98–99.

[11] Truman to Mary Jane Truman, 28 June 1947. Truman Papers, Post Presidential Papers, Memoirs File, Truman Library; and Clifford, *Counsel to the President,* 73.

[12] Truman, Address Before the NAACP, 29 June 1947, in *Public Papers of the President, Truman, 1947,* 311–13.

[13] Gross, "Truman Sees Rights Report as 'Human Freedom Charter,'" *Washington Post,* 30 October 1947.

[14] Truman, Annual Message to the Congress on the State of the Union, 7 January 1948, in *Public Papers of the Presidents, Truman, 1948,* 3.

[15] Gallup Organization, "How do you feel about Truman's Civil Rights Program?" 5 April, 1948.

[16] Truman personal writing, undated. Longhand Notes File, President's Secretary's Files, Truman Papers, Truman Library.

[17] See "Truman and the Vinson Court," in Gardner, *Harry Truman and Civil Rights,* 163–97.

[18] Quoted in Berman, *Politics of Civil Rights,* 110–11.

[19] Truman, Address in Philadelphia Upon Accepting the Nomination of the Democratic National Convention, 15 July 1948, in *Public Papers of the Presidents, Truman, 1948,* 408–9; and SR61-28, a sound recording of the speech, audiovisual collection, Truman Library.

[20] Gardner, *Harry Truman and Civil Rights,* 98–99.

[21] Ernie Roberts to Truman, [14 August 1948], and Truman to Roberts, 18 August 1948, Personal File, President's Secretary's Files, Truman Papers, Truman Presidential Library.

[22] Clifford, *Counsel to the President,* 234–35.

[23] Truman, Address in Harlem, New York, Upon Receiving the Franklin Roosevelt Award, 29 October 1948, in *Public Papers of the Presidents, Truman, 1948*, 923–25.

[24] *Henderson v. United States*, 339 U.S. 816 (1950).

[25] *Sweatt v. Painter*, 339 U.S. 629 (1950); *McLaurin v. Oklahoma State Regents*, 339 U.S. 637 (1950); and "Made Illegal by 3 Rulings," *Baltimore Afro-American*, 17 June 1950.

[26] *Brown v. Board of Education*, 347 U.S. 483 (1954), 5.

CLUTCHING AT CIVIL RIGHTS STRAWS
A Reappraisal of the Truman Years and the Struggle for African American Citizenship

Carol Anderson

In many ways, President Truman's record on civil rights, in an era of entrenched Jim Crow and lynching, is impressive. Entire books have been dedicated to understanding how a man who emerged from rural roots in a former slaveholding state with cities blackened by redlining and educational institutions left ignorant by racial segregation could have deigned to desegregate the military, ordered the integration of the federal bureaucracy, and commanded his Justice Department to support a series of lawsuits designed to break Jim Crow. Truman's stature is enhanced further when he is compared to his predecessor, Franklin Delano Roosevelt, whose dubious civil rights record left a trail of racial debris strewn from Claude Neal's branded, dismembered body to the internment camps of Manzanar. Truman becomes even more impressive when placed next to his Republican successor, Dwight D. Eisenhower, who "personally wished that the Court had upheld *Plessy v. Ferguson*" and reputedly said that the "biggest damn fool mistake" he had ever made was "the appointment of that dumb son of a bitch Earl Warren" as chief justice. Is it any wonder that Truman has emerged in a pantheon occupied by only Abraham Lincoln and maybe Lyndon Johnson?[1]

Yet, is the racially checkered history of Missouri, FDR, and Eisenhower really the appropriate baseline to use when assessing presidential commitment to safeguarding and protecting the constitutional rights of American citizens? What happens if the standard is set at a higher and more relevant level, such as ensuring the protection of constitutional rights and liberties for all American citizens, even those still bearing the scars of centuries of enslavement and more than fifty years of Jim Crow? That is to say, what happens if Truman's courage in the face of Southern opposition is viewed not in terms of the Dixiecrats' power, but in terms of the federal government wielding its power—the power it was so willing to use in Greece and Turkey—to ensure that the rights of American citizens, even those in Mississippi and South Carolina, were also protected? This fundamental assertion about the federal government's political, legal, and moral obligation to protect the civil rights of African Americans is not revolutionary or new. There had already been a long-standing belief among civil rights proponents, stretching back to antebellum days, that "African Americans had rights as national citizens, whether their states recognized them as state citizens or not."[2]

Of course, by the time Truman had assumed the presidency in April 1945, World War II had already transformed this long-standing belief into a firestorm of discontent within the African American community. Author Pearl S. Buck warned, "The deep patience of colored peoples is at an end. Everywhere among them is the same resolve for freedom and equality that white Americans...have, but it is a firmer resolve, for it includes the determination to be rid of white rule and exploitation and white race prejudice, and nothing will weaken this will." Buck had only articulated what Philleo Nash, an administrator in the Office of War Information and soon to be minority affairs expert in the Truman White House, reported. "Negroes," he warned, "are in a militant and demanding mood."[3]

Black Americans, already hardened by the false promises of World War I, were not going to be denied. Not this time. They were determined that World War II, unlike the previous one, would result in the total destruction of Jim Crow and the second- and third-class citizenship that came with it. They were determined that, after hundreds of years in the United States, they would finally gain their rightful place as American citizens. They had more than met the "obligation" requirements of citizenship by, at minimum, their service in the military and in the national defense industries. They had also clearly met the "being born on American soil" requirement. Thus, African Americans' concept of citizenship was not some theoretical, philosophical, epistemological exercise. Even "people unversed in legal complexity," historian Linda Kerber noted, "understand that they are entitled to free speech, to a right against self-incrimination, to religious freedom, to a jury trial, to the vote."

Civil rights advocate Harry T. Moore, who would eventually be killed by the Klan, was even more explicit: "We seek merely the fundamental rights of American citizenship, equality of opportunities, equal protection of the law, justice in the courts, and free participation in the affairs of our government."[4]

Coming out of World War II, however, black America was anything but equal. A series of lynchings, each seemingly more graphic and gruesome than the one before, bathed the United States in blood. Housing shortages, exacerbated by the mass migration of African Americans into the urban areas, piled one black body on top of the other in tightly segregated, geographically constrained, and decaying inner cities. And then there was the South, where nearly 75 percent of all black Americans still lived, but only a small number could even dare to vote.

Truman and his administrative team grasped, and even acknowledged, that there was a problem, a very serious problem. The president said that "we have only recently completed a long and bitter war against intolerance and hatred.... Yet, in this country today," he lamented, "there exists disturbing evidence of intolerance and prejudice similar in kind, though perhaps not in degree, to that against which we fought the war." Truman further confessed to former first lady Eleanor Roosevelt that the virulent racism coursing through the United States reminded him, in so many unsettling ways, of Nazi Germany.[5] He was not alone.

African Americans had earlier made that connection. They looked at Hitler's Germany and saw something distinctly, painfully familiar. In 1941, after reviewing a series of Nazi edicts on such issues as the sterilization of mulatto babies (the so-called Rhineland bastards) and the application of the discriminatory Nuremberg Laws to German's black population, *Pittsburgh Courier* journalist George Schuyler remarked that "what struck me...was that the Nazi plan for Negroes approximates so closely what seems to be the American plan for Negroes." Roy Wilkins, assistant secretary of the National Association for the Advancement of Colored People (NAACP), wrote in a nationally published editorial that "the South approaches more nearly than any other section of the United States the Nazi idea of government by a 'master race' without interference from any democratic process." Wilkins further believed that "the major difference between the racism of the two countries was that the national government of the United States did not use its machinery against blacks, it was merely indifferent toward their fate."[6]

With Truman now at the helm, however, that was supposed to change. The president stood before the NAACP at its 1947 annual convention and asserted that the United States had "reached a turning point" in guaranteeing the constitutional rights of "freedom and equality to all its citizens." The impetus for this change was clear. Nazi tyranny followed by the rapid onset of the Cold War and Soviet totalitarianism had made it "more important today than ever before to insure that all Americans enjoy these rights. And," Truman emphasized, "when I say all Americans—I mean all Americans." Truman then insisted that the "extension of civil rights today means, not [only] the protection of the people *against* the Government, but protection of the people *by* the Government. We must," he concluded, "make the Federal Government a friendly, vigilant defender of the rights and equalities of all Americans. And again I mean all Americans." He reaffirmed that commitment when he told the graduates at Howard University's commencement, "The full force and power of the federal government must stand behind the protection of rights guaranteed by our federal constitution."[7]

This would be no small feat. The federal government was, at its best, a disinterested bystander in the systematic denial of African Americans' constitutional rights. Unfortunately, in far too many instances, it was also a willing accomplice. To compound the problem, the arm of government that seemed the most likely candidate to become the "vigilant defender" that Truman envisioned, the Civil Rights Section of the Department of Justice, was structurally, philosophically, and, to some degree, legally ill-equipped to take on the job.

By 1950, the Civil Rights Section had "only six attorneys," which was the same staffing level it had "at its inception" a decade earlier. Yet these same six "received between 12,000 and 13,000 complaints" in 1950 alone and could easily expect up to 20,000 allegations of civil rights violations in any year. Moreover, the section had no independent investigative wing and, therefore, relied on the Federal Bureau of Investigation (FBI) to determine the veracity of the facts alleged in the complaints. The FBI, however, was the wrong agency, at the wrong time, at the wrong place, for the wrong job. Its director, J. Edgar Hoover, had an intense disdain for civil rights and blacks, and that antipathy shaped the culture and operating code of the bureau for decades. In addition, because the bureau "in most other aspects of its work...cooperated closely with local officials and was unwilling to alienate them," the FBI's investigations were often perfunctory and superficial, especially if the sheriff or police were named in the complaint. Finally, because much of the investigation "had to take place within the Negro community...the nearly all white FBI" had neither "a good rapport with the Southern black man" nor the necessary "training or experience in conducting" civil rights investigations to be effective. Indeed, in the late 1940s, the FBI "had only three black agents," none of whom were really G-Men.[8]

Adding to the section's structural weakness was its dependence on the apparatus of U.S. attorneys to prosecute cases. Because these lawyers, although officially tied to the Department of Justice, were political appointees chosen from the local areas, they often carried the value system of their community—even if that community was in defiance of the Constitution. Therefore, even when the section could build the type of airtight case that had become its standard for prosecution, the U.S. attorneys would, on far too many occasions, refuse to prosecute. As a result, during Truman's administration, of more than 13,000 complaints received annually, the Civil Rights Section only moved forward on an average of twenty per year.[9]

The section's efficacy was further undermined both by the limits of its statutory authority to protect civil rights and by its decidedly narrow interpretation of that authority. The first part of the problem was that only two statutes, created during Reconstruction, survived a series of Supreme Court decisions in the late nineteenth century. Those court decisions effectively gutted most of the laws Congress had passed to ensure political equality for the freedmen. One surviving statute, section 51, made "it a crime for two or more persons to conspire to 'injure, oppress, threaten, or intimidate any citizen in the free exercise or enjoyment of any right or privilege secured to him by the Constitution or laws of the United States.'" The other, section 52, made "it a crime for anyone, acting under color of law, willfully to subject any inhabitant to a deprivation of 'any rights, privileges, or immunities' secured or protected by the Constitution or laws of the United States or to different punishment, pains or penalties than are prescribed for the punishment of citizens." Section 51 was clearly aimed at a *conspiracy* to deprive citizens of their constitutional rights, and section 52 went after public officials, such as sheriffs and law enforcement officers, who violated the dictates of due process, equal protection, and other rights that all citizens enjoy. The Civil Rights Section staff, however, looked at these two statutes and saw only "'slender reeds upon which to lean' in the enforcement program." Those "slender reeds" were whittled down further when, in June 1948, sections 51 and 52 were replaced by sections 241 and 242. The point of tweaking the civil rights statutes, unfortunately, was not to strengthen these laws but to make them more palatable and acceptable to the South. Attorney General Tom Clark, therefore, further reinforced the staff's sense of ineffectiveness when he insisted that the federal government's ability to protect the rights of African Americans "hung on 'a very thin thread of law.'" One attorney in the section went on to explain why the results were so limited during the Truman years. The attorneys only had these "two small statutes to work with," she said, and because it was not clear which rights were protected under the Constitution anyway, the staff determined that the best way to proceed was with "caution and restraint." Unpersuaded and, frankly, outraged, Walter White, secretary of the NAACP, did not see caution and restraint in the Civil Rights Section's actions; he saw downright timidity. He railed that instead of using the authority it did possess, the "federal machinery for justice" demonstrated an uncanny ability to just "collapse" in the face of southern opposition.[10]

Nowhere was this opposition more consistent, more insistent, and more in direct violation of not only the Constitution but also the civil rights statues and the Supreme Court's *Yarbrough* and *Smith v. Allwright* decisions than in the denial to African Americans of the right to vote. Beginning in the 1890s, the South had erected a series of barriers that essentially blocked all but a relative handful of African Americans from voting. The extrication of black Americans from the voting process was designed to abrogate their citizenship and reassert legalized white supremacy. It was more than effective.

A lethal combination of poll taxes, election-day terrorism, white primaries, literacy tests, and "understanding" clauses had done their damage. The understanding clause, for example, permitted an often uneducated election official to reject potential African American voters because they could not interpret the state constitution to the registrar's satisfaction or answer a question such as "How many bubbles are there in a bar of soap?" Then there was the poll tax. States such as Mississippi and South Carolina had applied this financial screw so effectively that voter turnout rates there were nearly 50 percent *below* the national average in both the 1944 and 1948 presidential elections.[11]

The use of sheer terror was, of course, not out of the question either. The "South's white supremacists," historian Glenn Feldman noted, "were not about to surrender the region without a fierce struggle." Alabama, for example, had already passed the Boswell Amendment, a master compendium of understanding clauses and disfranchisement tools, but for white Alabamians it was still not enough. "Postwar Alabama was...tense," Feldman wrote. "Klan violence was part and parcel of a situation in which black assertiveness [and] voting registration efforts...clashed with determined white reaction." One elderly Southern man thus "greeted news of the [resurgence of the] Klan by saying 'This will teach the niggers to stay put in their place. If they don't we'll stack 'em up like cordwood.'"[12] That was no idle threat.

Georgia's gubernatorial candidate, Eugene Talmadge, for example, "campaigned largely on the issue of 'keep the niggers where they belong.'" He insisted that "if the good white people will explain it to the negroes around the state just right I don't think they will want to vote." Talmadge's clarion call, as intended, was deadly and resulted in at least five black corpses within a month.[13]

As a result of this cocktail of barely legal and extralegal disfranchisement, in 1944 there were no blacks registered as Democrats in the entire state of Florida. In Bilbo's Mississippi of 1946, where nearly half the population was black, the percentage of voting-age African Americans who actually went to the polls was barely .001. Mississippi was so bad and the problem had been allowed to fester for so long that the state "permitted fewer blacks to vote for Lyndon Baines Johnson in 1964 than had been eligible to vote for William McKinley in 1896." Given the unrelenting violence and "perils of democracy" faced by blacks determined to vote, one civil rights worker could only describe America's Mississippi as "the land of the tree and the home of the grave."[14]

When confronted with this vicious denial of constitutional rights, "the Negro could look only to Washington, where," unfortunately, "he found little help before 1965." In the late 1940s and early 1950s, the Civil Rights Section continually ran for cover behind the rationale that the Department of Justice had little or no statutory authority to intervene. Department officials insisted, "Under present laws...the Justice Department cannot prosecute until a voter has been denied the right to vote on Election Day. It cannot take civil action in advance against individual acts or conspiracies to deprive citizens of their voting rights." Thus, Bilbo's plan to keep blacks away from the polls the night *before* found more than sufficient legal cover in the Justice Department's interpretation of the law. This formula for inaction was tailor-made for ignoring reprisals—*after* the election—as well. Therefore, when a black man who had just voted had to flee the state of Florida and go into hiding after whites firebombed his home, the Justice Department held firm that "an investigation of this complaint has failed to disclose...any connection between this explosion and the attempted intimidation of the Negroes who voted" and, as a consequence, "no further action would be taken."[15]

As one scholar noted, African Americans' "only hope" to assert their franchise rights "lay in federal intervention, and for over eighty years the federal government had failed to act." This was despite the fact that President Truman had identified the protection of the vote against "organized terrorism" and "mob violence" as absolutely essential for a working democracy. This was also despite the fact that the President's Committee on Civil Rights (PCCR) asserted in its landmark report, *To Secure These Rights,* that "interference with the right of a qualified citizen to vote locally cannot today remain a local problem.... Can it be doubted that this is a right which the national government must make secure?" Yet, despite all this concern, which was buttressed by a recommendation from the PCCR that the Civil Rights Section be strengthened to meet its responsibilities, nothing of significance was done.[16]

The Civil Rights Section's studied inaction certainly undercut Truman's call to make the federal government a "vigilant defender" of the Constitution. Yet, when it came to the critical issue of housing and home ownership, the federal government threw off its sackcloth of timidity and impotence and became a strong, vigilant defender—of racial segregation, discrimination, and the creation of black, impoverished, resource-deprived slums.

During the Great Depression, when the private mortgage industry was on the verge of collapse because of the banking crisis, the federal government, under the New Deal, stepped in and created an agency to throw Washington's power and financial resources behind a plan to increase home ownership for Americans. In 1937, this agency was supplanted by the Federal Housing Administration (FHA), whose "mortgage insurance eliminated the lending institution's risk in providing mortgage financing for properties meeting FHA standards." This allowed for lower down payments, longer loan periods, and, thus, much more affordable monthly payments. "Within a year of its creation, FHA was insuring 40 percent of new home mortgages. Home building had doubled and mortgage costs were at an all-time low."[17]

There was a horrible downside to this success story, however. The FHA was "staffed by 'the very financial and real estate interests and institutions which led the campaign to spread racial covenants and residential segregation'" and their professional code of conduct was explicit in demanding the perpetuation of racially segregated neighborhoods: "A Realtor should never be instrumental in introducing into a neighborhood a character of property or occupancy, members of any race or nationality, or any individuals whose presence will clearly be detrimental to property values in that neighborhood." Thus, racial segregation and the undesirability of black people was the guiding principle of the FHA through, at least, the 1960s. In its 1939 *Underwriting Manual,* for example, the agency asserted that "if a neighborhood is to retain stability, it is necessary that properties shall continue to be occupied by the same social and racial classes." It was essential, the FHA continued, to not insert "inharmonious racial or nationality groups" into a community. Not surprisingly, then, "'Incompatible racial elements' was officially listed as a valid reason for rejecting a mortgage."[18]

This racialized vision of home ownership dictated the FHA's adoption of a four-tiered, color-coded rating system for neighborhoods, which made it clear where and under what circumstances lending institutions could expect to have their loans underwritten by the federal government. For example, those neighborhoods that had a majority of African American residents were automatically coded "red" and strictly off limits to FHA loans. Neighborhoods that abutted predominantly African American areas and appeared "in danger" of becoming black "virtually never received" federally underwritten loans. On the other hand, areas that were "new, homogenous"—that is, white—"and in demand in good times and bad" or areas that were stable and not threatened by black "invaders" consistently received federal support.[19]

Therefore, to maintain neighborhood stability and property values, the FHA, as part of its underwriting standard, demanded restrictive covenants. These covenants, which were enforced by the courts, required that white home owners could sell their homes only to other whites. That racial vise grip on the housing market was supposed to evaporate, however, under the heat of a searing Supreme Court decision in *Shelley v. Kraemer* (1948) in which the justices declared it unconstitutional to have the court system or other government authority enforce these racially restrictive covenants. Early on, the Truman administration weighed in on this decision as well, filing an amicus curiae brief in support of ending this discriminatory practice.[20]

Despite *Shelley,* restrictive covenants did not disappear. The FHA, the most important federal entity in shaping the residential housing market in the United States, deliberately ignored the ruling and "did not change" its open support of covenants until 1950. Even after that, the FHA still successfully adapted "an ongoing policy of racial separation" that allowed the agency to comply with the exact letter of the *Shelley* decision while defying the intent and spirit of the ruling.[21]

The FHA's actions redounded throughout America. Well into the 1960s, for example, "FHA procedures rendered whole cities ineligible for FHA-guaranteed loans simply because of a minority presence." Without the capital to upgrade or maintain properties, without the ability to find buyers who could afford to purchase a home without tapping into the largest, low-interest-rate mortgage pool in the nation, housing values plummeted "and a pattern of disrepair, deterioration, vacancy, and abandonment" came to define America's cities. The deteriorating housing stock and quality of life were, however, attributed directly to the black inhabitants of the area and served only to reify the FHA's rationale for redlining and white suburban home owners' convictions that the mere presence of African Americans drove down property values.[22]

Not only did private lenders follow the FHA's lead in mortgage lending, but so, too, did the Veterans Administration (VA). As a consequence, although Truman insisted, "We must house the veteran—and I mean every veteran," in 1950 nonwhites received only 2 percent of the VA's guaranteed mortgages. Thus, while the federal government, through the VA and FHA, "financed more than $120 billion worth of new housing between 1934 and 1962," less than 1 percent of all those loans went to African Americans.[23]

African Americans, on the other hand, expected that the "vigilant defender" in Truman's clarion call for justice would break them out of the rat-infested ghettoes that the FHA and VA had helped erect. Truman, in fact, was committed to addressing the serious housing shortage that plagued the United States after the war. That commitment resonated throughout his presidency, from his first State of the Union Address. He even issued executive orders "to the FHA to deny financial assistance to new housing projects with racial or religious restrictions."[24] Yet, just as the Civil Rights Section and the FBI were ill equipped to deal with the president's pledge to ensure the right to vote in the United States, so, too was the FHA unwilling to abide by Truman's directives for open housing.

Thus a public housing and urban renewal bill that was supposed to alleviate the housing crisis, particularly in the inner city, looked more like a "Negro removal" bill with "devastating" consequences. Faced with a growing throng of homeless, impoverished African Americans who had been uprooted and displaced by federal policy, the NAACP pushed Truman for a stronger and more effective executive order because the "problem was especially acute in several Southern and border-state communities where Negroes, displaced by slum clearance programs, could not find replacement dwellings." The White House's response was to ask for patience. The NAACP had none and went to its supporters in Congress for relief. The Truman administration immediately moved to block the NAACP's attempt to get fair housing legislation. The FHA, of course, had no intention of issuing any regulation that would provide for integrated housing and was characteristically "unresponsive."[25]

The Truman administration knew that the FHA was a problem—one that the administration had never truly dealt with. Nash wrote the president that "in 55 years [sic] of FHA operations, only 1.8 percent of FHA projects were available to Negroes, as compared to 35 percent of public housing projects." The results of FHA policy, Nash continued, were disastrous: "Washington is typical. Its suburbs are ringed with 'White Only' developments. Many of these are FHA financed. In the heart of D.C. is a handful of projects open to Negroes.... If this process is permitted to continue, our northern cities will grow into Negro 'downtowns' surrounded by white suburbs."[26]

No feature on the American scene, however, emphasized the bleakness, precariousness, and devaluation of black life more than the wave of lynching (legal and otherwise) that occurred after World War II. It was as if the usual suspects—Mississippi, Alabama, Georgia, South Carolina, Florida, Tennessee—rounded up their "usual suspects" and proceeded to try to push defiant, "uppity" African Americans back into their so-called proper, subordinate place in American society. Thus, when Leon McTatie was accused of stealing a saddle, six white Mississippians, reliving the glory days of the Old South, grabbed the wrongly accused man and "whipped [him] to death."[27] The brutality, of course, did not end there:

> In Alabama, when an African-American veteran removed the Jim
> Crow sign on a trolley, an angry streetcar conductor took aim and
> unloaded his pistol into the ex-Marine. As the wounded veteran

staggered off the tram and crawled away, the chief of police hunted him down and finished the job with a single bullet, execution style, to the head. In South Carolina, another veteran, who complained about the inanity of Jim Crow transportation, had his eyes gouged out with the butt of the sheriff's billy club. In Louisiana, a black veteran who defiantly refused to give a white man a war memento was partially dismembered, castrated, and blowtorched until his "eyes 'popped' out of his head and his light complexion was seared dark."[28]

As the body count soared, the NAACP demanded that the White House do something. If nothing else, these were veterans—men who had fought the Germans and the Japanese in the name and cause of democracy. Certainly, that democracy could now turn around and fight for them. But, once again, the Department of Justice could not discover that it had any jurisdiction in these cases.

Then came the unbelievable horror of Monroe, Georgia: four young African Americans—two couples—ambushed, defenseless, and facing a lynch mob armed with enough firepower for a small militia. The two black women became nothing more than collateral damage in a fatal lesson aimed at their husbands, whose behavior—one stabbed a white man for "messing" with his wife, while the other came back from the army thinking he was equal to any white man—spelled an unspeakable death. Historian Laura Wexler described the results after the mortician had done his best:

> At the far end of the row lay Roger Malcolm, his face pocked with the plaster of paris Dan Young [the mortician] had used to conceal the damage to his face. But nothing could hide the hole in Roger Malcolm's cheek. It was larger than a quarter, the result of a shotgun fired at close range. Dorothy's body lay next to Roger's, a bandage covering her face where the right side of her jaw had been blown away.... Next to Dorothy lay her brother George. His right was covered with a bandage—it had been shot out—and his right ear, which had been partially shot off, was attached by tape. And last in the row was Mae Murray Dorsey, whose...face, unlike the others, wasn't a record of her death.

Roger Malcolm was also castrated, "the privates halfway cut off, something kind of hanging." Mae Dorsey, who had miraculously kept her face, had her spine severed and her hands crushed as sixty bullets ripped through her body.[29]

Black America was shaken and outraged. African Americans understood the dogma of states' rights clearly enough; what was so difficult to understand, however, was the paralyzing limits that the federal government placed on itself even in its own domain. "Is not the South a part of the United States?" a Baptist minister angrily asked. Because surely there were some laws that even the South had to abide by when it came to the rights of American citizens. As far as the minister was concerned, the president acted as if he was "afraid to tell" the South "'that it is wrong to lynch human beings" and "helpless women." The Reverend Lyslee continued to seethe. "If we have a democracy what price do the Negroes have to pay for it?"[30]

The Department of Justice, however, was not up to the challenge. Two "assistant U.S. attorneys...visited Monroe on the day after the Moore's Ford lynching" to determine if sections 51 and/or 52 had been violated. When the sheriffs told them that they had no idea there was going to be a lynching, "the federal lawyers told a reporter 'they didn't think there had been a violation of any federal law. They didn't think the civil rights statutes would apply.'" Walter White warned Truman that "very dark days are ahead" because of the department's lackluster, abysmal performance. Getting away with murder, White explained, only emboldened those who preferred "the law of the jungle" to the rule of democracy.[31]

Truman was also outraged. This was not the democracy he knew and loved. He wanted the Justice Department to go back and investigate again. He ordered Attorney General Clark to "'push with everything you have' to determine if there has been a 'violation of any Federal statutes.'" Clark, however, returned empty-handed. They "just won't talk...we just couldn't get any citizens there to give us information, although we know they have it."[32]

It was at this point, disgusted by the killings in Georgia and "literally blue with anger when he heard that this returning veteran [Isaac Woodard] had been blinded on the way home from a camp from which he was discharged," that Truman ordered the creation of the President's Committee on Civil Rights. His administration assembled a high-powered team and an excellent support staff, who compiled an invaluable, detailed report. But that was pretty much the end of it. The PCCR did not have any authority, and its recommendations, for far too long, ended up in a Pandora's box surrounded by plagues, pestilence, and only a scintilla of hope.[33]

Few could ignore the horrific lynching of Willie Earle in South Carolina. Earle, epileptic and accused of stabbing a cab driver, was pulled out of a jail by more than twenty men, tortured, mutilated, and killed. "When the undertakers had finished," one journalist wrote, "I too found it hard to believe that a South Carolina mob, and not a gang of Nazis, had done this atrocious thing. Where there must have once been a right eye, there was only a socket.... Where once there was skin and bones on the left side of the face, there was only the undertaker's plaster trying to form a face."[34]

Once again the hue and cry for justice resounded all the way up Pennsylvania Avenue. Perhaps learning something from its initial sluggish response in Monroe, Georgia, when it took the president nearly a week to even mention the killings, the PCCR "immediately moved in on" the Willie Earle slaying, issued a press release, made it clear to the public that it was "'deeply concerned' over the lynching," and provided a progress report detailing the role of federal agents in investigating the case. Within a week of the killing, the PCCR chair reported, "State and local officers ha[d] arrested some twenty persons and ha[d] obtained confessions from twelve of these people." Because it was clear that "state authorities [were] making vigorous efforts to arrest and prosecute the guilty parties," the chairman of the PCCR offered that the Department of Justice would "make no effort to seek a federal indictment." Thus, although it seemed as if section 52 could come into play because Earle was pulled out of a jail, it was, in the PCCR's assessment, also clear that the deputy was "an elderly man" who did not appear to be a "party to a conspiracy." After all, the sixty-two-year-old jailer remarked, he was totally innocent of any wrongdoing. "They had shotguns and I danced to their music." So too, apparently, did the jury, which despite the grisly death, the detailed confessions, and the physical evidence, found all the murderers "not guilty."[35]

The fact that the verdict, which was "what one might have expected from twelve idiots in a madhouse," came shortly after Truman asked Congress for $400 million to bring democracy to Greece and Turkey, was more ironic and tragic than most could bear. Walter Reuther, the president of the United Auto Workers, denounced the jury's verdict as a "legal farce," one that would certainly come back to haunt the United States. "So long as lynch mobs are permitted to murder American citizens and go unpunished, these peoples of other nations will look with skepticism on our claim that we are the most democratic nation in the world." Once again, though, despite the high stakes, there was nothing the Justice Department could do.[36]

What so many understood as they watched the federal government's consistent inability to secure the vote, end housing discrimination, and protect American citizens, including veterans, from lynching, was that in contrast to the "caution and restraint" the Truman administration showed in dealing with the destructive forces engulfing the black community, its actions on the international stage were bold, innovative, and decisive. It was not as though the international problems ere less intractable, the opponents less formidable, or the goals more attainable. In fact, they were not. At that time, the international system was in absolute chaos. The old multipolar system, with Britain as power broker, was in rubble, and the wartime alliance with the Soviet Union had rapidly disintegrated. Faced with these seemingly insurmountable odds, Truman and his team devised strategies to cope with this new international situation. The administration not only did everything in its power to craft innovative programs, such as the Marshall Plan and the North Atlantic Treaty Organization (NATO), but it also removed ineffective or recalcitrant top administrators, such as Secretary of State James Byrnes and General Douglas MacArthur, and replaced them with those who shared the president's vision and determination to get things done and done right.

Except, of course, in the area of civil rights. There, helplessness, hopelessness, and mediocrity reigned. Not only were Truman's attorneys general—Tom Clark and J. Howard McGrath—lackluster, but they also shared many of the same traits, including a tendency to not "strain" themselves "in behalf of advancing Negro rights." Moreover, Truman's chief aide for minority affairs, David Niles, was also problematic. While he clearly saw his role as being the president's "ambassador" to liberal and Jewish organizations in New York, he was strikingly unconcerned about the condition of black Americans. The memos and letters that survived Niles's annual New Year's Day purge reveal a man who was contemptuous of African American leaders and the concerns they tried to bring to Truman's attention. In addition, Niles, from all accounts, had a "mania for anonymity" and "spent much of his time outside Washington." And when he was in the capital, he "slunk rather furtively around the corridors of the White House" and "alone among the senor Presidential assistants never attended HST's daily morning staff meeting." As a result, it was painfully "clear that the Minorities Office...was a rather isolated operation and, in that respect, rather different from the rest of the White House staff," which, Niles's key aide had to admit, "had its obvious disadvantages."[37] Yet, because the Cold War and black demands for citizenship had forced civil rights to the fore, the issue could not be totally ignored. Thus, "Negro affairs" became the province of Philleo Nash, who, unfortunately, did not have authority or access to make a significant impact. He therefore focused his efforts on working hard to develop among the black component of the New Deal coalition an "appreciation for the administration's 'good faith' efforts"—as opposed to actual accomplishments, which during the president's second term were virtually nil.[38]

At the end of his term as president, as he delivered his farewell address to the nation, Truman could only direct the nation's attention to the fact that his administration had at least put the issue of civil rights on the nation's agenda and had established the groundwork for change. "We have made progress in spreading the blessings of American life to all of our people," Truman asserted. There has been a tremendous awakening of the American conscience on the great issues of civil rights—equal economic opportunities, equal rights of citizenship, and equal educational opportunities for all our people, whatever their race or religion or status of birth." Yet, in truth, while there may have been some level of consciousness-raising, the actual attainment of civil rights, given the persistence of disfranchisement, lynching, and housing discrimination, left those facing the onslaught of Jim Crow wondering when this vaunted "progress" would finally catch up to them.[39]

In 1968, a group of scholars came together to discuss the Truman legacy on civil rights and met, by sheer happenstance, the day after Martin Luther King Jr. was assassinated and America's urban landscape became a smoldering inferno. Against this hellish backdrop the scholars discussed what Truman had accomplished and the various reasons he could not have done more. These included the power of the southern Democrats and the fact that, above all else, he was a "party man" and realized that to push too hard for civil rights would destroy the Democratic Party. But one scholar, acknowledging the external pressures on Truman, kept asking why the president did not do more in those areas where he had greater control. Why were there no appointments in the Department of Justice where the need was obviously so great? Why, Professor Flint Kellogg kept asking, did Truman seemingly find "it easier to move to integration in the armed forces than he did within the administration itself? What was the block here? Usually you'd think that would cause less uproar if he moved within administrative agencies than within the armed forces."[40]

In 1948, the labor secretary of the NAACP, Clarence Mitchell, had asked virtually the same question. But because Truman had at least done what no other modern president had, the association leadership decided that the man from Missouri, "though far from perfect," was still the best that black people could get under the circumstances.[41] That tendency to accept less and to clutch at civil rights straws as if they are the silk threads of democracy has created an anomaly in American society in the area of civil rights (and only in the area of civil rights), where the mere act of trying—and not necessarily succeeding—becomes more than enough. At some point, as a democracy, we must realize it is not.

Notes

[1] Ambrose, *Eisenhower,* 2:190.

[2] Michael Les Benedict, *The Blessings of Liberty* (1996), quoted in Kerber, "The Meanings of Citizenship," 835n6.

[3] Buck quoted in Lauren, *Evolution of International Human Rights,* 154; Philleo Nash to Jonathan Daniels, December 16, 1943, OWI Files, Alphabetical File—Race Tension—Jonathan Daniels File—Memoranda Nash to Daniels, 1942-45; and "Attachment No. 1: Factors affecting Negro attitudes towards the war," Fragment of report, Box 55, WH Files—Minorities—Negro Attitudes Toward War, Nash Papers, Truman Library.

[4] Wynn, "Impact of the Second World War on the American Negro," 44, 49; Sugrue, "Crabgrass-Roots Politics," 551-78; Moore quoted in Emmons, "'Somebody Has Got to Do That Work,'" 238; Cox, "Programs of Negro Civil Rights Organizations," 354; Hale, *Making Whiteness,* 19; Ottley, *New World A-Coming,* 306-26.

[5] Truman to Charles G. Bolte, August 28, 1946, Official File 93, May–December 1946 [2 of 2], Truman Papers, Truman Library; Truman to Eleanor Roosevelt, December 12, 1945, File Harry S. Truman, 1945-1948, Papers of Eleanor Roosevelt, Franklin D. Roosevelt Presidential Library, Hyde Park, NY.

[6] Quoted in Grill and Jenkins, "Nazis and the American South in the 1930s," 690, 675, 689.

[7] President Truman's Speech before the Annual Convention of the NAACP, press release, June 28, 1947, Official File 413 (1945-1949), Truman papers (emphasis in original); and commencement statement quoted in Johnson, "Vinson Court," 221-22.

[8] Washington, "Program of the Civil Rights Section," 343-44; Lichtman, "Federal Assault," 348-49; O'Reilly, *Racial Matters,* 29.

[9] *To Secure These Rights,* 120-22; and Washington, "Civil Rights Section," 344-45.

[10] Washington, "Civil Rights Section," 335-38; Clark quoted in Dray, *Hands of Persons Unknown,* 452; Eleanor Bontecou oral history, Truman Library; Washington, "Civil Rights Section," 342-43; Walter White to Mrs. (Marian Wynn) Perry, October 4, 1946, Box B112, File Perry, Marion Wynn, 1945-1949, Legal, NAACP Papers; and Walter White to Truman, telegram, June 15, 1946, Official File 93, May–December 1946 [1 of 2], Truman Papers. I thank professor of law and former attorney in the Civil Rights Division of the Department of Justice Michael Middleton for his help with and insight on the statutes.

[11] Lewis, "Negro Voter in Mississippi," 338; *To Secure These Rights,* 38; and Anderson, *Eyes Off the Prize,* 80.

[12] Feldman, "Soft Opposition," 756, 757.

[13] Talmadge quoted in Anderson, *Eyes Off the Prize,* 63; and "Resolution on Terrorism in the South: Adopted by Pacific States Council of Furniture Workers," August 10-11, 1946, Official File 93a, Truman Papers.

[14] Emmons, "'Somebody Has Got to Do That Work,'" 235; Lewis, "Negro Voter in Mississippi," 333; McMillen, "Black Enfranchisement in Mississippi," 352, 354.

[15] McMillen, "Black Enfranchisement," 354; Justice officials quoted in Lewis, "Negro Voter in Mississippi," 349; and Emmons, "'Somebody Has Got to Do That Work,'" 240.

[16] Lichtman, "Federal Assault," 346; Harry Truman to Walter White, June 6, 1946, File N (Folder 1), Nash Files, Truman Papers; and *To Secure These Rights,* 101.

[17] Orfield, "Federal Policy, Local Power, and Metropolitan Segregation," 785.

[18]Brown, "Access to Housing," 68; Massey and Denton, *American Apartheid,* 54; and Orfield, "Federal Policy," 786.

[19]Massey and Denton, *American Apartheid,* 51; Vaughan, "The City and the American Creed," 57.

[20]Kluger, *Simple Justice,* 252–53; and Dudziak, "Desegregation," 101, 105–6, 118.

[21]Brown, "Access to Housing," 66; and Orfield, "Federal Policy," 788.

[22]Massey and Denton, *American Apartheid,* 54–55; and Sugrue, "Crabgrass-Roots Politics," 561.

[23]Truman to Walter White, June 6, 1946, Gile N (Folder 1), Nash Files, Truman Papers; Orfield, "Federal Policy," 785, 788–89; Lipsitz, *Possessive Investment in,* 6; and Conley, *Being Black, Living in the Red,* 37.

[24]McCullough, *Truman,* 468, 470, 532, 586, 591, 628, 634, 642, 651, 666, 758, 915.

[25]Orfield, "Federal Policy," 788; Pika, "Interest Groups," 665–66.

[26]Pika, "Interest Groups," 665–66.

[27]"Lynching Record for 1946: Chronological Listing," n.d., File Lynching: Lynching Record, 1946–1952, NAACP Papers.

[28]Anderson, *Eyes Off the Prize,* 58.

[29]Wexler, *Fire in a Canebrake,* 87–88; and Anderson, *Eyes Off the Prize,* 59.

[30]Sammye T. Lewis to Truman, telegram, July 27, 1946; and Rev. Wm. Lyslee to Harry S. Truman, telegram, July 26, 1946, Official File 93a, Lynching of (4) Negroes at Monroe, GA, July 25, 1946, Truman Papers.

[31]Wexler, *Fire in a Canebrake,* 111; Walter White to Truman, telegram, July 26, 1946, Official File 93a, Lynching of (4) Negroes at Monroe, GA, July 25, 1946, Truman Papers; and Walter White to Eleanor Roosevelt, telegram, September 18, 1946, File NAACP, 1945-1947, Roosevelt Papers.

[32]Anderson, *Eyes Off the Prize,* 61; and "Tom Clark's Testimony to the President's Committee on Civil Rights," Record Group 220, Papers of the President's Committee on Civil Rights, Truman Library.

[33]*Conference of Scholars on the Truman Administration and Civil Rights,* 20.

[34]"Negro Veteran Mutilated by Mississippi Mob," March 6, 1947, WH Files—Minorities—Negro—General—Lynching—Newsclipping—1946-1947; and B. M. Phillips, "Mob Victim's Mother Sobs Out Tale of Woe," [Baltimore] *Afro-American,* March 1, 1947, WH Files—Minorities—Negro—General—Lynching—Newsclipping—Willie Earle South Carolina, Feb.-Mar. 1947, Nash Papers, Truman Library.

[35]Wexler, *Fire in a Canebrake,* 113; David K. Niles to Matt [Connelly], memo, February 19, 1947, Civil Rights/ Negro Affairs 1945-June 1947, Niles Papers; "President Truman's Civil Rights Committee Watches S.C. Lynching: Closest Attention Being Given, Chairman States," [Atlanta] *Daily World,* February 23, 1947, WH Files—Minorities—Negro—General—Lynching—Newsclipping—Willie Early South Carolina, Feb.-Mar. 1947, Nash Papers; Robert K. Carr to All Members of the President's Committee on Civil Rights, memo, February 21, 1947, Civil Rights/Negro Affairs 1945-June 1947, Niles Papers; and "South Carolina Negro First Lynch Victim of 1947," *P.M.,* Feb.-Mar. 1947, WH files—Minorities—Negro—General—Lynching—Newsclipping—Willie Earle South Carolina, Feb.-Mar. 1947, Nash Papers.

[36]Ted Le Berthon, "White Man's Views: Wrong for Acquitted Lynchers to Believe They are Christians," *Pittsburgh Courier,* June 21, 1947, WH Files—Minorities—Negro—General—Lynching—Newsclipping—Willie Earle South Carolina, Feb.-Mar. 1947, Nash Papers; and Walter Reuther to the President, telegram, May 27, 1947, Official File 93a, Truman Papers.

[37] Kluger, *Simple Justice,* 277; Pika, "Interest Groups," 651–52; Heller, *Truman White House,* 52–56; David K. Niles to Matthew J. Connelly, January 6, 1947 [*sic*], Official File 93, 1948 [1of 3], Truman Papers; and Stephen J. Spingarn to Donald R. McCoy, memo, April 4, 1969, Civil Rights File—Civil Rights Correspondence Regarding—under Truman Administration, Spingarn Papers, Truman Library.

[38] Heller, *White House,* 54; Pika, "Interest Groups," 665; McCoy and Ruetten, *Quest and Response,* 148–49, 171–200; Berman, *Politics of Civil Rights,* 137–81; G. L. Bishop to Truman, July 8, 1949, Official File 93b, July–December 1949 [2 of 2], Truman Papers; "The 40th Annual NAACP Conference," by Edward Strong and William Taylor, and Roy Wilkins to Officers of Branches/State Conference/Youth Councils and College Chapters, memo, October 21, 1949, Edward Strong Papers, Moorland-Spingarn Research Center, Howard University, Washington DC; and Walter White, press release, April 3, 1952, Official File 413 (1950–1953), Truman Papers.

[39] King, *Where Do We Go From Here,* 8.

[40] *Conference of Scholars,* ed. McCoy, Ruetten, and Fuchs, 10, 18, 22, 25, 28, 32–34.

[41] Clarence Mitchell to Walter White, May 20, 1948, File Harry S. Truman, 1946-1949, and Alfred Baker Lewis to Walter White, December 19, 1947, File Wallace, Henry A.—General, 1945-1948, NAACP Papers; Claude Barnet to Channing Tobias, April 10, 1948, and Channing Tobias to Philleo Nash, March 29, 1948, File T (Folder 1), Nash Files, Truman Papers; and Oral history interview with William H. Hastie, January 5, 1972, Truman Library.

TRUMAN LAID THE FOUNDATION FOR THE CIVIL RIGHTS MOVEMENT

Ken Hechler

Harry Truman was conditioned by his youthful environment and family influence to grow up as a racist. Both of his grandfathers, Anderson Shipp Truman and Solomon Young, were unabashed slaveholders who used their slaves as cheap labor on their farms. Truman's mother, Martha Ellen, whom he adored and who taught him to love music and good literature, hated the Great Emancipator, Abraham Lincoln, and always regarded John Wilkes Booth as a hero, feelings resulting from her horrifying experiences during the Civil War, when her family's farm in Jackson County, Missouri was raided several times and her family was put in an internment camp.

When Truman first entered politics in the early 1920s as a candidate for judge (county commissioner) for the eastern district of Jackson County, Missouri, he thought at first he would join the politically powerful Ku Klux Klan, but then refused when the Klan recruiter tried to make him sign a pledge not to hire Roman Catholics. Truman had learned during his time as captain of Battery D during World War I to respect the rowdy Catholic boys from Kansas City who served under him. He would sign no pledge that would have excluded them from getting jobs.

Once he became county judge, and thus also an agent of the Pendergast political machine that ruled Kansas City, Truman was moved by the condition of the poverty-stricken African Americans whom he recruited as political cannon fodder who would vote as they were told to vote by the Pendergast machine. Even so, he was apparently content that blacks were segregated into a slum known as Nigger Neck in his home town of Independence, Missouri, and he apparently used the word "nigger" routinely, probably following the custom of most of his friends and neighbors. He probably also routinely used other words that today would be regarded as ethnic slurs, and he once wrote to his future wife, Bess Wallace, that he was "strongly of the opinion that negroes ought to be in Africa, yellow men in Asia, and white men in Europe and America."[1] Yet despite his racist background, Harry Truman emerged as a champion of civil rights who during his presidency accomplished much and foreshadowed much more.

Southern Democrats who had supported Truman's candidacy for vice president in 1944 were shocked when, shortly after becoming president on 12 April 1945, he wrote a public letter to the House Rules Committee seeking release of a bottled-up bill to make the wartime Fair Employment Practices Committee (FEPC) permanent. In this letter, Truman stated bluntly, "Discrimination in the matter of employment against properly qualified persons because of their race, creed, or color is not only un-American in nature, but will lead eventually to industrial strife and unrest."[2]

Any remaining doubts regarding Truman's position on civil rights were removed by his hard-hitting, sixteen-thousand-word message to Congress on 6 September 1945. Among a great many proposals for legislation contained in this message, Truman spelled out his strong and continued support for a permanent FEPC. Calling attention to the committee's wartime effectiveness in helping to remove or prevent "many of the injustices based upon considerations of race, religion, and color," he requested the Congress to take action "to continue this American ideal." The reaction was hostile, as most Republicans joined with racist Southern Democrats to block the legislation.[3] Congress also declined to pass legislation that would realize Truman's proposals to raise the standards of education, employment, health care, and housing for all Americans. These proposals, reformulated and resubmitted to later Congresses, would come collectively to be known as the "Fair Deal."

Truman suffered another serious setback to his program ambitions during the 1946 midterm elections. Chafing under wartime controls, labor unrest, and meat shortages, voters rallied to the Republican slogan of "Had enough? Vote Republican!" and dealt President Truman and his party a stinging defeat. Republicans captured control of both the House of Representatives and the Senate for the first time since 1928. Still, a month after the election, on 5 December 1946, Truman demonstrated his unflagging support for civil rights by issuing Executive Order 9808, which established the President's Committee on Civil Rights.

What inspired Truman to take this action? On 19 September 1946, he had met with a delegation of African American leaders representing the recently formed National Emergency Committee Against Mob Violence. These men described for Truman several horrifying incidents of lynching and racial violence against black veterans, in particular the beating and blinding of Isaac Woodard only three hours following his honorable discharge from the army. Woodard was attacked by Lynwood Lanier Shull, the police chief of Batesburg, South Carolina, who bragged publicly about what he had done. On 20 September 1946, the day after his meeting with the committee leaders, Truman wrote to his attorney general, Tom Clark, expressing alarm at "increased racial feeling all over the country" that was leading to violent incidents such as that involving Isaac Woodard. Six days later, Clark announced that criminal charges had been filed against Shull. In the end, however, an all-white jury acquitted Shull after deliberating for only thirty minutes."[4]

Truman was worried about more than this one terrible episode. In his 20 September letter to Attorney General Clark, he expressed his belief that dealing with acts of racial violence one at a time was not an effective strategy.

> I have been very much alarmed at the increased racial feeling all over the country, and I am wondering if it wouldn't be well to appoint a commission to analyze the situation and have a remedy to present to the next Congress....
>
> I think it is going to take something more than the handling of each individual case after it happens—it is going to require the inauguration of some sort of policy to prevent such happenings.[5]

Truman took several steps to ensure that the President's Committee on Civil Rights could be established and would be effective. Knowing Congress would not pass a law to authorize a civil rights committee, he created the committee by executive order and paid for it from his contingency fund. He appointed as chairman Charles E. Wilson, president of General Electric, who had been recommended to him by Walter White, head of the National Association for the Advancement of Colored People (NAACP). White felt that Wilson had a passion for good race relations. Truman appointed others to the committee who shared this passion, but no one who could be expected to be a defender of Jim Crow segregation. The members came from varied backgrounds, including business and labor leaders, two bishops, a rabbi, two college presidents, and a no-nonsense activist named Sadie Alexander.   An African American attorney from Philadelphia, Alexander could be depended upon to give the committee a firsthand, unvarnished account of racial atrocities and to point out the sure path to reform. Truman made it abundantly clear at the committee's first meeting on 15 January 1947 that he expected it to produce a conclusive analysis of civil wrongs and to recommend meaningful measures for correcting the evils identified. Recalling his clash with the Ku Klux Klan in the early 1920s, Truman said that in Jackson County, Missouri, "there was an organization...that met on hills and burned crosses and worked behind sheets. There is a tendency in this country for that situation to develop again, unless we do something tangible to prevent it." He told the committee, "I want our Bill of Rights implemented in fact. We have been trying to do this for 150 years."[6]

About six months after getting the President's Committee on Civil Rights under way, Truman delivered a landmark address to the annual meeting of the NAACP, assembled dramatically at the base of the Lincoln Memorial in Washington DC. The first president to address the NAACP, Truman knew he was departing from the dictates of his upbringing. On the day before his speech, he wrote his sister to admit that his prejudiced mother "won't like what I say because I wind up by quoting old Abe. But I believe what I say and I'm hopeful we may implement it."[7]

In his address, Truman enunciated a revolutionary role for the federal government in the area of civil rights. Pointing out that the framers of the U.S. Constitution were concerned with protecting citizens against the tyranny of government, he added, "We must keep moving forward with new concepts of civil rights to safeguard our heritage. The extension of civil rights today means, not protection of the people *against* the government, but protection of the people *by* the government." He proclaimed forcefully, "There is no justifiable reason for discrimination because of ancestry, or religion, or race, or color." Truman made clear that his concept of civil rights went far beyond merely the right to vote. He condemned what he termed the

limitations on any of our people and their enjoyment of basic rights which every citizen in a truly democratic society must enjoy. Every man should have the right to a decent home, the right to an education, the right to adequate medical care, the right to a worthwhile job, the right to an equal share in making the public decisions through the ballot, and the right to a fair trial in a fair court.[8]

Following his address, Truman remarked to Walter White that he "meant every word" in the speech and stressed, "I'm going to prove that I do mean it."[9] Truman recognized the international implications of his NAACP address, which was delivered only three months after he had unveiled what came to be known as the Truman Doctrine, in which he pledged American support to free people seeking to remain free. The NAACP address was widely broadcast and also translated, so that several hundred million people around the world heard it.

Truman reiterated his civil rights themes in his 1948 State of the Union address, delivered before a joint session of Congress on 7 January. "Any denial of human rights," he said, "is a denial of the basic beliefs of democracy and of our regard for the worth of each individual."[10] He also announced that he would send a special message to Congress requesting legislation to implement the recommendations of the President's Committee on Civil Rights (presented in their final report, *To Secure These Rights,* issued 29 October 1947).

Truman sent the promised message to Congress on 2 February 1948. It was the first special message on civil rights ever sent by a president to Congress. Truman reiterated his conviction that the federal government must play a leading role in guaranteeing civil rights for all Americans without respect to race, religion, or color. In detailing "the basic civil rights which are the source and the support of our democracy," Truman emphasized that the American people "believe that all men are entitled to equal opportunities for jobs, for homes, for good health and for education." He described the rights due all Americans very broadly. "We cannot be satisfied," he said, "until all our people have equal opportunities for jobs, for homes, for education, for health, and for political expression, and until all our people have equal protection under the law."

Truman went on to request that Congress enact legislation to accomplish ten specified objectives: a permanent Commission on Civil Rights, a Joint Congressional Committee on Civil Rights, and a Civil Rights Section in the Department of Justice; strengthening of existing civil rights statutes; federal protection against lynching; protection of the right to vote; a permanent Fair Employment Practices Commission; prohibition of discrimination in interstate transportation facilities; home rule and suffrage in presidential elections for the people of the District of Columbia; statehood for Hawaii and Alaska and a greater measure of self government for the country's island possessions; equal opportunity for residents of the United States to become naturalized citizens; and settlement of the claims of Japanese Americans for compensation due to their internment during World War II.[11]

Some critics have charged that Truman failed to pursue the broad goals regarding jobs, housing, education, health care that he put forward in this special message, that he defined "equal opportunity" too narrowly as only the right to vote. For Truman, though, the broad goals of good jobs, good housing, good education, and good health care were also civil rights goals. They were the essence and core of what he labeled the Fair Deal. To charge that Truman should have done more to achieve these broad goals specifically for African Americans and other minorities is to ignore both the constitutional structure of American government and the political reality of the seniority system, which insured that long-serving segregationist members of the House and Senate chaired almost all the congressional committees. Given the constitutional prerogatives of the executive and legislative branches, the separation of powers, and the checks and balances of the constitutional system, there is a limit to what a president could accomplish without the approval of Congress.

Truman acted against political advice in fighting for a civil rights program. Why should he do so? Unlike the later era of Martin Luther King Jr., there were no 1960s-style race riots when Truman was championing civil rights, no sit-ins in restaurants and other public facilities to protest whites-only service, no freedom riders. There was no black caucus in Congress; in fact, there were only two African Americans in Congress: Adam Clayton Powell, whom Truman did not respect, and William Dawson, who did not make any particular effort to get civil rights reform moving. It was not pressure from such men that caused Truman to act. He certainly did not act because of public pressure, either; a contemporary Gallup poll revealed that 82 percent of those polled were opposed to Truman's civil rights program. Civil rights was a dangerous political issue for Truman, especially in the election year of 1948. The Democratic National Committee pointed out that no Democrat since the Civil War had won the presidency without the support of the "Solid South." The outpouring of outrage from Southern political leaders and the Southern press reached such a crescendo following Truman's civil rights message that it was clear the South's support for him would not be solid, and that some Southern states might completely bolt the ticket. All this sound and fury did not deter Truman from his firm determination to go forward with his civil rights program, though he probably, during these months, turned frequently to the Mark Twain quotation he kept on his Oval Office desk: "Always do right. This will gratify some people and astonish the rest."

Truman tried to hold the Democratic Party together. At the national convention held in Philadelphia in mid-July 1948, he favored including in the platform the same civil rights plank as in the 1944 platform. This did not satisfy some of the liberals in the party; after a colorful floor fight led by Hubert Humphrey, a stronger plank was adopted. This restored the enthusiasm of those liberals who had opposed Truman's candidacy, but confirmed the fears of Southern Democrats, and resulted in delegates from Mississippi and Alabama walking out of the convention. As South Carolina governor J. Strom Thurmond was leading the dissidents off the convention floor, a reporter approached and asked him to explain why he was leaving the party when President Truman was only following the same civil rights policies Roosevelt had advocated. "I agree," Thurmond said, "but Truman really means it."[12] Two days after the conclusion of the Democratic National Convention, Thurmond became the presidential candidate of the States' Rights Party, whose adherents were popularly known as Dixiecrats. This party was designated the official Democratic Party in four Southern states: Alabama, Mississippi, Louisiana, and South Carolina. Thurmond carried these four states in the election.

Truman formally accepted his party's nomination at two in the morning on 15 July 1948. It had been a difficult convention, and the Democratic Party's chances for victory in November looked dim. In the steamy convention hall, without air conditioning, Truman came up to the podium dressed in an immaculate white linen suit. He exuded an air of confidence. Thanking the delegates for choosing him as the party's nominee, he accepted the nomination and then said, "Senator Barkley [the vice presidential candidate] and I will win this election and make these Republicans like it—don't you forget that!" The delegates loved Truman's bravado and rose to their feet with enthusiastic applause.[13]

Then Truman began to dissect the various planks in the Republican Party's platform, which they had approved at their convention a few weeks earlier. It was a liberal platform, and their candidate for president, Thomas E. Dewey, was a liberal. Truman began to contrast these convention promises with the opposition of Republicans in Congress to every liberal measure he had advocated. When he came to the Republican civil rights plank, he said, "Everybody knows that I recommended to the Congress the civil rights program. I did that because I believed it to be my duty under the Constitution. Some of the members of my own party disagree with me violently on this matter. But they stand up and do it openly! People can tell where they stand. But the Republicans all professed to be for those measures. But Congress failed to act."[14]

Then, in a master stroke, Truman called the Congress back into special session to give the Republicans a chance to vote for those measures their platform claimed they favored. This presented Dewey with two problems with respect to civil rights. First, he could not call attention to his good civil rights record during his term as governor of New York without also calling attention to the hidden conspiracy of the Republicans in Congress who had teamed up with Southern racists to block any progress on civil rights. Second, he would have to demonstrate some real leadership in the area of civil rights over a party dominated by figures such as Senator Robert A. Taft of Ohio, who pronounced that Truman's special session was all politics and resolved that nothing would be done during it. Truman's ploy also diverted attention away from the Southern Democrats' own sorry record on civil rights, making it seem that all the fault lay with the hypocritical Republicans.

On 26 July 1948—the very day that Congress assembled to begin its special "Turnip Day" session—President Truman issued two blockbuster executive orders. Executive Order 9980 ordered that "all personnel actions taken by Federal appointing officers shall be based solely on merit and fitness; and such officers are authorized and directed to take appropriate steps to insure that in all such actions there shall be no discrimination because of race, color, religion, or national origin." This order established departmental fair employment officers and a Fair Employment Board to ensure that hiring for federal jobs was done without discrimination. Executive Order 9981 stated, "It is hereby declared to be the policy of the President that there shall be equality of treatment and opportunity for all persons in the armed services without regard to race, color, religion or national origin." The new policy would be "put into effect as rapidly as possible, having due regard to the time required to effectuate any necessary changes without impairing efficiency or morale." The order established the President's Committee on Equality of

Treatment and Opportunity in the Armed Services to help guarantee the integration of the armed forces.[15]

Some historians have contended that A. Philip Randolph, the aggressively outspoken head of the Brotherhood of Sleeping Car Porters, pressured Truman into ordering the desegregation of the armed forces in 1948 by threatening African Americans' mass refusal to serve in a Jim Crow army. However, according to George M. Elsey, a member of Truman's White House staff who had a major role in advising Truman on the civil rights issue and who helped draft his major civil rights statements, including Executive Order 9981,

> A. Philip Randolph did not meet with any of the members of the White House staff who drafted the February 2, 1948, message to Congress nor did he have any contact with them as they worked on the two executive orders of July 26. Any "threat" he might have made when he was a member of a delegation calling on Truman on March 22, 1948, was unknown to the White House staff. If Randolph made a "threat," Truman never mentioned it in the numerous discussions with staff on the contents of his speeches, communications with the Congress, or the timing and the content of the two executive orders. Randolph's "pressure" is simply not discernable.[16]

Truman did not make civil rights a focus of his 1948 presidential campaign. He did, however, insist that when he made one of his few trips into the South to campaign in Texas, his rallies must be integrated. He also declared that his inaugural ceremonies would be open to all, without regard to race.[17]

If there were some Democrats who believed that Truman after his election victory would attempt to heal the breach with the South, they were sadly mistaken. In his State of the Union address of on 5 January 1949, the president made clear that he would press his civil rights program on the new Congress.

> The driving force behind our progress is our faith in our democratic institutions. That faith is embodied in the promise of equal rights and equal opportunities which the founders of our Republic proclaimed to their countrymen and to the whole world.
>
> The fulfillment of this promise is among the highest purposes of government. The civil rights proposals I made to the 80th Congress, I now repeat to the 81st Congress. They should be enacted in order that the Federal Government may assume the leadership and discharge the obligations clearly placed upon it by the Constitution.

I stand squarely behind those proposals.[18]

Faced with the threat of filibusters in the Senate that would kill his civil rights proposals, Truman decided to launch a frontal assault on Rule XXII by modifying it to restrict the ability to filibuster. When, on 11 March 1949, the Senate voted 46 to 41 to reject the proposed modification of Rule XXII, Truman knew that almost no civil rights legislation could possibly get through Congress. Even so, his proposed civil rights legislation was introduced into Congress on 28 April 1949.

Truman knew his legislative initiatives were doomed, so he took executive action wherever he could to advance his program. On 15 October 1949, he nominated William H. Hastie, former dean of Howard University Law School and a prominent black attorney, to a seat on the Third Circuit Court of Appeals. Judge Hastie later said that Truman's "accomplishments in the field of race relations and the treatment of the Negro by the Government were in my view precedent-making; they paved the way for, and made very much easier the things that President[s] that succeeded him did."[19] Two months after Truman appointed Judge Hastie, the Federal Housing Administration announced that it would refuse to provide financial assistance to projects that discriminated against African Americans.

In his State of the Union address on 4 January 1950, President Truman once again urged Congress to enact the civil rights legislation he had first requested in his special message of 2 February 1948. He also continued to press for all his Fair Deal proposals, which would have codified his contention that good jobs, education, housing, and health care for all Americans, regardless of race, were an inseparable component of civil rights.

On 2 February 1951, Truman issued Executive Order 10210, which established civil rights employment protection for work awarded by government contracts. The order stated explicitly

> there shall be no discrimination in any act performed hereunder against any person on the ground of race, creed, color or national origin, and all contracts hereunder shall contain a provision that the contractor and any subcontractors thereunder shall not so discriminate.[20]

Truman issued a second order on the subject of federal contracts on 3 December 1951. Executive Order 10308 sought to enforce compliance with the nondiscriminatory provision of his earlier order. It established a Committee on Government Contract Compliance with responsibility to

> confer and advise with the appropriate officers of the various contracting agencies and with other persons concerned with a view toward the prevention and elimination of such discrimination, and [to] make to the said officers recommendations which in the judgment of the Committee will prevent or eliminate discrimination.[21]

On 2 November 1951, Truman vetoed HR 5411, which would have mandated segregated schools on federal military installations throughout the South. In his memorandum of disapproval, Truman stated, "This proposal, if enacted into law, would constitute a backward step in the efforts of the Federal Government to extend equal rights and opportunities to all our people." He warned that such a law could damage the country's credibility in the world: "We should not impair our moral position by enacting a law that requires a discrimination based on race. Step by step we are discarding old discriminations; we must not adopt new ones."[22]

When Truman delivered his seventh State of the Union address on 9 January 1952, he once again asked Congress to make civil rights a reality for all Americans. "As we build our strength to defend the freedom in the world," he said, "we ourselves must extend the benefits of freedom more widely among all our own people. We need to take action toward the wider enjoyment of civil rights. Freedom is the birthright of every American." The executive branch, he pointed out, had done its part to make civil rights a reality for everyone; now the Congress must do something. "The executive branch has been making real progress toward full equality of treatment and opportunity—in the Armed Forces, in the civil service, and in private firms working for the Government. Further advances require action by Congress, and I hope that means will be provided to give the Members of the Senate and the House a chance to vote on them."[23]

In a commencement address delivered at Howard University on 13 June 1952, Truman stated that all Americans "should enjoy equal political rights. And they should have equal opportunities for education, employment, and decent living conditions. This is our belief and we know that it is right." After reviewing civil rights achievements since 1947, Truman acknowledged that such progress "does not mean we have reached the goal or that we can stop working. Much remains to be done." He again asked Congress to help him. "We still need the legislation that I recommended to the Congress in

1948. Only two of the recommendations I made in my Civil Rights Program have been adopted so far. I shall continue, in office and out, to urge Congress to adopt the remainder."[24]

Frustrated by the unwillingness of Congress to pass his civil rights legislation, Truman turned to the Supreme Court to further the cause of civil rights. The court was headed during most of Truman's term by Chief Justice Fred Vinson, one of Truman's closest friends. Like Truman, Vinson came from a former slave state, Kentucky, but had a strong sense of justice that overcame much of the traditional prejudice of his region. Truman appointed Vinson chief justice on 6 June 1946; by 1950, he had appointed three other Supreme Court justices—Harold Burton, Tom Clark, and Sherman Minton—all of whom had been exposed to Truman's unwavering insistence that ending discrimination was a moral imperative. With the participation of these four justices, the Vinson court made a number of landmark decisions during Truman's presidency. These in turn paved the way for the historic 1954 ruling in *Brown v. Board of Education,* which overturned the court's 1896 ruling in *Plessy v. Ferguson* that had validated the principle of "separate but equal" in schools and public facilities.

Truman influenced the series of decisions by the Vinson court that advanced civil rights. He ordered his attorney general, Tom Clark, to submit a series of hard-hitting amicus curiae briefs that served as persuasive guides to the court in the framing of its decisions. Like the great double-play combination enshrined in baseball lore—Tinker to Evers to Chance—for several years the great double-play combination for civil rights was Truman to Clark to Vinson.

The Justice Department briefs frontally attacked the *Plessy v. Ferguson* ruling. In the cases of *Shelley v. Kraemer* and *Hurd v. Hodge,* they cited Truman's ringing words in his 1947 address to the NAACP, which Chief Justice Vinson had attended. "We must make the Federal Government a friendly, vigilant defender of the rights and equalities of all Americans," President Truman had said, "Our National Government must show the way." The amicus brief submitted for *Henderson v. United States* again attacked *Plessy v. Ferguson* by pointing out that segregated interstate travel might provide separate facilities, but not equal ones. The brief stated bluntly, "The phrase 'equal rights' means the same rights." In its decisions in all these cases, the Supreme Court ruled unanimously and foursquare against discrimination. In the cases of *Sweatt v. Painter* and *McLaurin v. Oklahoma State Regents,* the amicus briefs helped the Vinson court to arrive at two unanimous decisions that ended long-standing practices of segregation in state-sponsored higher education.[25]

On 2 December 1952, Truman's Justice Department sent its final civil rights amicus brief to the Supreme Court. Again the brief concerned *Plessy v. Ferguson,* specifically its effect on education. It was for the combination of five cases that was known by the title, *Brown v. Board of Education.* Though *Brown* was argued before the Vinson court on 9 December 1952, Chief Justice Vinson died in September 1953, before the case was decided. It was his successor, Chief Justice Earl Warren, who issued the final ruling, which was announced on 17 May 1954.

Truman's last address dealing primarily with civil rights was delivered to sixty-five thousand people in Harlem on 11 October 1952. Reflecting on his civil rights address of 2 February 1948, he proclaimed, "We pledged ourselves that day to a great enterprise—the end of racial injustice and unfair discrimination. I am here to say to you now that fight will never cease with me as long as I live."[26]

In his final State of the Union address, delivered on 7 January 1953, President Truman, looking back on civil rights advances during his administration, said that the barriers of prejudice and discrimination were coming down "in our armed forces, our civil service, our universities, our railway trains, the residential districts of our cities—in stores and factories all across the Nation—in the polling booths as well." The country was experiencing, he said, "a great awakening of the American conscience on the issues of civil rights." This progress was ongoing, not yet at any stage of completeness, he admitted, but it demonstrated that the American people intended "to live up to the promises of equal freedom for us all."[27]

President Truman did everything within his constitutional power to ensure that it was public policy to guarantee civil and human rights to all Americans, without respect to race, religion, or any other limitations. He fully recognized that only the Congress, dominated by racist committee chairmen, could pass the laws he repeatedly and publicly advocated to achieve his goals. He went as far as he could to carry forward his objectives through executive orders and the actions of his Department of Justice, including the submission of amicus briefs in important civil rights cases. It was impossible to do more under the U.S. Constitution.

When Martin Luther King Jr. sent Truman a copy of his first book, *Stride Toward Freedom: The Montgomery Story* (1958), he wrote an on an inside page: "To President Harry Truman, in appreciation for your humanitarian concern, and the positive stand that you have always taken in the area of civil rights. With warmest regards, Martin L. King Jr."[28]

Notes

[1] Harry Truman to Bess Wallace, 22 June 1911, in Ferrell, *Dear Bess,* 39–40. Other letters in this collection document Truman's conventionally racist attitudes toward African Americans and other minorities.

[2] Letter to the Chairman, House Rules Committee, Concerning the Committee on Fair Employment Practice, 5 June 1945, in *Public Papers of the Presidents, Truman, 1945,* 104–5. See also Philleo Nash, interview, 29 November 1966, 572–73.

[3] Truman, Special Message to the Congress Presenting a 21-Point Program for the Reconversion Period, 6 September 1945, in *Public Papers of the Presidents, Truman, 1945,* 282. This message outlined the essence of what would later be called the "Fair Deal" program, which sought to raise the standards of education, employment, health care, and housing for all Americans, black and white.

[4] Gardner, *Harry Truman and Civil Rights,* 16–18.

[5] Truman to Tom C. Clark, 20 September 1946, Niles Papers, Truman Presidential Library.

[6] Truman, Remarks to Members of the President's Committee on Civil Rights, 15 January 1947, in *Public Papers of the Presidents, Truman, 1947,* 98–99.

[7] Truman to Mary Jane Truman, 28 June 1947, Truman Papers, Post-Presidential Papers, Memoirs File, Truman Presidential Library.

[8] Truman, Address Before the NAACP, 29 June 1947, in *Public Papers of the Presidents, Truman, 1947,* 311–13.

[9] White, *A Man Called White,* 348.

[10] Truman, Annual Message to Congress on the State of the Union, 7 January 1948, in *Public Papers of the Presidents, Truman, 1948,* 3.

[11] Truman, Special Message to the Congress on Civil Rights, 2 February 1948, in *Public Papers of the Presidents, Truman, 1948,* 121–26.

[12] Truman, *Memoirs,* 2:183.

[13] McCullough, *Truman,* 642.

[14] Truman, Address in Philadelphia Upon Accepting the Nomination of the Democratic National Convention, 15 July 1948, in *Public Papers of the Presidents, Truman, 1948,* 406–10.

[15] Executive Order 9981, Code of Federal Regulations, Title 3, The President, 1943-1948 Compilation, 720–22.

[16] George M. Elsey, personal correspondence with author, 31 October 2006.

[17] Gardner, *Harry Truman and Civil Rights,* 128–29.

[18] Truman, Message on the State of the Union, 5 January 1949, in *Public Papers of the President, Truman, 1949,* 6.

[19] Hastie, interview, 5 January 1972, 78.

[20] Executive Order 10210, Code of Federal Regulations, Title 3, The President, 1943-1948 Compilation, 390–92, quote at pt. 1, par. 7.

[21] Executive Order 10210, Code of Federal Regulations, Title 3, The President, 1943-1948 Compilation, 837–38.

[22] Truman, Memorandum of Disapproval of Bill Requiring Segregation in Certain Schools on Federal Property, 2 November 1951, in *Public Papers of the Presidents, Truman, 1951*, 616–17.

[23] Truman, Annual Message to the Congress on the State of the Union, 9 January 1952, in *Public Papers of the Presidents, Truman, 1952*, 16.

[24] Truman, Commencement Address at Howard University, 13 June 1952, in *Public Papers of the Presidents, Truman, 1952–3*, 420–24.

[25] Gardner, *Harry Truman and Civil Rights*, 172–97.

[26] Trumam, Address in Harlem, New York, Upon Receiving the Franklin Roosevelt Award, 11 October 1952, in *Public Papers of the Presidents, Truman, 1952*, 797–802.

[27] Truman, Annual Message to the Congress on the State of the Union, 7 January 1953, in *Public Papers of the Presidents, Truman, 1952–1953*, 1117.

[28] Truman's inscribed copy of King's book is in the Harry S. Truman Presidential Library.

TRUMAN'S CIVIL RIGHTS LEGACY: A GRAPHIC ESSAY

President Truman's parents, John and Martha Ellen (Young) Truman, on their wedding day, 28 December 1881. The Trumans and the Youngs were both from Kentucky, and before that from Virginia. Truman's grandparents on both sides owned slaves. His Young grandparents suffered a raid by Unionist guerrillas and several confiscations of property by Union soldiers. In August 1863, the Young family was interned and then resettled by the occupying Union army. Truman's mother retained strong and bitter memories of these things all her life, and impressed on her children her animosity toward the North and Abraham Lincoln and all they stood for. (TL 62–360)

President Truman meeting with African American leaders who want more African Americans in important positions in agencies involved in the administration's defense program. The President's prominent visitors include Mary McLeod Bethune, president emeritus of the National Council of Negro Women, Lester Granger, executive secretary of the National Urban League, Tobias Channing, director of the Phelp-Stokes Foundation, and Walter White, executive secretary of the NAACP. 28 February 1951. (TL 65–3630)

The most notorious racist statement Truman ever committed to paper is in a letter to Bess Wallace, dated 22 June 1911. A portion of his racist outburst is shown in this illustration. On the next page of the letter, Truman admits to being prejudiced and says "I am strongly of the opinion that negroes ought to be in Africa, yellow men in Asia, and white men in Europe and America." He also, in this letter, proposed to Bess Wallace. She refused the proposal, but presumably not because her suitor had prejudices that she probably shared. Historians have sometimes expressed surprise that a man who had once felt such prejudice and probably retained some degree of racial prejudice his entire life, could, during his presidency, undertake with apparent conviction a serious civil rights program. (Family, Business, and Personal Papers, Truman Papers, Truman Library.)

White and African American soldiers participating in interracial solidarity training at a bomber base in Italy, circa early March 1945. The armed services, despite training exercises such as these, were segregated institutions at the end of World War II. Of all the services, the Army was most resistant to President Truman's order to desegregate. The determined efforts of President Truman and members of the President's Committee on Equality of Treatment and Opportunity in the Armed Services, together with the influence on the Army of three years of combat in Korea, brought an end to segregation in the Army by 1954. (TL 75–3952)

Informal Remarks of the President to the Members
of the President's Committee on Civil Rights

January 15, 1947, 11.35 a.m..e.s.t.

. . . . .

~~Well, I tried to line up chairs enough so everybody~~
~~could sit down, but didn't have enough in here, and I didn't~~
~~have an auditorium because~~ Congress took the money away from
me to build it. (laughter) I save the money now, you know.

~~But~~ you have, ~~in my opinion,~~ a vitally important
job. We are none of us entirely familiar with just how far
the Federal Government under the Constitution has a right to
go in these matters, ~~and~~ (Civil rights) ~~In my opinion~~ ~~Our Government is~~ by the
~~the only one in the whole world today that absolutely, by~~
~~constitutional right, puts the right of the individual~~ above
~~the right of any group or any state to oppress them.~~

I want ~~that~~ our Bill of Rights implemented, in fact, ~~as~~
~~well as on paper.~~ We have been trying to do this for 150 years.
We are making progress, but we are not making progress fast enough.
This country could very easily be faced with ~~another~~ situation
~~as it was~~ similar to the one with which it was faced in
1922. That was ~~so thoroughly~~ date impressed on my mind because in
1922 I was running for ~~the~~ my first elective office ~~to which I~~
~~was ever elected --~~ County Judge of Jackson County -- and there
was an organization in that county that met on hills and

The first page of a transcription of President Truman's informal remarks to the first meeting of the members of the President's Committee on Civil Rights, January 15, 1947. Truman's remarks were taken down in shorthand by the White House official reporter. The edited transcript was released by the White House press secretary and later published in the Public Papers of the Presidents. The segments of Truman's remarks that were edited out have been largely forgotten. "...In my opinion," Truman says in one of these segments, "our Government is the only one in the whole world today that absolutely, by constitutional right, puts the right of the individual above the right of any group or any state to oppress them." Another deleted segment concerns Truman's belief that the federal government shouldn't exercise dictatorial powers over local authorities, but should protect Constitutional rights that are not being enforced at the local level. "I want to find out just how far we can go," he tells the committee. (White House Official Reporter Files, Truman Papers, Truman Library)

September 20, 1946

Dear Tom:

I had as callers yesterday some members of the
National Association for the Advancement of
Colored People and they told me about an incident
which happened in South Carolina where a negro
Sergeant, who had been discharged from the Army
just three hours, was taken off the bus and not
only seriously beaten but his eyes deliberately
put out, and that the Mayor of the town had bragged
about committing this outrage.

I have been very much alarmed at the increased
racial feeling all over the country and I am wondering if it wouldn't be well to appoint a commission
to analyze the situation and have a remedy to present to the next Congress - something similar to
the Wickersham Commission on Prohibition.

I know you have been looking into the Tennessee and
Georgia lynchings, and also been investigating the
one in Louisiana, but I think it is going to take
something more than the handling of each individual
case after it happens - it is going to require the
inauguration of some sort of policy to prevent such
happenings.

I'll appreciate very much having your views on the
subject.

Sincerely yours,

Honorable Tom C. Clark
Attorney General
Washington, D. C.

cc x David K. Niles
Administrative Assistant to the President

*On 20 September 1946, the day following a meeting with African American leaders in
which the rising level of violence against African Americans was discussed, Truman
wrote to Attorney General Tom Clark to express his alarm at this racial violence and
suggest that a presidential commission might have to be appointed to do something
about it. Truman sent a copy of his letter to his minority affairs assistant David Niles. "I*

THE WHITE HOUSE
WASHINGTON

September 20, 1946

MEMORANDUM FOR: David K. Niles
                 Administrative Assistant
                 to the President

FROM: The President

I am attaching copy of a letter I have just sent to Tom Clark.

I am very much in earnest on this thing and I'd like very much to have you push it with everything you have.

HST.

Enclosure

am very much in earnest on this thing and I'd like very much to have you push it with everything you have," he told Niles. About ten weeks later, Truman issued Executive Order 9808, which created the President's Committee on Civil Rights. (Niles Papers, Truman Library.)

Truman addressed the 38th annual conference of the National Association for the Advancement of Colored People on 29 June 1947. He was the first president to speak to a meeting of the NAACP and he did so in grand surroundings, from the steps of the Lincoln Memorial, with the Reflecting Pool and the Washington Monument stretching out into the distance. The president's message matched the grandeur of the occasion and surroundings. "It is my deep conviction," he said, "that we have reached a turning point in the long history of our country's efforts to guarantee freedom and equality to all our citizens…. We can no longer afford the luxury of a leisurely attack upon prejudice and discrimination." Historians disagree about the importance of Truman's civil rights program and about the degree of his commitment to it, but they would probably agree that he employed strong rhetoric on behalf of civil rights. (TL 73–2561)

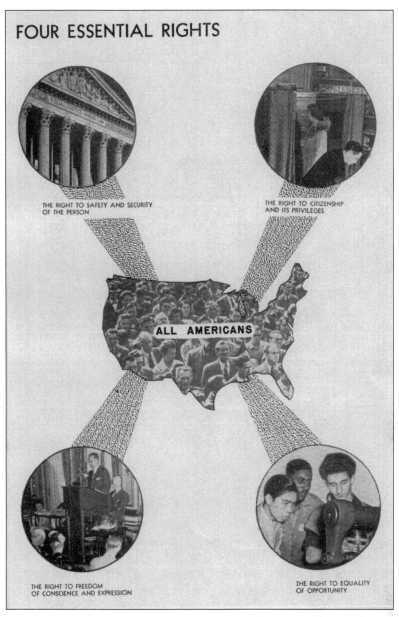

FOUR ESSENTIAL RIGHTS

THE RIGHT TO SAFETY AND SECURITY OF THE PERSON

THE RIGHT TO CITIZENSHIP AND ITS PRIVILEGES

ALL AMERICANS

THE RIGHT TO FREEDOM OF CONSCIENCE AND EXPRESSION

THE RIGHT TO EQUALITY OF OPPORTUNITY

The report of the President's Committee on Civil Rights, To Secure These Rights, *began by identifying four rights that were "essential to the citizen in a free society." This illustration from the report depicts the four rights: the right to safety and security of the person, the right to citizenship and its privileges, the right to freedom of conscience and expression, and the right to equality of opportunity. "We believe that each of these rights is essential to the well-being of the individual and to the progress of society."*

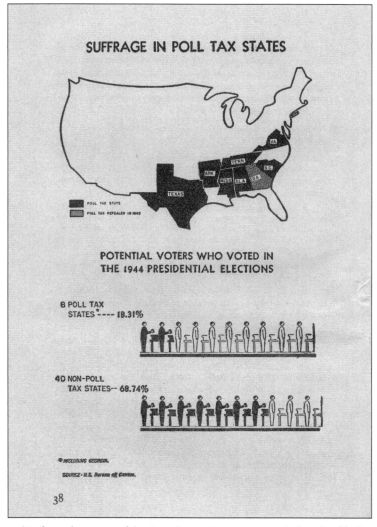

This graphic from the report of the President's Committee on Civil Rights, To Secure
These Rights, depicts the drastic effect poll taxes had on the ability to exercise the right
to vote. According to To Secure These Rights (39) the poll tax was administered in a
discriminatory manner and "has been very effective as an anti-Negro device." The
Fifteenth Amendment to the Constitution, ratified in 1870, gave African American men
the right to vote, but Southern states instituted a number of devices, including the poll
tax, to effectively take the right away. Eleven states enacted poll tax laws; by the time To
Secure These Rights was issued in 1947, seven states still had these laws. In his civil
rights message of 2 February 1948, President Truman asked Congress to outlaw poll
taxes, but Congress did not do so. Poll taxes were outlawed in federal elections by the
Twenty-fourth Amendment, which was ratified in 1964. The 1966 Supreme court
decision, Harper v. Virginia Board of Elections, outlawed the imposition of poll taxes in
state elections.

FOR WHITE MEN AND WOMEN EVERYWHERE

For the sake of our COUNTRY and the SOUTH I plead that you READ the following:

In 1944 genuine Democrats made the first serious move to eliminate from the real Democratic Party the alleged Negro-LOVING, pink and red MONGRELS who FALSELY called themselves Democrats—True, we were whipped and humiliated and on election day 1944 real Democrats found themselves with no place to go. BUT, THE SEED OF OUR STRENGTH HAD BEEN PLANTED!

Since then the scalawag, carpet-bagger Northern bosses of the New Deal Party kept adding shame and degradation to our lot—smugly sure there was no end to what loyal Democrats would endure for party harmony—Late in 1947—after Chairman McGrath of the Democratic National Committee showed RIDICULE and SCORN for our Constitutional State Rights—GOVERNOR BEAUFORD JESTER of Texas sounded the first warning that the SOUTH and good Democrats everywhere would not forever give BLIND OBEDIENCE to renegade, FALSE and Negro Democrats.

The warnings of Governor Jester gained wide public approval in the genuine Democratic newspapers and meeting places of the SOUTH and the entire nation—But New Deal spokesmen SCOFFED and POOH-POOHED the warning of Governor Jester—they laughed at the Texas spark as something they could STOMP out with the greatest of ease—they had the usual CONTEMPT for "IN THE BAG" Southern Democrats.

BUT THE TEXAS SPARK DID NOT DIE and since then FIRES have broken out in Mississippi, Oklahoma, South Carolina, Alabama, Florida, Louisiana—sparks are flying all over the South—Now, GOVERNOR FIELDING WRIGHT, backed by the almost unanimous support of the entire Democracy of Mississippi, has challenged the Democrats of the South and Nation to work with his state to put an end to the delivery of the Democratic Party to the Negroes, the C. I. O., the Pinks and Reds who control and ride herd over these minority groups.

On Thursday, January 29, 1948, senior U. S. SENATOR JAMES EASTLAND of Mississippi told a joint session of both houses of the Mississippi legislature that "THE SOUTH HAD ITS BACK TO THE WALL", and that unless we defended the real Democratic Party we would soon be completely governed by a collection of "MONGRELS."

Senator Eastland said that, "In good times or in bad, the bone, sinew, the flesh and the constancy of the Democratic Party was found below the Mason and Dixon Line"

Instantly! Democrats asked "THEN, WHY NOT A DEMOCRATIC CONVENTION BELOW THE MASON AND DIXON LINE??!!"

Congressional delegations from several Southern states are talking the situation over—At last! Political leadership have ears to the ground, waiting for "We the People" to stomp and speak.

If you are tired of the threat of FEPC—sick of the Wallaces, Hannegans, McGraths and Peppers—weary of C. I. O. and the Reds who want to MARRY us into the WILLING ARMS of the Negro! You can now do something about it before it is too late!

WE MUST HAVE A DEMOCRATIC CONVENTION BELOW THE MASON - DIXON LINE.

Five million white men and women of the South must get a message of approval to the thirteen governors of the Southern States—five million people must sign their name and address to one of these circulars and mail or carry it to their governor, ASKING FOR A DEMOCRATIC CONVENTION BELOW THE MASON-DIXON LINE.

Your political leaders are waiting to HEAR FROM YOU—if you fail it will not be their fault. "THE HOPE OF THE NATION RESTS WAY DOWN SOUTH IN DIXIE!"

Cordially, John U. Barr,
P. O. Box 86—New Orleans 6, La.

In Louisiana mail to Gov. Designate Hon. Earl K. Long, Winnfield, La.

Permission is granted to reproduce this or our printer can furnish additional copies at 75c per hundred delivered to you.

President Truman's civil rights program caused many in the South to oppose both the program and the president, as this virulently racist open letter suggests, and caused some southern political leaders to lead a rebellion within the Democratic Party. Several copies of this open letter were apparently sent to Truman by four African Americans, who assured the president in a statement titled "The Black South Speaks" that they would fight against such bigotry and for their just rights. "The American Negro is going to continue to fight on all fronts—religious, economic, political and educational," they wrote. "His goal is complete equality without reservation. As an American he intends to enjoy democracy for which he has given so much." (Official File 596, Truman Papers, Truman Library)

EXECUTIVE ORDER

_____

ESTABLISHING THE PRESIDENT'S COMMITTEE ON
EQUALITY OF TREATMENT AND OPPORTUNITY IN
THE ARMED SERVICES

WHEREAS it is essential that there be maintained in the armed services of the United States the highest standards of democracy, with equality of treatment and opportunity for all those who serve in our country's defense:

NOW, THEREFORE, by virtue of the authority vested in me as President of the United States, by the Constitution and the statutes of the United States, and as Commander in Chief of the armed services, it is hereby ordered as follows:

1. It is hereby declared to be the policy of the President that there shall be equality of treatment and opportunity for all persons in the armed services without regard to race, color, religion or national origin. This policy shall be put into effect as rapidly as possible, having due regard to the time required to effectuate any necessary changes without impairing efficiency or morale.

2. There shall be created in the National Military Establishment an advisory committee to be known as the President's Committee on Equality of Treatment and Opportunity in the Armed Services, which shall be composed of seven members to be designated by the President.

3. The Committee is authorized on behalf of the President to examine into the rules, procedures and practices of the armed services in order to determine in what respect such rules, procedures and practices may be altered or improved with a view to carrying out the policy of this order. The Committee shall confer and advise with the Secretary of Defense, the Secretary

Executive Order 9981, signed by President Truman on 26 July 1948, is arguably one of the most important executive orders ever issued. It declared that the president's policy was "that there shall be equality of treatment and opportunity for all persons in the armed services without regard to race, color, religion or national origin," and it established a committee charged with bringing this policy into effect "as rapidly as possible…without impairing efficiency or morale." The committee negotiated with the

- 2 -

of the Army, the Secretary of the Navy, and the Secretary of the Air Force, and shall make such recommendations to the President and to said Secretaries as in the judgment of the Committee will effectuate the policy hereof.

4. All executive departments and agencies of the Federal Government are authorized and directed to cooperate with the Committee in its work, and to furnish the Committee such information or the services of such persons as the Committee may require in the performance of its duties.

5. When requested by the Committee to do so, persons in the armed services or in any of the executive departments and agencies of the Federal Government shall testify before the Committee and shall make available for the use of the Committee such documents and other information as the Committee may require.

6. The Committee shall continue to exist until such time as the President shall terminate its existence by Executive order.

Harry Truman

THE WHITE HOUSE,
July 26, 1948.

sometimes resisting armed services to bring about desegregation, and Truman supported the committee's work with energy and conviction, with the result that the armed services became fully integrated by 1954. The original order, signed by President Truman, is in the records of the Department of State, National Archives and Records Administration.

August 18, 1948

Dear Ernie:

I appreciated very much your letter of last Saturday night from Hotel Temple Square in the Mormon Capital.

I am going to send you a copy of the report of my Commission on Civil Rights and then if you still have that antibellum proslavery outlook, I'll be thoroughly disappointed in you.

The main difficulty with the South is that they are living eighty years behind the times and the sooner they come out of it the better it will be for the country and themselves. I am not asking for social equality, because no such thing exists, but I am asking for equality of opportunity for all human beings and, as long as I stay here, I am going to continue that fight. When the mob gangs can take four people out and shoot them in the back, and everybody in the country is acquainted with who did the shooting and nothing is done about it, that country is in pretty bad fix from a law enforcement standpoint.

When a Mayor and a City Marshal can take a negro Sergeant off a bus in South Carolina, beat him up and put out one of his eyes, and nothing is done about it by the State authorities, something is radically wrong with the system.

On the Louisiana and Arkansas Railway when coal burning locomotives were used the negro firemen were the thing because it was a backbreaking job and a dirty one. As soon as they turned to oil as a fuel it became customary for people to take shots at the negro firemen and a number were murdered because it was thought that this was now a white-collar job and should go to a white man. I can't approve of such goings on and I shall never approve it, as long as I am here, as I told you before. I am going to try to remedy it and if that ends up in my failure to be reelected, that failure will be in a good cause.

On 14 August 1948, Ernie Roberts, an old friend, wrote to Truman warning him that what he called the "Equal Rights Bill" would cause him to lose the South in the upcoming election. Then he offered some advice: "You, Bess and Margaret, and shall I say, myself, are all Southerners and we have been raised with the Negros [sic] and we know the term 'Equal Rights.' Harry, let us let the South take care of the Niggers, which they have done, and if the Niggers do not like the Southern treatment, let them come to Mrs. Roosevelt." He closes with an only superficially humorous warning. "You put equal rights in Independence and Bess will not live with you, will you Bess[?]" Truman

- 2 -

I know you haven't thought this thing through and that you do not know the facts. I am happy, however, that you wrote me because it gives me a chance to tell you what the facts are.

Sincerely yours,

HARRY S. TRUMAN

Mr. E. W. Roberts
c/o Faultless Starch Company
Kansas City, Missouri

Note in longhand --

This is a personal & confidential communication and I hope you'll regard it that way - at least until I've made a public statement on the subject - as I expect to do in the South.

HST

(Envelope marked - Personal and Confidential)

Report enclosed - "To Secure These Rights" --
"The Report Of The President's Committee On Civil Rights"

answered Roberts on 18 August. "I am not asking for social equality, because no such thing exists, but I am asking for equality of opportunity for all human beings and, as long as I stay here, I am going to continue that fight." He talks about the violence African Americans are suffering and says he is going to do everything he can to remedy the situation, "and if that ends up in my failure to be reelected, that failure will be in a good cause." (Personal File, President's Secretary's Files, Truman Papers, Truman Library)

Robert M. Marshall assists Chief Justice of the United States Fred M. Vinson to put on his judicial robe. Vinson was appointed chief justice by President Truman in June 1946. He presided over a series of Supreme Court decisions from 1948 to 1950 which invalidated discriminatory practices in housing, interstate transit, and higher education, and which challenged, but did not definitively overturn, the separate-but-equal doctrine of Plessy v. Ferguson. The Truman administration submitted amicus curiae briefs on behalf of the plaintiffs in some of these cases. Some historians give President Truman credit for appointing justices to the Supreme Court who shared his belief that civil rights must be accorded to all Americans. (TL 99-1249)

African American supporters meeting with President Truman aboard the Ferdinand Magellan, his campaign car, in Des Moines, Iowa, on 18 September 1948. As a result of African American migration from the South into northern cities, the African American vote was important to Truman in 1948, and political considerations influenced his civil rights program. (TL 2006–208)

Truman with White House employee Sam Jackson on his retirement day, 31 December 1950. Truman genuinely liked the African Americans on the White House staff who cared for many of his daily needs, and the staff would sometimes talk to him on a personal level. "I wonder why nearly everyone makes a father confessor out of me," Truman wrote in his diary after a White House butler came to him, "scared stiff and almost crying," and asked how to deal with a personal problem. Truman helped the man. "The rule around here is that no one may speak to the President. I break it every day and make 'em speak to me." (TL 58–355)

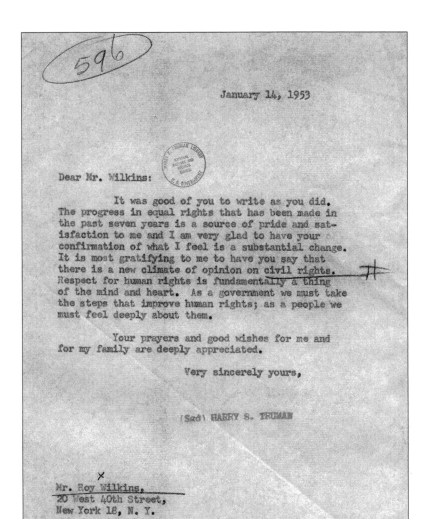

January 14, 1953

Dear Mr. Wilkins:

It was good of you to write as you did.
The progress in equal rights that has been made in
the past seven years is a source of pride and satisfaction to me and I am very glad to have your
confirmation of what I feel is a substantial change.
It is most gratifying to me to have you say that
there is a new climate of opinion on civil rights.
Respect for human rights is fundamentally a thing
of the mind and heart. As a government we must take
the steps that improve human rights; as a people we
must feel deeply about them.

Your prayers and good wishes for me and
for my family are deeply appreciated.

Very sincerely yours,

(Sgd) HARRY S. TRUMAN

Mr. Roy Wilkins,
20 West 40th Street,
New York 18, N. Y.

PN:bj

*On 12 January 1953, in the last days of Truman's presidency, NAACP assistant
secretary Roy Wilkins sent a remarkable three page letter to the outgoing president. He
thanked Truman for all he had done to realize civil rights for all Americans. "As you
leave the White House," he wrote, "you carry with you the gratitude and affectionate
regard of millions of your Negro fellow citizens who in less than a decade of your
leadership, inspiration and determination, have seen the old order change right before
their eyes." Truman, in his response of January 14, thanked Wilkins for confirming his
belief that "there is a new climate of opinion on civil rights." He added that respect for
human rights must come from the mind and heart. "As a government we must take the
steps that improve human rights; as a people we must feel deeply about them." (Official
File 596, Truman Papers, Truman Library)*

Independence, Missouri
December 11, 1957

Executive Order No. 9808, which created the President's Committee on Civil Rights, said, in part:

"Freedom from fear is more fully realized in our country than in any other on the face of the earth. Yet all parts of our population are not equally free from fear. And from time to time, and in some places, this freedom has been gravely threatened. It was so after the last war, when organized groups fanned hatred and intolerance . . . .

"The preservation of civil liberties is a duty of every government -- state, Federal and local. Wherever the law enforcement measures and the authority of Federal, state and local governments are inadequate to discharge this primary function of government, these measures and this authority should be strengthened and improved."

I asked fifteen prominent Americans to serve as the President's Committee on Civil Rights, in the conviction that if the American people were given a clear picture, they themselves would be quick to remedy those practices shown to be out of keeping with our heritage of freedom. I am happy indeed that the record of the past ten years bears out my confidence.

Twice before in American history, as the Committee's Report recalled, this nation took stock of its freedoms. The first came soon after the Constitution was ratified -- and resulted in the first ten amendments we know as the American Bill of Rights.

The War between the States brought the next appraisal -- "the new birth of freedom" which President Lincoln predicted, marked by the Emancipation Proclamation and the 13th, 14th and 15th amendments to the Constitution.

Truman was asked in 1957 to make a statement on the tenth anniversary of his civil rights committee presentating him their report, To Secure These Rights. *He expressed in his statement his optimistic conviction, in 1957 as well as 1947, that "if the American people were given a clear picture, they themselves would be quick to remedy those*

-2-

The Committee pinpointed the danger points where freedom was lagging: Segregation in the nation's capital; racial and religious discrimination in employment, housing and education; infringements of the right to vote, to serve in the armed forces, to enjoy equal justice under law.

Given the facts, the American people soon moved into action. Civic and religious organizations, veterans groups, labor unions and business associations, women's clubs, youth council -- men and women in every walk of life and in every section of our land joined to close the gap between our ideals and our practices.

Given the facts, the American people will always lead the way.

Harry S. Truman

practices shown to be out of keeping with our heritage of freedom. I am happy indeed," he concludes, "that the record of the past ten years bears out my confidence.... Given the facts, the American people will always lead the way." (Secretary's Office File, Post Presidential Papers, Truman Papers, Truman Library)

WESTERN UNION TELEGRAM

Independence, Missouri
March 24, 1960

EDWARD M TURNER PRESIDENT
ARTHUR L. JOHNSON EXECUTIVE SECRETARY
DETROIT BRANCH NAACP
DETROIT MICHIGAN

YOUR TELEGRAM REGARDING THE STATEMENT WHICH I MADE ABOUT SIT DOWNS

IN THE RESTAURANT IS CORRECT. I WOULD DO JUST WHAT I SAID I WOULD.

NAACP IS AN ORGANIZATION WHICH HAS BEEN WORKING FOR GOOD WILL AND

COMMON SENSE IN THIS SITUATION WITH WHICH WE ARE FACED. WHEN THEY

DO THINGS THAT CAUSE PEOPLE WHO HAVE BEEN AS FRIENDLY TO THEM AS

I HAVE BEEN TO FEEL THAT THEY ARE DOING THE WRONG THING THEY ARE

LOSING FRIENDS INSTEAD OF MAKING THEM.

IF I WERE IN DETROIT I WOULD SAY THE SAME THING TO YOU PERSONALLY FOR

ALL THE NEWSPAPERS AND TELEVISIONS IN THE COUNTRY. I CAN'T COME TO

DETROIT BECAUSE OF ILLNESS IN THE FAMILY BUT IF I WERE THERE I WOULD

TELL YOU EXACTLY WHAT I AM SAYING NOW. THIS IS NOT PERSONAL NOR

CONFIDENTIAL

HARRY S TRUMAN

Truman didn't like the civil disobedience tactics employed by activists in the 1950s and 1960s. When protestors used sit-in tactics to oppose lunch counter segregation in Detroit, Truman was reported in the press to say, "If anyone came into my store and tried to stop business I'd throw him out.... The Negro should behave himself and show he's a good citizen." When two NAACP officials sent Truman a telegram, asking to meet and explain to him why civil disobedience was necessary, the former president declined the meeting and said, "Your telegram regarding the statement which I made about sit downs in the restaurant is correct. I would do just what I said I would." (Secretary's Office File, Post Presidential Papers, Truman Papers, Truman Library)

CONSIDERING TRUMAN'S CIVIL RIGHTS ACHIEVEMENTS

TRUMAN'S SPEECH TO
THE NAACP, 29 JUNE 1947

Raymond Frey

Most Americans have heard of Dr. Martin Luther King Jr.'s inspiring "I Have a Dream" speech, delivered at the Lincoln Memorial during the March on Washington on 28 August 1963. Few recall, however, that President Harry S. Truman delivered a no less important and historic speech at that same spot, sixteen years before. Truman had been invited to speak to the closing session of the thirty-eighth annual conference of the National Association for the Advancement of Colored People on 29 June 1947. He would become the first president of the United States to address the NAACP since its founding in 1909. More importantly, Truman would become the first modern president to make an open and public commitment to civil rights.

Acts of domestic violence at home had turned the president's attention to civil rights during 1946. One incident in particular prompted Truman to act. On 19 September 1946, a delegation from the National Emergency Committee Against Mob Violence came to the White House to inform the president that acts of violence against blacks in the South had become a serious problem. They told him the story of a black veteran named Isaac Woodard. Discharged from the army a few hours earlier and still in his military uniform, Woodard was riding a Greyhound bus on the night of 13 February 1946 from Camp Gordon, Georgia, to his home in Winnsboro, South Carolina. In Batesburg, South Carolina, Woodard got off the bus to use the segregated washroom and took more time than the bus driver thought he should. The driver called the police. Chief of Police Lynwood Shull confronted Woodard and reportedly did not like the soldier's attitude. He beat him severely and poked out Woodard's eyes with his nightstick, leaving him totally blind.[1] When Truman was told about this and similar incidents of violence against African Americans during the meeting with the Committee Against Mob Violence, he was stunned and outraged, and he told the African American leaders that something had to be done to prevent further acts of violence.

The next day, Truman sent a letter to Attorney General Tom C. Clark. He referred to the Woodard incident and then wrote: "I have been very much alarmed at the increased racial feeling all over the country, and I am wondering if it wouldn't be well to appoint a commission to analyze the situation and have a remedy to present to the next Congress." Truman sent a copy of this letter to White House assistant David K. Niles, who handled issues relating to minorities. "I am very much in earnest on this and I'd like very much to have you push it with everything you have," he instructed Niles.[2]

Having suffered a crushing Democratic defeat in the 1946 congressional elections, and with 47 percent of the American people saying in a national poll that they disapproved of the president's leadership, Truman nevertheless decided to take on the politically explosive issue of civil rights. In December 1946 he signed an executive order creating the President's Committee on Civil Rights. Acutely aware of the threat to the nation's security posed by the emerging Cold War with the Soviet Union, he had come to the conclusion that world peace and the checking of totalitarianism depended upon protecting the civil rights of American citizens, regardless of race, creed, or color.[3] He believed that combating racism at home would improve America's image abroad, especially in emerging third-world nations.

The NAACP did not have great expectations that a president who was born and raised in a former slave state would do very much for African Americans, but it nonetheless extended an invitation to Truman to speak to the closing session of its annual conference, to be held at the Lincoln Memorial. Recognizing the growing importance of the NAACP and aware that the President's Committee on Civil Rights would issue its report in a few months, Truman decided to accept the invitation.

The day before the speech, on 28 June 1947, Truman sat down to write a letter to his sister, Mary Jane Truman, who lived with their mother in Grandview, Missouri. He was in a thoughtful mood, and the speech he was to give the next day was on his mind. He wrote, "I've got to make a speech to the Society [sic] for the

Advancement of Colored People tomorrow. Mamma won't like what I say because I wind up by quoting old Abe. But I believe what I say and I'm hopeful we may implement it."[4]

The sentences in this letter that refer to NAACP executive secretary Walter White and Eleanor Roosevelt are rarely quoted but extremely significant. Here, as in some other of Truman's personal letters, Truman's racial prejudices are evident. Some scholars have interpreted these documents to mean that Truman never overcame the prejudices of his Missouri upbringing and was pursuing a civil rights program in order to win African American votes in 1948. However, his comments to his sister about his speech to the NAACP suggest something else. He was clearly, in this letter, the same old Harry his sister had always known, prejudices and all. But he also makes it clear he is now the president of the United States, and as such he has to speak for the nation, which means quoting Abraham Lincoln and supporting civil rights for all Americans. Perhaps, too, he was using this letter, as he sometimes used writings not intended for public viewing, to help himself understand how he felt and what he believed. Understood in this way, Truman wrote the letter to his sister partly to reassure himself that he was doing right, and that as president he *had* to say what he would say to the NAACP the next day.

As for the black vote, Truman was certainly aware of its increasing importance, but he must also have been aware that he risked political suicide if he alienated the Southern white Democratic vote. By pushing his civil rights agenda, by saying the things to the NAACP that he would say the next day, he accepted this risk. When later, at the time of the Democratic National Convention in July 1948, some Southern politicians approached Truman and offered their support and that of other Southerners if he would soften his views on civil rights, Truman said, "My forebears were Confederates. ... Every factor and influence in my background ... would foster the personal belief that you are right. But my very stomach turned over when I learned that Negro soldiers, just back from overseas, were being dumped out of army trucks in Mississippi and beaten. Whatever my inclinations as a native of Missouri might have been, as President I know this is bad. I shall fight to end evils like this."[5] This statement, like the words addressed to his mother and sister regarding what he would say to the NAACP—"I believe what I say and I'm hopeful we may implement it"—suggests that political opportunism was not the driving force of Truman's civil rights program.

The Sunday of the NAACP speech, 29 June 1947, was a cloudy, warm, and humid day in Washington. The hour-long program at the Lincoln Memorial was to begin at 4:00 PM, but people began gathering near the Reflecting Pool and on the sidewalks in front of the memorial long before the scheduled starting time. By four o'clock, 612 official NAACP delegates from forty-five states, approximately 900 invited guests sitting in folding chairs, and about 3,000 additional people standing on walkways or sitting on the grass were ready for the program.[6]

The program included a performance by African American contralto Carol Brice, who had sung at President Roosevelt's third inauguration in 1941. She was accompanied by the United States Marine Band. The opening invocation was given by the Reverend Stephen G. Spottswood, a prominent black leader and civil rights activist who would later become a bishop in the AME Zion Church and a board chairman of the NAACP. Seated on the platform and to the president's left were Walter White, Eleanor Roosevelt, Senators Wayne Morse of Oregon and Arthur Capper of Kansas, Admiral Chester W. Nimitz, Attorney General Tom C. Clark, and Chief Justice Fred M. Vinson (who would later write the Supreme Court's decisions in a number of important civil rights cases).[7]

Senator Morse spoke first. Nicknamed the "Tiger of the Senate" for his outspoken and controversial views, he was an early champion of civil rights. He told the audience that it was fitting they should be "gathered at a great national shrine of human beings who recognize no distinctions in our democracy because of race, sex, creed or class." He went on to say that "bigotry and democracy cannot be reconciled," and called for "more men in government who did more than pay lip service to democracy.... We need to put the dignity of the individual above the dignity of the state."[8]

Eleanor Roosevelt spoke next. She said that the United States must rid itself of "the blot of lynching" in order to make democracy work. "We are now under the eyes of the whole world, which sees us as a nation built upon the contributions of many peoples."[9] Walter White then recalled the story of William English Walling, a white Southerner, who witnessed a race riot in Springfield, Illinois, the old home of President Lincoln, in 1908. A year later, he became one of the founders of the NAACP. Since the day of its founding, White said, "the association has carried to the Supreme Court twenty-four cases involving fundamental human rights, winning twenty-two. As a result, no man in this country can legally be denied the right to vote in a primary election, to secure education in a tax-supported school, to ride first-class travel in return for a first-class fare, or be denied, because of color, the right to work."[10]

President Truman came to the podium at 4:30 PM. His speech, which was carried by the four radio networks of the day, would run about twelve minutes. His fourth typewritten draft of the speech, preserved at the Truman Presidential Library, clearly shows his determination in taking a strong stand for civil rights.[11]

"It is my deep conviction," he declared, "that we have reached a turning point in the long history of our country's efforts to guarantee freedom and equality to all our citizens. Recent events in the United States and abroad have made us realize that it is more important today than ever before to insure that all Americans enjoy these rights." Truman then read a line he had penciled in himself during the writing process. "When I say all Americans I mean all Americans." He emphasized this point soon after when he said, "We must make the Federal Government a friendly, vigilant defender of the rights and equalities of all Americans"—and here another penciled-in addition—"and again I mean all Americans."

Truman later went on to say, "If this freedom is to be more than a dream, each man must be guaranteed equality of opportunity." The speechwriters had written "have equality of opportunity," but Truman had changed this to "be guaranteed," making clear his assertion that the federal government would take the role of providing this guarantee.

In one of the most powerful and frequently quoted lines of the speech, he said, slowing down and speaking with special clarity, "There is no justifiable reason for discrimination because of ancestry, or religion, race, or color."[12] He followed with an expansive definition of the concept of civil rights: "Every man should have the right to a decent home, the right to an education, the right to adequate medical care, the right to a worthwhile job, the right to an equal share in making the public decisions through the ballot, and the right to a fair trial in a fair court." Truman then delivered another line that he had added to the speechwriters' draft: "To these principles, I pledge my full and continued support."

The country could no longer afford "the luxury of a leisurely attack upon prejudice and discrimination" by states and local governments. Rather, Truman insisted, the federal government must take the lead. "Federal laws and administrative machineries must be improved and expanded.... We must strive to advance civil rights wherever it lies within our power."

Walter White later reflected that after Truman sat down at the conclusion of the speech, he showed absolutely no signs of fear of the impending political firestorm that was certain to come quickly his way. White told the president that he thought it was an excellent speech, and Truman assured him, "I said what I did because I mean every word of it—and I am going to prove that I do mean it."[13]

The initial response to the speech was mixed. The *Christian Science Monitor* gave a cautiously favorable review. "Few are the Americans, we think, who will find fault with the ideals of human rights and freedom to which President Truman pledged himself the other day as he stood on the steps of the Lincoln Memorial," the *Monitor* reported on 1 July 1947. "We trust Mr. Truman does fully understand not only that this is, as he says, 'a difficult and complex undertaking' but also how difficult and how complex an undertaking it really is."[14] Reaction among African Americans was understandably less guarded. The NAACP's monthly journal, *Crisis,* called the speech "the most comprehensive and forthright statement on the rights of minorities in a democracy and the duty of the government to secure safeguards that has ever been made by a President of the United States."[15]

Most of those who heard Truman's NAACP speech were taken by surprise. No one expected this of the former haberdasher, born and raised in a state that had largely sympathized with the Confederacy, the only president of the twentieth century who had never gone to college, the product of a corrupt Kansas City political machine, who had come to Washington bringing with him all of the prejudices of his rural Missouri upbringing. No one expected it would be this man who would be the first president to publicly advance a bold civil rights agenda for America.

Some people believed that Truman's strong civil rights stand was all but destroying his chances for election in 1948. In late 1947, White House aide Clark Clifford sent Truman a memorandum outlining a political strategy for the 1948 presidential campaign. Predicting correctly that the Republicans would nominate Governor Thomas E. Dewey of New York for president and that former vice president Henry Wallace would launch a third-party challenge, the memorandum also predicted that "the South, as always, can be considered safely Democratic."[16]

By the time Truman sent his civil rights legislation to Congress in February 1948, his disapproval rating in the South had reached 57 percent and nationally, only 6 percent of Americans approved of his civil rights program.[17] Mississippi governor Fielding L. Wright claimed that Truman's proposals were designed to do nothing less than "to wreck the South and its institutions."[18] On 20 January 1948, Governor James "Big Jim" Folsom of Alabama said to the white people of his state: "Right now, you're living under a dark cloud.... Who is running our party in Washington? The head of our party is a nice man. But he's not running our party any more. And he's not running our country."[19]

"I felt that any other course would be inconsistent with international commitments and obligations," Truman later wrote about his civil rights program in his memoirs. "We could not endorse a color line at home and still expect to influence the immense masses that make up the Asian and African peoples. It was necessary to practice what we preached, and I tried to see that we did it." Truman also wrote that he was following the civil rights policy articulated in every Democratic Party platform since 1932. "When the Southerners saw in 1948 that I meant to put it [that policy] into effect, they bolted the party." He also told the story about Strom Thurmond's comment to a reporter as he was leading mutinous Southern delegates out of the Democratic National Convention in July 1948. The reporter asked why Thurmond was doing this: "Isn't President Truman only following the platform that Roosevelt advocated?" Thurmond replied, "I agree, but Truman really *means* it."[20]

As an ardent student of both American history and the U.S. Constitution, Truman clearly understood his role and responsibilities as president. Being president of the United States, he often said, meant being president of *all* the people. Truman deeply believed this. Being president meant that one must sometimes put aside personal beliefs and prejudices, as well as future political ambitions, to do what is in the best interests of the country—the entire country and all its citizens.

At the time Truman made his speech to the meeting of the NAACP at the Lincoln Memorial, Washington DC was a segregated city. Schools in the United States were also segregated, as were the armed forces. Jim Crow laws were the norm throughout the South, and lynchings were all too commonplace. The Ku Klux Klan was a prominent force in Southern culture, justice, and politics. Truman ignored opinion polls, stood up to white Southern Democrats, and put his presidency on the line because he believed the time had come for America to start living up to its constitutional promises. This was well before any organized civil rights movement, before any action by Congress or the Supreme Court required a president to take such a stand. If the other two branches of government would not act, he would. Standing virtually alone, risking his presidency, acting on basic moral principles, Truman forged ahead on civil rights.

Harry S. Truman left office with one of the lowest approval ratings in American history, but he never cared much for polls anyway. "I wonder how far Moses would have gone," he once said, "if he had taken a poll in Egypt."[21] But his deep knowledge of history taught him that the decisions a president makes affect the country far into the future. It took a few more decades to prove Truman correct on civil rights, but unfortunately his pioneering role is all but forgotten. Although Truman's NAACP speech did not contain the soaring prose of King's "I Have a Dream" speech and has been largely forgotten by Americans, it retains an important place in the history of civil rights in America. Walter White said it was a more important speech than Lincoln's Gettysburg Address "in its specific condemnation of evils based upon race prejudice which had too long disgraced America, and its call for immediate action against them."[22] For Harry Truman, the speech was simply what had to be said, it was the simple truth about what was right and had to be done, and, as he was fond of saying, "That's all there is to it."

Notes

[1]Lawson, *To Secure These Rights,* 8; and Gardner, *Truman and Civil Rights,* 16.

[2]Truman to Tom C. Clark, 20 September 1946, and Truman to David K. Niles, 20 September 1946. Niles Papers, Truman Presidential Library.

[3]Gross, "Truman Holds Civil Rights a Key to Peace," *Washington Post,* 30 June 1947.

[4]Truman to Mary Jane Truman, 28 June 1947. Truman Papers, Post-Presidential Papers, Memoirs File, Truman Presidential Library.

[5]Truman, Margaret, *Harry S. Truman,* 392.

[6]Gross, "Truman Holds Civil Rights a Key to Peace." *Washington Post,* 30 June 1947.

[7]McFadden, "Bishop Spottswood of NAACP Dies," *New York Times,* 3 December 1974. For seating arrangement on platform, see phograph 59–1386-2, audiovisual collection, Truman Library.

[8]Streator, "Truman Demands We Fight Harder to Spur Equality," *New York Times,* 30 June 1947.

[9]Streator, "Truman Demands We Fight Harder." See also "Racial Wall U.S. Peril, Truman Says," *Los Angeles Times,* 30 June 1947.

[10]Streator, "Truman Demands We Fight Harder."

[11] Address Before the National Association for the Advancement of Colored People, 29 June 1947, Public Papers of the Presidents, Truman 1947, 311–313. See also the fourth draft of the speech, showing changes made by Truman, Truman Papers, President's Secretary's Files, Speech File, Truman Library.

[12] Sound Recording SR 64–54, audiovisual collection, Truman Library.

[13] White, *A Man Called White*, 348–49.

[14] "Not What, But How." *Christian Science Monitor*, 1 July 1947.

[15] Berman, *Politics of Civil Rights*, 64.

[16] Clark M. Clifford to Harry S. Truman, 19 November 1947, Clifford Papers, Truman Library, cited in Hamby, *Man of the People*, 430–31.

[17] Hamby, *Man of the People*, 435.

[18] Wright speech in V. O. Key, *Southern Politics in State and Nation* (New York: Alfred A. Knopf, 1949), 330, cited in Karabell, *Last Campaign*, 47–48.

[19] Folsom speech in Truman Papers, official File 299E, Truman Library, cited in Karabell, *Last Campaign*, 47–48.

[20] Truman, *Memoirs*, 2:183.

[21] Longhand note by Harry S. Truman, Truman Papers, President's Secretary's Files, Longhand Notes File, Truman Library, cited in McCullough, "Harry S. Truman," 52.

[22] White, *A Man Called White*, 348.

POLITICAL PRAGMATISM AND CIVIL RIGHTS POLICY
Truman and Integration of the Military

Richard M. Yon and Tom Lansford

Harry S. Truman was in many ways an unlikely advocate for civil rights in the United States. He was a product of a culture that was deeply segregated. Truman himself would later be faulted for his use of racist language and his attitude toward the tactics of the civil rights movement during the 1960s. Nonetheless, as president, Truman helped launch the modern civil rights movement by enacting antisegregationist policies and by adopting controversial, and often politically unpopular, stances in regard to racial equality. He became the first American president to develop a comprehensive civil rights program and thereby established a political precedent that future chief executives would follow. One of the most important and influential actions undertaken by Truman was his decision to integrate the military. The ultimate success of Truman's military integration policies undermined the political and social arguments against broader societal integration and emboldened the leaders of the African American community to seek further advances in desegregation.

Truman's military integration policies resulted from a combination of political courage and pragmatism. This essay explores the seeming contradictions between Truman's personal background and his military desegregation policy in the context of the obstacles and challenges faced by the administration as it sought to integrate the U.S. armed services. Specifically, the essay explores the personal, political, and practical reasons that prompted Truman to seek integration of the military. It also analyzes the main institutional, political, and popular constraints Truman and the administration confronted as they sought to implement new polices, expand opportunities for African Americans, and more effectively utilize African American personnel in the armed forces. Finally, the essay surveys the immediate and long-term results of Truman's policies.

The first tentative steps toward integration of the U.S. armed forces occurred during World War II. The army and navy made limited efforts at integrating some units and commissioned a range of surveys to study desegregation. In September 1945, Secretary of the Army Robert P. Patterson appointed a board to undertake a comprehensive review of the Army's treatment of African Americans. In April of the following year, the Gillem Board (named after its chair, Lieutenant General Alvan C. Gillem Jr.) issued its recommendations under the title "Utilization of Negro Manpower in the Postwar Army Policy." Specifically, the report advised the army to adopt a number of initiatives, including "expanding the range of army jobs available to Negroes, mixing Negroes and whites in duty assignments in overhead (house-keeping) installations, increasing the types of Negro units, and steadily reducing the size of Negro units and assigning them to larger white units."[1] The board's recommendations were accepted and implemented, but they marked only minor progress toward integration.

In 1947, in the aftermath of the Gillem report, two Truman administration panels, the President's Advisory Committee on Universal Training and the President's Committee on Civil Rights, criticized continued segregation in the armed forces and called for increased integration. By January 1948, Truman had decided to use an executive order rather than going through Congress to end segregation in the armed forces because he believed Southern politicians would block legislation to achieve this end.[2]

On 2 February 1948, in a major civil rights speech, Truman announced to Congress that he had ordered the Secretary of Defense to integrate the military "as rapidly as possible." On 26 July 1948, Truman issued Executive Order 9981, which stated, "It is hereby declared to be the policy of the President that there shall be equality of treatment and opportunity for all persons in the armed services without regard to race, color, religion or national origin. This policy shall be put into effect as rapidly as possible, having due regard to the time required to effectuate any necessary changes without impairing efficiency or morale."[3] In order to implement the order, Truman established the President's Committee on Equality of

Treatment and Opportunity in the Armed Services (known as the Fahy Committee after its chair, Charles Fahy, a former U.S. solicitor general). Truman charged the committee with developing the necessary procedures, rules, and evaluations to ensure integration. Truman stated, "I want it done in such a way that it is not a publicity stunt. I want concrete results—that's what I'm after—not publicity on it."[4]

The committee sought to work with the military to achieve integration without controversy, but many senior officers publicly opposed the effort.[5] The navy and the air force moved relatively quickly and had their integration plans approved by June 1949. The army, however, had to revise its plan several times and was not able to develop an acceptable plan until January 1950. It was not until 1953 that the army could report that 95 percent of African Americans were serving in integrated units.

The desegregation of the armed forces had its origin in conditions that developed following World War II. After the war, Truman sought to refocus the nation's political attention on domestic issues and both complete and expand the New Deal programs begun by his predecessor, Franklin D. Roosevelt.[6] However, throughout Truman's presidency, world events forced him to spend considerable time and energy on foreign policy. The military was one of several areas where domestic and foreign policy intersected. In order to confront the growing security challenges posed by the onset of the Cold War, Truman implemented dramatic reorganizations of the nation's defense and military structures, including the creation of the U.S. Air Force and the Department of Defense. In his memoirs, Truman stated that his intention was to create "an integrated military program and budget; greater economies through unified control of supply and service functions; improved co-ordination [sic] between the military and the rest of the government; the strongest means for civilian control of the military; creation of a parity for air power; systemic allocation of the limited resources for scientific research and development; and consistent and equitable personnel policies."[7]

One component of Truman's efforts at more equitable personnel policies was the creation of greater opportunities for African American service members. During the war, the navy developed a program that allowed limited integration on some ships, while the marines and the army resisted even limited efforts at integration.[8] Truman's subsequent policies were designed to maximize the assets and capabilities of the military in order to free resources for domestic programs while maintaining the nation's necessary security commitments. The motivations behind his military integration policies combined a range of factors and were testament to the complexity of Truman's character.[9]

At the core of Truman's practical considerations regarding military integration was efficiency. Segregation meant redundancy and repetition, since the military had to operate dual training programs and maintain dual housing and base facilities. In addition, because of segregation, the best and most capable officers were not always given commands appropriate to their abilities. For instance, in the army, only about one in ten African American soldiers who scored in the top two categories of entrance tests became officers; for white soldiers, the figure was one in four.[10] Studies conducted by the military services also noted that the failure to adequately train African American soldiers had undermined the efficiency and morale of their units.[11] The President's Committee on Civil Rights bolstered these arguments when it reported that "by preventing entire groups from making their maximum contribution to the national defense, we weaken our defense to that extent and impose heavier burdens on the remainder of the population."[12]

Truman had personal reasons for promoting military integration. For instance, his own experiences with African American troops led him to believe that the main factor in past poor performance was not ability, but leadership. During World War I, Truman served alongside the African American 92nd Division. This segregated division performed poorly in combat, but another African American unit, the 93rd Division, fought well. After the war, Truman was curious about the differences in the two units and investigated their history. He found that the 92nd had only white officers, but the 93rd, which was under French command, had an integrated officer corps. Truman later recalled that the incident convinced him that integration was the only way to ensure that officers were chosen on the basis of skill and ability, and that the services would have the best possible leaders.[13] In a speech to the National Colored Democratic Association in 1940, Truman quoted the commander of American forces in Europe in World War I, General John J. Pershing: "I cannot commend too highly the spirit shown among the colored combat troops, who exhibit fine capacity for quick training and eagerness for the most dangerous work." In the speech, Truman declared that "the Negroes' flag is our flag, and he [sic] stands ready, just as we do, to defend it against all foes from within and without."[14]

Presidential advisor Clark Clifford recalled that Truman was deeply bothered by the dichotomies inherent in segregation:

> President Truman believed segregation in the armed forces under-mined American values and acted against the nation's best inter-ests. He thought it was outrageous that men could be asked to die for their country but not be allowed to fight in the same units because of their color. He knew that in the military, where argu-ments over equipment and privileges were a way of life, white sol-diers inevitably took precedence over blacks.[15]

Truman knew that limited integration within the military had proven successful during World War II. He was impressed that the army's integration of its officer training corps during World War II had been successful, in spite of intense opposition from Southern pol-iticians who especially objected to integrated living quarters for the officers. Army historian Morris J. MacGregor Jr. concluded in his study of the integration of the armed forces that "officer candidate training was the Army's first formal experiment with integration" and that "blacks and whites lived together with a minimum of fric-tion, and, except in flight school, all candidates trained together."[16]

Truman believed that the treatment accorded African American veterans after World War II was unacceptable. Many who had served in combat units during the war were relegated to service and logisti-cal units once the fighting stopped.[17] Truman was especially moved by the violent receptions that awaited some African American veter-ans when they returned home after the war. In February 1946, one such veteran, Isaac Woodard, was attacked and blinded by police-men in Batesburg, South Carolina. In July, two African American veterans and their wives were shot to death by a white mob near Monroe, Georgia. The latter incident prompted Truman to order Attorney General Tom Clark to determine whether any federal stat-utes could be used against the mob leaders.

The violence against returning African American veterans led civil rights leaders to establish the National Emergency Committee Against Mob Violence. A delegation from the group met with Tru-man on 19 September 1946 and presented evidence of the atrocities being committed. The delegation's spokesman, Walter White, described in his memoirs Truman's reaction when he was told about the violence being suffered by African American veterans: "The President sat quietly, elbows resting on the arms of his chair and his fingers interlocked against his stomach as he listened with a grim face to the story of the lynchings.... When I finished, the President exclaimed in his flat, midwestern accent, 'My God! I had no idea it was as terrible as that! We've got to do something!' "[18]

Truman's reaction underscores his recognition that whatever his personal beliefs were, he had to take action on civil rights. This was a longstanding characteristic of Truman's political career—he had supported civil rights for African Americans while continuing to hold racist beliefs. Before he became president, Truman supported civil rights legislation in the Senate, including a 1939 act to increase appropriations for the investigation of violations of civil rights and civil liberties.[19] In the speech, which opened his campaign for reelection to the Senate, given in Sedalia, Missouri in the summer of 1940, Truman explained why he felt he had to support civil rights for African Americans. "In giving Negroes the rights which are theirs we are only acting in accord with our own ideals of a true democracy," he said. "If any class or race can be permanently set apart from, or pushed down below the rest in political and civil rights, so may any other class or race when it shall incur the displeasure of its more powerful associates, and we may say farewell to the principles on which we count for our safety."[20]

This appreciation of the importance of equality before the law would underlie Truman's civil rights policies. In a ceremonial letter to the annual conference of the National Urban League, dated 12 September 1946, he made an unusually strong statement for such an occasion: "If the civil rights of even one citizen are abused, government has failed to discharge one of its primary responsibilities."[21] On 6 December 1946, he launched his civil rights program by appointing the President's Committee on Civil Rights.

Truman's personal considerations in his push for military integration existed concurrently with very real and concrete political motivations. On the domestic level, he was acutely aware of the importance of the African American vote to the Democratic Party.[22] On the international level, he also understood the necessity of mobilizing all components of American society in order to successfully wage the Cold War.

After the Republican capture of both houses of Congress in the 1946 midterm elections, Truman's aides turned their attention to the 1948 election. In late 1947, Clark Clifford sent Truman a forty-three page memorandum that prescribed an election strategy emphasizing, among other things, the need for the president to take strong action on civil rights. Clifford warned that Republicans in Congress

planned to introduce antilynching legislation and measures to curb
the poll tax. By doing this, Clifford warned, the GOP could conceiv-
ably regain the strong African American support it had historically
enjoyed before the New Deal. Presidential aide George Elsey con-
curred with Clifford and emphasized the importance of the African
American vote in states such as New York, New Jersey, Illinois, and
California.[23]

William L. Batt, a researcher and strategist for the Democratic
Party, underscored the recommendations of Clifford and Elsey and
voiced concern about the potential loss of African American votes to
third-party candidate Henry A. Wallace, who was campaigning on a
platform that included a strong civil rights plank. Batt argued that
Wallace might capture as much as 20 to 30 percent of the African
American vote, and he pointed out that some New York ward leaders believed African American voters in their districts might support
Wallace. He advised Truman to integrate the military as a means to
appeal to African Americans and erode support for Wallace.[24]

A range of political figures and groups advised Truman to integrate the military in order to assure victory in the upcoming presidential elections. In a letter dated 22 July 1948, Leon Henderson,
chairman of Americans for Democratic Action (a group that
included Hubert Humphrey and Franklin D. Roosevelt Jr.), urged
Truman to "issue an Executive Order declaring it our national policy that there shall be no segregation or discrimination in the armed
forces."[25] Henderson's letter was received the same day that the Students for Democratic Action sent the White House a letter calling
on Truman to desegregate the military in order to deal Henry Wallace "a heavy blow."[26]

African American voters did prove crucial in the 1948 election.
In California, Illinois, and Ohio, African American votes helped
provide Truman the margin of victory in the closely contested presidential race. Truman noted in his memoirs, "Without Ohio and California, I would have been assured of only 254 electoral votes, twelve
less than the required 266."[27] Truman's actions on behalf of civil
rights, including his issuance of Executive Order 9981, helped ensure
that African Americans would remain loyal to the Democratic
Party.

One final political consideration for Truman was the perception
of the United States held by the rest of the world. Truman recognized the implicit dichotomy between America's promotion of
democracy abroad and its practice of segregation at home. In his

memoirs, he wrote that any course other than integration "would be inconsistent with international commitments and obligations. We could not endorse a color line at home and still expect to influence the immense masses that make up the Asian and African peoples. It was necessary to practice what we preached, and I tried to see that we did it."[28]

As the Cold War intensified, Truman needed African Americans to support the national effort to counter Soviet expansionism. According to army historian MacGregor, "the black community represented 10 percent of the country's manpower, and this also influenced defense planning. Black threats to boycott the segregated armed forces could not be ignored, and civil rights demands had to be considered in developing laws relating to selective service and universal training."[29] Truman needed the support of African Americans to accomplish his national security objectives, and African American leaders such as A. Philip Randolph and Grant Reynolds were demanding that the armed forces be integrated. In November 1947, Randolph and Reynolds organized the Committee against Jim Crow in Military Service and Training, which was dedicated to the desegregation of the military and the expansion of opportunities for African Americans. The group originally lobbied to include an amendment against discrimination in legislation on the military draft; when this effort failed, it concentrated on pressuring Truman to issue an executive order to force integration.

In March 1948, twenty-two African American organizations joined together at a meeting in New York to issue a demand that segregation in the armed services be abolished. In a letter to Truman dated 29 June 1948, Randolph and Reynolds threatened that African American youth would boycott the draft if Truman did not provide an executive order to abolish segregation. "In light of past official civil rights pronouncements," Randolph and Reynolds wrote, "it is our belief that the President, as Commander-in-Chief, is morally obligated to issue an order now."[30] These groups applied significant political pressure on Truman that, combined with other considerations, caused him to issue Executive Order 9981. With the promulgation of 9981, Randolph and Reynolds ended their call for a boycott of the draft.

The armed forces were not instantly integrated when Truman issued Executive Order 9981, as many obstacles remained. Truman's political dexterity served him well as he carefully maneuvered between groups opposed to and in favor of integration. He employed his legendary political courage to deflect public criticism away from the military itself and away from others in the integration process. Truman also deftly utilized both force and compromise to achieve his goals without sacrificing the nation's military efficiency or capability.

Truman's decision to integrate the military was not uniformly popular. A Gallup poll conducted in 1948 found that 82 percent of those interviewed opposed Truman's civil rights policies. Many opponents of military integration sent angry letters to Truman.[31] Newspaper editorials throughout the South condemned Truman's order to integrate and some commentators invoked state sovereignty and talked of possible revolt. Many newspapers asserted that the timing of the executive order was designed to erode support for Wallace and alleged that Truman's action was undertaken for the basest political reasons. Other newspapers supported Truman's decision. For instance, both the Republican-leaning *Pittsburgh Courier* and the Democratic *Chicago Defender* supported Truman in editorials.[32]

Statements by some of the country's leading military figures provided substantial ammunition to anti-integration forces. Testifying before Congress, General Dwight D. Eisenhower argued that the military reflected society and should not be used to promote social change. He stated, "I do believe that if we attempt merely by passing a lot of laws to force someone to like someone else, we are just going to get into trouble." General Omar Bradley made a similar statement. The day after Truman issued Executive Order 9981, Bradley argued that the military was no place for "social experiments" and that desegregation would only be successful in the army when the rest of the country was integrated. Bradley later publicly apologized to Truman for his comments. Besides Eisenhower and Bradley, other prominent officers, including George C. Marshall and Mark W. Clark, also expressed opposition to integration. These pronouncements would be used repeatedly by those who were opposed to integration.[33]

Negative public opinion with respect to civil rights had an effect on Truman's program. Historian Barton J. Bernstein has argued that Truman consistently limited his efforts on behalf of civil rights because he and his advisors feared a public backlash.[34] The Korean War intensified this caution, as some in the administration did not want to appear to be interfering with military efficiency. Furthermore, the rise of McCarthyism damaged hopes for further advances in civil rights by causing some prominent African Americans, such as the performer Paul Robeson, to be perceived as sympathetic to the Soviet Union. Historian Kevern Verney argues that while Truman made important progress in the area of civil rights, the rise of McCarthyism delayed the full emergence of the civil rights movement until the 1950s.[35]

McCarthyism and the Korean War also eroded Truman's personal popularity. In 1951 and 1952, his approval rating fell below 30 percent. His unpopularity and his growing sense of political and personal isolation constrained his ability and his willingness to exert pressure on the military to complete the process of integration. Nonetheless, he continued to urge the army, the most recalcitrant of the services, to achieve nearly full integration during the last years of his presidency.

Southern members of Congress tried in several different ways to blunt the effect of Executive Order 9981. On the eve of the order's issuance, Senator Richard B. Russell of Georgia tried to insert language into the draft order that would have allowed enlistees the option of choosing to serve in units of their own race. When Congress tried to pass legislation to eliminate a 10-percent quota system for African American enlistees, Southern politicians consistently blocked the effort and the quota system as it applied to the draft was only ended through an administrative decision by the Selective Service Commission.[36] Truman was forced to veto a bill in 1951 because it contained a clause requiring schools on federal military bases to conform to the education laws of the state in which the base was located. This would have caused schools on military bases in the South to be resegregated.[37] In one important instance, the segregationists were successful: the army made no effort for several years to force states to integrate their National Guard units, many of which remained segregated into the 1960s.

The most significant congressional opposition to Executive Order 9981 came from the support Congress gave to attempts by the army to delay integration. Anti-integration senators and representatives routinely met with Army officials to coordinate efforts to slow integration. E. W. Kenworthy, executive secretary of the Fahy Committee, recalled that the committee often faced officers who had been encouraged to mislead the committee. In addition, in a foreshadowing of the tactics used by anti-integration groups following the Supreme Court's 1954 *Brown v. Board of Education* decision, opponents of military integration seized on the phrase in Executive Order 9981 which stated that desegregation should occur "without impairing efficiency or morale" in the military. Secretary of the Army Kenneth Royall believed that the order did not necessitate "swift" integration if it harmed morale. He continued to resist the integration of the army throughout his tenure as secretary.[38]

On 11 May 1949, Secretary of Defense Louis Johnson approved the air force's integration plan but ordered the army and navy to revise theirs. A new navy plan was accepted on 7 June 1949, but the army continued to present plans that were unacceptable. At the core of the army's plans were continued segregation in some units, mainly combat units, and the maintenance of a 10-percent enlistment quota for African Americans. Both of these policies were vehemently opposed by the Fahy Committee.[39]

Truman took great interest in the workings of the Fahy Committee and insisted on being kept informed of its work. The committee appealed to him on a number of occasions to pressure the army toward integration. In its interim report of 11 October 1949, for instance, the committee suggested that the president "may wish to advise the Secretary of Defense that the Committee's recommendations [with respect to the integration of the army] conform to the requirements of Executive Order 9981." The committee also threatened to release to the press statements critical of the army.[40] In response, Truman pressured both the committee and the army to work together to resolve the impasse. When the army developed another revised plan, Truman instructed senior officers that his acceptance would be based on the approval of the Fahy Committee.[41] On 14 January 1950, the committee and the army agreed on an integration plan that still contained the quota for African American recruits. On 1 February, Truman informed the army that the Fahy Committee would remain in existence until the army ended its 10 percent recruitment quota. In March, the army surrendered and announced it would drop the quota the following month.[42]

Once the 10-percent quota was ended, African American enlistments rose. By August 1950, African Americans constituted 11.4 percent of army personnel, and enlistments continued to grow as a percentage of the total. By early 1953, African Americans constituted 16.1 percent of army personnel. In January 1951, the main army command in Korea began unofficially to integrate all units. Meanwhile, the rush of new African American recruitments meant that all branches of the service had to desegregate basic training, and the Department of Defense made an announcement to this effect on 18 March 1951. On the third anniversary (26 July 1951) of Executive

Order 9981, the army announced that all units in the Asian theater would be integrated within six months.[43]

Truman's commitment to civil rights, and perhaps most significantly his desegregation of the armed forces, brought him important political benefits. For one thing, most African Americans who voted supported Truman in 1948. Perhaps most significantly, Truman's desegregation of the armed forces helped offset negative perceptions of the Democratic Party caused by Southern segregationists in Congress and elsewhere, and it helped prevent the Republican Party from regaining its pre–New Deal level of support among African Americans. In the 1960s, Democratic presidents would take up the cause of civil rights again, with such success that African Americans became firmly bound to the Democratic Party.

Integrated military bases, including desegregated base housing, had a ripple effect on civil rights in local communities. In some areas, especially in the West and upper South, an increased measure of integration seeped into communities located close to military bases.[44] Nonetheless, many servicemen and their families continued to face discrimination in off-base housing and other accommodations. Efforts to end these practices through the use of federal economic sanctions were resisted by Congress and by the Department of Defense until the passage of the 1964 Civil Rights Act.

The successful integration of the armed forces was probably the most important civil rights achievement of the Truman administration. The Korean War, which gradually forced the army to integrate, greatly discouraged any further progress in Truman's other civil rights initiatives. The Democratic Party lost seats in the 1950 elections, partly because of the war's negative affect on Truman's popularity; neither house of Congress would even consider any of his major civil rights initiatives in the final two years of his presidency. Still, the desegregated military survived under succeeding presidents, and its existence and example helped inspire many in the country, including many leaders within the Democratic Party, to fight for a good and just society for all Americans, regardless of race.

Notes

[1]Billington, "Freedom to Serve," 268.

[2]Shull, *American Civil Rights Policy,* 122.

[3]Executive Order 9981.

[4]Memorandum, Meeting of the President and the Four Service Secretaries with the President's Committee on Equality of Treatment and Opportunity in the Armed

Services, 12 January 1949, attached to C.G.R. [Charles G. Ross] to Donald Dawson, 17 January 1949. Truman Papers, Official File 1285-O, Truman Library. Most of the original documents cited in this essay are available at the Truman Library's online document collection, "Desegregation of the Armed Forces," www.trumanlibrary.org.

[5] Nichols, *Breakthrough on the Color Front,* 89–90.

[6] See Hamby, *Beyond the New Deal.*

[7] Truman, *Memoirs,* 2:67.

[8] For more on the navy's program, see Nelson, *Integration of the Negro into the U.S. Navy.*

[9] Pauly, *Modern Presidency and Civil Rights,* 36.

[10] Ginzberg, *Negro Potential,* 85.

[11] E. W. Kenworthy to Charles Fahy, 10 March 1949. Record Group 220, Records of the President's Committee on Equality of Treatment and Opportunity in the Armed Services, Truman Library.

[12] President's Committee on Civil Rights, *To Secure These Rights,* 162.

[13] Nichols, *Breakthrough on the Color Front,* 83–85.

[14] Truman, "New Deal for the Negro," in Horton, *Freedom and Equality,* 7.

[15] Clifford, *Counsel to the President,* 208.

[16] MacGregor, *Integration of the Armed Forces,* Chapter 2, World War II: The Army.

[17] MacGregor, *Integration of the Armed Forces,* Chapter 2, World War II: The Army.

[18] White, *A Man Called White,* 330–31.

[19] Truman, *Memoirs,* 1:177.

[20] Quoted in Daniels, *Man of Independence,* 339–40.

[21] Truman to L. B. Granger, 12 September 1946. Truman Papers, President's Personal File 2685, Truman Library.

[22] Vaughn, "Truman Administration's Fair Deal for Black America," 291–305.

[23] McCullough, *Truman,* 590.

[24] Gropman, *Air Force Integrates,* 106–8.

[25] Leon Henderson to Harry S. Truman, 22 July 1948. Truman Papers, Official File 93-B, Truman Library.

[26] Richard A. Givens to John R. Steelman, 22 July 1948. Truman Papers, Official File 93-B, Truman Library.

[27] Truman, *Memoirs,* 2:257.

[28] Truman, *Memoirs,* 2:257.

[29] MacGregor, *Integration of the Armed Forces,* Chapter 12, The Present Resident Intervenes.

[30] Grant Reynolds and A. Philip Randolph to Harry S. Truman, 29 June 1948, attached to Matthew J. Connelly to James V. Forrestal, 7 July 1948. Truman Papers, Official File 93-B, Truman Library.

[31] Gardner, *Truman and Civil Rights,* 106, 119.

[32] Dalfiume, *Desegregation of the U.S. Armed Forces,* 158; Berman, *Politics of Civil Rights,* 118–19; and MacGregor, *Integration of the Armed Forces,* Chapter 13: Service Interests Versus Presidential Intent.

[33] Quoted in Nichols, *Breakthrough on the Color Front,* 167, 172. See also Edgerton, *Hidden Heroism,* 164.

[34] Bernstein, "America in War and Peace."

[35] Reddick, "Negro Policy of the American Army," 208; and Verney, *Black Civil Rights in America.*

[36] Reddick, "Negro Policy of the American Army," 202, 210.

[37] McCoy and Ruetten, *Quest and Response,* 244.

[38] Gardner, *Truman and Civil Rights,* 112; and Nichols, *Breakthrough on the Color Front,* 92, 89.

[39] Billington, "Freedom to Serve," 266–67, 269.

[40] Charles Fahy, Memorandum for the President, 11 October 1949, and Further Interim Report to the President, 11 October 1949, both attached to David Niles to the President, n.d.. Truman Papers, President's Secretary's Files, Truman Presidential Library; and Charles Fahy to David K. Niles, 30 November 1949, and E. W. Kenworthy to Charles Fahy, 19 December 1949. Record Group 220, Records of the President's Committee on Equality of Treatment and Opportunity in the Armed Services, Truman Library.

[41] Billington, "Freedom to Serve," 271–73; and McCoy and Ruetten, *Quest and Response,* 230.

[42] Dalfiume, *Desegregation of the U.S. Amred Forces*, 196–98.

[43] Dalfiume, *Desegregation of the U.S. Armed Forces*, 205, 209, 211; McCoy and Ruetten, Quest and Response, 233; MacGregor, *Integration of the Armed Forces*, Chapter 17, The Army Integrates.

[44] Gropman, *Air Force Integrates,* 141.

TRUMAN, DESEGREGATION OF THE ARMED FORCES, AND A KID FROM THE SOUTH BRONX

Colin Powell

Of all the many domestic challenges President Truman faced in 1948, none was greater than the need to move the nation's civil rights agenda forward. The reality of life in America in 1948 was that during the eighty years since the Civil War ended slavery, America had designed and implemented a system of apartheid, almost as evil as slavery and far more duplicitous. The Reconstruction period that flourished briefly after the Civil War ended abruptly before much progress could be made toward full citizenship for African Americans. Reconstruction died, and the nation, so soon after the promise of the Emancipation Proclamation, sank into Jim Crow and the concept of separate but equal. Black Americans were disenfranchised, black Americans were lynched, courts in the South were closed to black Americans. Education, unions, trade, political life—all were closed to black Americans. Blacks were excluded systematically from legislative or executive power at almost every level of government. In 1948, fourscore years after the Civil War, the sad, troubling, disgraceful traditions of our past continued.

This is our history. It is cold to recite these facts, but we must understand them if we want to understand where we are and where we have to go. The reality of our history is that president after president, Congress after Congress, Supreme Court session after Supreme Court session continued to read our Declaration of Independence's glorious conception of inalienable rights as not applying to black Americans. The Constitution was similarly interpreted. When it was written in 1787, blacks were counted as only three-fifths of a white person, with zero-fifths of the rights of citizenship. Separate but equal, racism and discrimination, resulted in a colossal system of preferences that were declared to be constitutional.

By 1948, things were beginning to change. The country was on the verge of a second period of reconstruction. A movement was growing that held that no nation so gloriously conceived in liberty as the United States could continue the degradation that was being perpetrated against one group of citizens. How could such a nation hold itself up to the rest of the world as a model of freedom, of democracy, of the protection of the God-given rights of men and women? How could the United States dare, if this degradation of black people continued, to assert its moral superiority to people of color in the third world? So things began to change. African Americans began to apply political pressure. Wartime migration of blacks to the North resulted in more political power in the northern cities. There was a push for voter registration in the South. Organizations such as the National Association for the Advancement of Colored People (NAACP) and the National Urban League protested and demonstrated. Great leaders came forward, such as Roy Wilkins, Thurgood Marshall, A. Philip Randolph, and many others. White Americans of conscience joined in the battle. Clark Clifford, one of President Truman's closest advisers, kept telling him, "Do the right thing, do the right thing, Mr. President." This pressure fit into the president's plans to run for reelection on a strong civil rights plank. He promised as much in a speech to the NAACP. (He was the first president to address a convention of the NAACP.) But Harry Truman was no raving integrationist. In fact, in later years, he would speak out against some of the tactics of the 1960s civil rights movement. He did not like the sit-ins. He was from a border state, and his biographers will tell you that, on occasion, he used words referring to race and ethnicity that would not be used today, that would be considered very objectionable. But despite Truman's at least partly Southern background, he believed to the depth of his heart that all citizens in this country were entitled to their constitutional rights. Otherwise, we were living a lie as a nation. Truman acted on this belief. On 2 February 1948, he became the first president to deliver a civil rights message to Congress. In his typical simple language, he said this: "We cannot be satisfied until all our people have equal opportunities for jobs, for homes, for education, for health, and for political expression, and until all our people have equal protection under the law.... There is a serious gap between our ideals and some of our practices. This gap must be closed."[1] Our country, Truman was insisting, cannot have two sets of rules, two sets of principles, two sets of ideals.

President Truman also saw the political pragmatism of moving forward on a strong civil rights agenda. Henry Wallace's new party was drawing away liberal supporters. Mayor Hubert Humphrey of Minneapolis was pushing civil rights on the left wing of the Democratic Party. The Republican Party was promoting a strong civil rights platform. Truman needed a strong platform for the campaign that was coming up. He needed the African American vote, because African American political power was now making a difference in America. Truman was willing to go for that vote even if it meant the loss of the Dixiecrats, who were totally opposed to any form of civil rights legislation. Truman could not delay. A. Philip Randolph of the Brotherhood of Sleeping Car Porters was getting ready to undertake a campaign of massive civil disobedience, to tell Negroes not to register for the draft. After all the fighting African Americans had done for their country, he said, still they were treated as tenth-class citizens; they would no longer sign up to serve in a segregated army. Truman knew he had to act.

Harry Truman was deeply moved in a very human and personal way by some of the things that happened after the war. The black veterans who had fought on foreign battlefields came home to discover nothing had changed on the battlefields at home. Truman was shattered by the story of two black veterans in uniform in Georgia who were pulled out of their car with their wives and murdered on the spot. Principle, pressure, pragmatism, politics—all came to bear and all caused Truman to sign Executive Order 9981 on 26 July 1948. The heart of the order says this: "It is hereby declared to be the policy of the President that there shall be equality of treatment and opportunity for all persons in the armed services without regard for race, color, religion or national origin."[2] The order also set up a committee to implement Truman's instructions.

Why did Truman act by executive order rather than ask Congress to pass a law? Because the Congress of the United States in 1948 would not have passed a law containing the simple language that was in Executive Order 9981.

Old Harry was deadly serious. He meant what he wrote. When the committee he set up—the President's Committee on Equality of Treatment and Opportunity in the Armed Services, called the Fahy

Committee after its chairman—met for the first time, Truman spoke to them. "Concrete results, that's what I'm after, not publicity on it," he said, and then he promised that, if it was necessary to get the job done, he would "knock somebody's ears down."[3] One does not hear that kind of talk in Washington enough these days.

The day after Truman signed Executive Order 9981, the chief of staff of the army, General Omar Bradley, not knowing the order had been signed, told an audience casually that he believed segregation in the army would probably continue for a long period of time. (The word "desegregation," by the way, was not used in the order; the phrase used was "equality of treatment and opportunity.") The following day, Truman gave a press conference. One of the reporters asked if General Bradley's statement was consistent with Executive Order 9981. When Truman said he knew of no statement by General Bradley about segregation in the army, the reporter asked if Truman's advocacy of "equality of treatment and opportunity" in the armed forces envisioned the end of segregation. He put Truman right on the spot, but the president did not blink. "Yes," he said, simply and bluntly.[4] The next day, General Bradley apologized to President Truman for his indiscreet statement. Bradley soon after became the first chairman of the newly created Joint Chiefs of Staff.

At about the time all this was happening, a future chairman of the Joint Chiefs of Staff was an eleven-year-old kid who had been born in Harlem and was growing up in the South Bronx. He was a happy-go-lucky kid, not a particularly good student, trying his best to get out of the sixth grade any way he knew how. He was a black kid and he knew it. He knew his country considered him to be different. He knew his country considered him a second-, third-, fourth-, or tenth-class citizen. He knew there were places he could not go, opportunities he could not have. There were dreams he dared not dream. But he was being taught, all the while, to love his country with all his heart and soul because it was a good place. It was unlike anywhere else on earth and it was founded on beliefs and principles that would eventually become reality. All you had to do was believe this was so, and work to make it come true. This kid was proud to be an American. He shared everyone's joy when World War II ended and there were block parties all over the South Bronx. But it was sometimes hard and confusing to understand why things were the way they were.

Just a year earlier, in 1947, a black man for the first time stepped out onto a baseball field to play with a group of white men. Jackie

Robinson became a hero, even as he was being cursed from the bleachers. At the same time, movies portrayed people who looked like the kid in the South Bronx as servants and buffoons who spoke poorly and were shiftless or ignorant. The occasional Ralph Bunche or Roy Wilkins or General B. O. Davis or Willie Mays did little to dispel that "Old Man River" image Hollywood presented to America. The little boy heard about a wonderful place called Levittown, a new development out on Long Island, not too far from where he lived. The government was providing low-interest loans so veterans could buy new homes there, but not black veterans. The little boy's Uncle Vic came home from Europe where he had served in the Fourth Armored Division, and he could not buy a home in Levittown.

The boy heard what it was like in the South—lynchings, Jim Crow, no rights, always in the back of movie theaters, buses, restaurants, always in the back if they let you in at all. He recited the Pledge of Allegiance in school every day, ending with those beautiful words, "with liberty and justice for all," but he was just beginning to grasp that these words did not apply to African Americans.

Many years later when he became chairman of the Joint Chiefs of Staff, he would be asked by inquisitive reporters who had forgotten their history, "Well, General Powell, when you were growing up in the South Bronx, did you ever think or dream that you would grow up to become chairman of the Joint Chiefs of Staff of the Armed Forces of the United States? And I would smile patiently and say, "No," because such a dream would have been impossible for that eleven-year-old kid. But that kid didn"t know that President Truman had just signed an executive order that would permit such a dream to come true. And the dream did come true, not just because President Truman signed an executive order, but also because after he signed the order, he went about the task of knocking the ears off the Pentagon to make it happen.

It took another six years of hard work. We had to go through the Korean War and realize that our soldiers would work better, fight better, serve this country better if they were in integrated units. On 30 October 1954, the army reported that all its units were finally integrated; the same thing was true then for the other services as well. That was a month after the black kid joined the Reserve Officers Training Corps (ROTC) at the City College of New York. Four years later he got out of college and joined an army in which blacks had served proudly throughout the nation's history, all the way back to the Revolutionary War. The military was the only institution in all of America—because of Harry Truman—where a young black kid, now twenty-one years old, could dream the dream he dared not think about at age eleven. It was the one place where the only thing that counted was courage, where the color of your guts and the color of your blood was more important than the color of your skin.

Black Americans had always been willing to serve, whether they were the Buffalo Soldiers or the Tuskegee Airmen or the navy's Golden 13—the first thirteen black officers allowed into the navy—or the Montford Point Marines—the first blacks allowed into the Marine Corps. All were willing to serve because they believed in something Frederick Douglass had once said: "Once let the black man get upon his person the brass letters 'U.S.,' let him get an eagle on his buttons and a musket on his shoulder and bullets in his pocket, and there is no power on earth which can deny that he has earned the right to citizenship in the United States."[5]

It took almost two hundred years for that expectation to come true, but it did come true. It happened not just because Truman signed an order or because the black kid entered an integrated army. It also happened because the U.S. Army and the other services knew that it was not enough just to sign an order. An environment had to be created, an atmosphere that was based on ability, an atmosphere that had been washed clean of discrimination and racism and all of the legal or informal barriers to performance. It was an atmosphere in which the armed services reached out through equal opportunity and affirmative action to find qualified people. Only when you go out and work the problem, only when you make sure that, through these programs, you are knocking down all barriers and allowing access into the system, only then can you promote and reward on the basis of ability and performance. A level playing field does not come into being by declaration, it comes by building it and maintaining it. That is what the armed forces of the United States did.

The army I love has made great progress since 1948, but even in the early years of my career in the late 1950s and 1960s, we still had difficulties throughout the country. As a captain, after I had gone away and fought for my nation in Vietnam, I came home to find my father-in-law guarding my wife and infant son in Birmingham, Alabama, because of the disturbances there and Bull Connor and his police dogs. Even after serving my country in Vietnam in the early 1960s, I came home and had difficulty finding a home for my family, and I still found many places in America where I could not even get a hamburger. So when I talk about these things and I try to take people back to 1948, it is for the purpose of showing that this is not ancient history—this is my generation. In this generation that started in 1948, this second reconstruction period that started in 1948 with Executive Order 9981, there has been much progress. I was able to rise to the top of the armed forces because of those who went ahead and proved we could do it, and because of Harry Truman, who gave me the opportunity to show I could do it. I think President Truman would be very pleased about that. I think President Truman would also be pleased to see how far the nation has gone beyond the modest civil rights agenda that he set forth in 1948.

It took struggles, it took the death of martyrs, it took marches, it took the marriage of principles and politics fused together with pressure, and it took a lot of goodwill. And the progress has not just been in the military. Black men and women now excel in every field of human endeavor—in politics, in the arts, in industry, in business and sports, in medicine and the sciences and education, anywhere the elements of success are nothing more than hard work and ambition and a dream, and where opportunity exists.

No other country on the face of the earth has done for its minority population what the United States has done. What is so wonderful is that, with each passing year, it gets better. We get closer and closer to the more perfect union that our founders spoke of. All Americans, black and white, should be proud of this progress and give credit to the redemptive spirit and system of government that we have here in this nation. But at the same time that we rejoice in our progress, we cannot say that the journey is over. The historical legacy of our past still confronts and conditions the present. We have not yet overcome.

That would be the easiest thing in the world for me to say: We have overcome. But I can't say that and go back to Washington DC, or many other major metropolitan areas in this country and see school systems that still look like part of a system of apartheid. I can't say that and still see people of color confronted with redlining from banks and discrimination in housing, discrimination in education or in jobs. The second reconstruction period is not yet over, and we must not quit too early this time. Too much is at stake. The military has learned that without vigilance, you can slip back. We've got to keep working at it. We also learned that removing barriers was not enough if people were not prepared, once the barriers were down, to march past them. And that is why I have spent so much of my time with young people: to educate them, to put hope in their hearts again, put discipline in their hearts again, put structure in their lives again, teach them the good way of living, the difference between right and wrong, the importance of hard work and education, of having self-respect and keeping away from all the things that will drag them down. I want to teach them too that there is no country like the country they live in. The opportunities available today are wonderful. People have fought for these opportunities, but what was the point of fighting if the new generation coming along behind us is not preparing itself to take advantage of them? That has to be our charge for the twenty-first century. The civil rights struggle is now moving in new directions. We have the laws we need; our hearts are changing. We must now educate *all* of our children to judge each other only on the content of their character. The armed forces, I am proud to say, led the way. President Truman gave us the order to march with Executive Order 9981.

Not too many years ago, the USS *Harry S. Truman* made its first voyage. I wish President Truman could have visited with its crew on that day, because the men and women of that crew would have matched his dream of what he wanted the armed forces to be. When the USS *Harry S. Truman* went to sea, every color of America, every accent of America, all of America the Beautiful was reflected in that crew—all five thousand sailors and marines, working together as members of a family. And it is like that as well in the army and the air force and the coast guard. It's going to be like that throughout this whole country, if we just keep working on it.

Notes

[1] Truman, Special Message on Civil Rights, 2 February 1948, in *Public Papers of the Presidents, Truman, 1948,* 121–26.

[2] Executive Order 9981.

[3] Meeting of the President and the Four Service Secretaries with the President's Committee on Equality of Treatment and Opportunity in the Armed Services, 12:15 P.M.—12 January 1949—Cabinet Room, White House, Truman Papers, Offical File 1285-0, Truman Library.

[4] President's News Conference, 29 July 1948, in *Public Papers of the Presidents, Truman, 1948,* 422.

[5] Ward, *Civil War,* 246.

TRUMAN'S CONCEPTION OF
ECONOMIC RIGHTS AS CIVIL RIGHTS
The Case of Health Care

Michael Dukakis

President Truman was an extraordinary man who displayed a great
deal of courage during his presidency. He was the first president in
the history of the United States who not only stood up for civil
rights, but asked Congress to pass an economic bill of rights. President Franklin D. Roosevelt had talked about the Four Freedoms,
but it was President Truman who first took serious action. He
knew, as we all understand now, that it is not enough to talk about
political liberties and political rights if people do not have economic
opportunity and so, in September 1945 he sent Congress a proposal
for an economic bill of rights.[1] No president had ever done that.

When I was in high school in the late 1940s and early 1950s, the
United States was racist and anti-Semitic. When I was a kid in Boston, I never saw an African American behind the counter at a
department store. I lived in Brookline, the first suburb west of Boston. There were four African American students in our high school
of twenty-six hundred, and three of them were the children of jani-
tors. Somehow Africa Hayes's family—her father was Roland
Hayes, the great concert singer—managed to live in Brookline. They
broke the rule that if you were black, you did not live on the Boston
side of the railroad tracks. African Americans normally could not
live in Brookline.

After high school in Brookline, I went to Swarthmore College
in Pennsylvania, just nine miles south of Philadelphia. It was a small
Quaker college and had a liberal reputation, but it had only just

begun to enroll its first black students shortly before I arrived. Most of them came from Nigeria, not from the United States. These black students could not get their hair cut in the local barbershops. This was not Birmingham or Montgomery—it was nine miles southwest of Philadelphia. In fact, in the City of Brotherly Love in 1944 (seven years before I came to Swarthmore), when the Philadelphia Transportation Company hired its first black bus driver, nine thousand white guys went on strike. They refused to work with a black man.

In the spring of 1952, a buddy of mine and I hitchhiked to Miami Beach. We had never been out of the North, and we wanted to find out what it was like to enjoy summer in wintertime. We hitchhiked down to Florida with our sleeping bags and thirteen egg-salad sandwiches, and we slept on the beach in front of a dog track, way down at the southern end of Miami Beach. African Americans could not be on these same streets after dark without a pass from their employer. This was happening in the United States of America, which was telling everyone it was "the capital of the free world."

When I went to Washington DC in 1954 to attend a semester at American University, the nation's capital was as segregated as Johannesburg, South Africa. The buses had been desegregated by this time—but not the schools, which were segregated by act of Congress—and not the restaurants or public facilities generally. I remember that one of my fellow students and I went to New Orleans the next year during our spring vacation. On the bus, there was a wooden sign with two spikes that went into the bar of the bus seat; if you happened to be white, you were supposed to put that thing behind you to separate yourself from the black passengers. As a small act of defiance, my buddy and I, when the bus driver wasn't looking, pulled the thing out, stuck it in our bag, and took it home. A small victory for civil rights.

This was the country I grew up in, which is why, in my judgment, Truman's civil rights legacy is so remarkable. The fact that we have advanced as far as we have has much to do with this president, who believed he had to do the right thing no matter what.

One of the right things that Truman committed himself to was the proposition that every American ought to have basic health security and comprehensive health insurance. He presented this idea for the first time in November 1945 as part of his proposed economic bill of rights.[2] Today the United States, alone among the advanced industrialized nations of the world, is still unable or unwilling to do what

Harry Truman urged the country to do so many years ago. His program would have guaranteed all Americans basic health security. Today (in 2004), however, forty-four million Americans don't have a dime of health insurance. Overwhelmingly, these are working people. They are not loafing, they are working, but they have no health insurance.

Harry Truman believed that health care was a basic civil right. Because the health care gap is still a major issue, just as it was in Truman's time, we do well to review and reflect on the history of efforts—so far unsuccessful—to provide all Americans with comprehensive health care, and especially the courageous role President Truman played during the years of his presidency. His actions as president with respect to health care are as relevant today as they were then. Furthermore, he is largely responsible for the fact that those of us who are sixty-five years old and older or severely disabled today have universal and reasonably comprehensive health coverage.

The history of efforts to provide all Americans with comprehensive health insurance goes back long before President Truman's arrival in the Oval Office. It begins in the early twentieth century when American reformers, largely social workers and members of the Progressive movement, emboldened by the social insurance programs in Germany and some other European nations, enthusiastically began to embrace the notion of social insurance here in the United States. They started with worker's compensation, which was first put in place in Massachusetts and then spread rapidly to other states from about 1910 to 1920.[3] This was an enormous breakthrough, and so the reformers decided to try to achieve other social insurance goals. They were encouraged by an electrifying speech by Louis Brandeis, delivered in 1911 to the National Conference on Charities and Correction. Brandeis urged the assembled gathering of social workers and political reformers to push beyond worker's compensation and to demand comprehensive social insurance that covered "sickness, accident, invalidity, premature death, or premature old age."[4]

For a few brief years, it looked as if the reformers would achieve their goals, as social insurance legislation was introduced in over a dozen states and politicians took up the cause. Teddy Roosevelt endorsed the idea during his Bull Moose campaign in 1912. In 1916, the Republican candidates for governor and lieutenant governor of Massachusetts, Samuel McCall and Calvin Coolidge, supported universal health insurance in their state. An initiative providing for universal health insurance was on the ballot in California in 1918, but it was defeated. In 1921, New York Governor Al Smith proposed universal health insurance. It passed the New York senate, but failed in the more conservative lower house. Even the American Medical Association (AMA), later to become the leading opponent of Harry Truman's health insurance program, was supportive of state efforts early in the century.[5]

Ultimately these early attempts failed. Curiously, it was Samuel Gompers, the longtime leader of the American Federation of Labor, who emerged as one of universal health insurance's principal opponents. When Gompers joined forces with the leaders of the insurance industry and others who were fighting universal health insurance, it proved fatal to the reform efforts. Gompers apparently believed that his unions, through the collective bargaining process, should lead the effort to insure workers and their families. It was not until the late 1930s that organized labor changed its tune, when Bill Green took over as head of the American Federation of Labor.[6]

The entry of the United States into World War I had not helped the reformers' cause, since the idea of social insurance, and particularly health insurance, had first appeared in Germany. The opponents of universal health insurance used this tie to the nation's wartime enemy as an argument against such a program.

Later, in the 1940s, the AMA and other determined opponents of President Truman's universal health proposal used similar tactics in comparing his plans with Soviet and Communist medicine, outrageous though such a comparison was.

When the United States fell into the Great Depression in the 1930s, President Franklin Roosevelt may have considered making universal health insurance an important part of his New Deal agenda. Harry Hopkins, Roosevelt's assistant and a professional social worker, was a very enthusiastic supporter of universal health insurance; early in Roosevelt's administration Hopkins predicted confidently that unemployment compensation and universal health insurance would be combined in the same package and would be passed by Congress within a year and a half. In 1934, President Roosevelt asked Secretary of Labor Frances Perkins, also a professional social worker, to head a special commission on the subject of social insurance. Unfortunately, despite the commission's strong recommendations of universal health insurance, Roosevelt refused to make it a part of the New Deal. His refusal was a calculated political judgment. Given everything he was trying to accomplish, he decided he could not take on the AMA, which strongly opposed health insurance—even voluntary health insurance—at this time.[7]

Some progress was made in expanding health care during the New Deal years through the Farm Security Administration, which provided care in rural areas, and the Works Progress Administration, which provided care to its workers. But Roosevelt did not embrace universal health care until his campaign for reelection in 1944 and he died before he could make a formal proposal to Congress. Congress had already been confronted with the issue; in 1943, Senator James Murray of Montana, Senator Robert Wagner of New York, and Congressman John Dingell of Michigan sponsored the so-called Wagner-Murray-Dingell Act, which would expand social security to include health insurance for everyone. The new program would be paid for by a small increase in the payroll tax, which, at a time when health care constituted a much smaller percentage of gross domestic product than it does now, would have been enough to support the program. This Wagner-Murray-Dingell Act of 1943-1944 failed to become law. Successor bills were introduced in 1945 and 1947 which incorporated President Truman's health care proposals.

President Roosevelt had been forced to confront an increasingly conservative congressional majority made up of a coalition of Republicans and conservative Southern Democrats. Under the seniority system of those days, this coalition controlled the congressional committees and, even during World War II, had stopped a number of Roosevelt's key initiatives. It was clear that President Truman would face the same obstacles as the nation emerged from war. In fact, the coalition would block Truman every time he tried to get his universal health care bill through the Congress.

Truman had been in the Oval Office less than six months when, on 6 September 1945, he sent his message to Congress advocating a broad economic bill of rights consisting of decent jobs, full employment, good housing, excellent education, and universal and comprehensive health insurance for all Americans. Two months later, on 19 November 1945, he sent Congress the most sweeping blueprint for the health of the nation and its people ever proposed by an American president.

As with many of the things Truman advocated, the beliefs underlying his health plan were rooted in his experiences earlier in life, before he was elected to the United States Senate in 1934. While he was very proud of his service in World War I and of those who served with him and under his command, he was not proud of the fact that many who volunteered for his unit could not pass their physical. He was not proud either that, during World War II, fully 30 percent of the men called up for active duty in the armed forces were unfit for service.

His experience in county government in the 1920s and 1930s also had a profound effect on him. In a speech he gave in May 1948 to the National Health Assembly, he recalled his time as county judge (county commissioner) in Jackson County, Missouri:

> It was my duty...to pass, with the other two judges, on the sanity of the people who would come before the judges and court, who would be tried for mental cases. Those [dozens of] cases ran over an 8-year period while I was in the court.... A most horrifying situation. It was our duty to send those people to the State hospitals for care.... That did not include the people who were in private institutions. I became aware of what that situation means in a community and what it means to future generations.
>
> It was also my duty at that time to see that poor people were properly taken care of from a health standpoint. We had two medical men in that county at that time who devoted their whole time to the health and welfare of those people, who couldn't afford to pay for medical care. We [also] had an excellent county home. ... And Kansas City had a hospital...[for] people who could not afford medical care in any other way.

Truman then made a deeply significant observation: "I found out with that experience that the people at the indigent bottom of the scale and the people at the top of the scale were the only ones who can afford adequate hospital care and medical care."[8] It was the folks in the middle that Harry Truman cared about, not just the poor. And it is mostly the folks in the middle—working people or members of working families—who even today lack health insurance.

Truman went on to state in that speech to the National Health Assembly, "When I came to the Senate of the United States, I did not need to be sold on Social Security and the health and welfare of the nation."[9] And when he assumed the presidency, he very quickly became the first in that office to address seriously the federal government's responsibility for the health of its citizens.

Truman's 1945 message to Congress is not only remarkable in and of itself, but much of it is as relevant and important today as it was back then. "Our new Economic Bill of Rights," he said, "should mean health security for all, regardless of residence, station, or race—everywhere in the United States." He went on to outline five basic problems requiring the nation's attention. The first of these was the number and distribution of doctors and hospitals. Of the twelve hundred counties in the nation, 40 percent of the total, with some fifteen million people, had either no local hospital or none that met minimal professional standards.[10]

The second problem was the need for public health services and maternal and child health care. Local health departments needed support; communities needed safe and sanitary water and sewage systems. "Our streams and rivers must be safeguarded against pollution," he insisted, twenty-five years before the first Earth Day. He also wanted the federal government to get involved in local efforts to provide services for expectant mothers, health care for "crippled or otherwise physically handicapped" children, and widespread immunization for all American children.[11]

Truman also proposed major investments in medical research, professional education for future health professionals with particular emphasis on cancer research, and research into the causes and treatment of mental illness, especially "much more research to learn how to prevent mental breakdown."[12] He wanted new social insurance to cover wages lost by workers as a result of sickness, even when their illness was not job-connected. And finally and most importantly, he asked Congress to pass legislation that would provide health insurance for all Americans.

Anticipating his critics, Truman insisted that he was not proposing a system of socialized medicine. He stated,

> People should remain free to choose their own physicians and hospitals. The removal of financial barriers between patient and doctor would enlarge the present freedom of choice. The legal requirement on the population to contribute involves no compulsion over the doctor's freedom to decide what services his patient needs....
>
> Likewise physicians should remain free to accept or reject patients. They must be allowed to decide for themselves whether they wish to participate in the health insurance system full time, part time, or not at all.... Physicians must be permitted to be represented through organizations of their own choosing, and to decide whether to carry on in individual practice or to join with other doctors in group practice in hospitals or in clinics.
>
> Our voluntary hospitals and our city, county, and state general hospitals, in the same way, must be free to participate in the system to whatever extent they wish. In any case they must continue to retain their administrative independence....
>
> I repeat—what I am recommending is not socialized medicine.

> Socialized medicine means that all doctors work as employees of government. The American people want no such system. No such system is here proposed.[13]

And so began President Truman's fight to accomplish something that continues to elude America and its political, medical, and business leadership—the enactment of a plan for comprehensive health insurance for all Americans. Truman was a stubborn and tenacious man. The election of a Republican Congress in 1946 was a setback for much of his agenda, and particularly for universal health care. Senator Robert Taft in particular became a strong opponent of Truman's proposal. But in typical Truman fashion, he did not give up. He kept coming at the Congress and he made universal health insurance a key issue in the 1948 presidential campaign. That election returned him to office, and also returned Congress to Democratic control.

It was not just congressional Republicans who fought Truman's health care program. The nation's physicians, represented by the AMA, opposed Truman and made his health plan the focus of one of the most skillful and well-financed lobbying and public relations efforts that has ever been launched against a presidential initiative. The word went out to doctors across the nation that "the final showdown on [this] collectivist issue" had begun. "Do not underestimate the crisis. If you are willing to fight for personal freedom and professional independence, send us [an] emergency contribution...to make possible maximum nationwide efforts."[14] The AMA said that President Truman's legislation was more socialistic than any medical program in any country, except maybe the Soviet Union, and would turn doctors into clock-watchers and slaves. I remember the AMA-sponsored pamphlets in my father's office on Huntington Avenue in Boston with titles such as *Showdown on Political Medicine.* Such alarmist literature was in offices like his all across the country, and doctors were urged to give them out to every single one of their patients.

Along the way, unfortunately, the AMA picked up a lot of allies. The American Hospital Association, the American Bar Association, the Protestant and Catholic Hospital Associations, editorial writers for the nation's newspapers, and scores of others weighed in against the plan. Even after Truman's stunning victory in 1948, the assault continued. It got worse as anticommunist hysteria began to play a greater and greater role in the attacks on his plan. In fact, a congressional investigating subcommittee at the time ended a report with what it called "a firm conclusion that American Communism holds this program as a cardinal point in its objectives, and that known Communists and fellow travelers within federal agencies are at work diligently with federal funds in furtherance of the Moscow Party line."[15]

Congressional and public support of Truman's plan steadily declined in the face of the assaults upon it. Although the president did succeed in persuading the AMA to support his hospital construction program—the Hospital Survey and Construction Act became law in 1946—and by 1948, to end its opposition to private voluntary health insurance, the AMA and its allies poured millions into the fight against universal health insurance. They hired Whitaker and Baxter, the same public relations firm that had helped to defeat Governor Earl Warren's plan for universal health insurance in California in 1946 and 1947. They pilloried Oscar Ewing, the head of Truman's Federal Security Administration, calling him a dangerous radical, refusing to support the president's plan for turning Ewing's agency, now called the Department of Health and Human Services, into a cabinet-level department. They finally forced the administration to retreat somewhat and to propose during Truman's last year in office a modified version of his original plan that would only have insured people sixty-five years of age and older and the dependants who survived them. Even this new plan did not satisfy the AMA camp, which proceeded to use the same arguments with which they had opposed the universal plan. But at least by advocating health coverage for seniors, Truman and Ewing were setting the stage for what ultimately became Medicare some thirteen years later.[16]

Congress was still wary about health insurance for older Americans in the 1960s. President John Kennedy could not even get his Medicare bill onto the House floor for a vote, thanks to the opposition of conservative Democrats who controlled the Rules Committee. He finally managed to get a vote in the Senate, but the measure was defeated. It was not until after Kennedy's assassination, after the 1964 election produced huge Democratic majorities in Congress, that Medicare finally passed, and even then President Johnson had to make two very significant compromises. He agreed to allow the insurance companies to be the fiscal intermediaries, which they still are, and he agreed to allow doctors to charge their usual and customary fees. In one of the great examples of political irony, it was President Ronald Reagan who finally imposed rate regulation on the doctors and on the hospitals because Medicare costs began getting

out of control. Reagan was a conservative, but he was also a pragma-
tist. He saw those costs going up and so decided to control costs.

It has been almost sixty years since Harry Truman had the fore-
sight to propose that all Americans be guaranteed basic health security for themselves and their families. Two succeeding presidents,
one a Republican named Richard Nixon and one a Democrat named
Bill Clinton, tried unsuccessfully to do the same in their own way.
They failed for many of the same reasons that made it impossible for
President Truman to implement his health care program: in all three
instances, special interest groups with a stake in the outcome spent
millions to convince the American people that a universal health
insurance program was not in their best interest.

Even so, we are closer today to Truman's goal than we were
when he proposed his economic bill of rights and the universal
health insurance that went with it. Eighty-four percent of us have
health coverage, much of it provided through two government programs, Medicare and Medicaid. The U.S. Department of Veterans
Affairs has an extensive network of clinics and hospitals providing
good health care for millions of veterans (ironically through a system that is, in fact, socialized medicine, paid for out of general reve-
nue funds, whose hospitals are part of the government and whose
doctors are government employees). And, of course, life expectancy
today is a lot longer than it was sixty years ago and infant mortality
is about one-fifth of what it was when Truman was president.

But if Harry Truman were with us today, I think he would be
asking a lot of the same questions that millions of Americans are asking about the future of the health care system. Why are forty-four
million Americans still uninsured? Why are we spending much
more on health care than any other advanced industrialized nation
of the world even though millions in America have no health insurance? What sense is there in a health care system that ties up doctors
and hospitals in a maze of private bureaucracy called managed care?
Why is 20 to 25 percent of the premium dollar being spent on
administrative overhead under our existing system? Why are health
care costs rising at five to six times the rate of inflation? And why do
we seem to be so singularly incapable of taking care of ourselves in
ways that ensure good health?

President Truman did not take his famous morning walks solely
because he enjoyed them. He understood the importance of keeping
fit and the critical role of fitness in good health, particularly for
older people. In his speech to the National Health Assembly in May

1948, he had this to say about individual responsibility for one's health: "When I was 21 years old, I voluntarily joined the National Guard of the United States...[a]nd I learned what to do to take care of myself physically. That is what a great many of us need to do.... [T]he reason we are not physically fit is because we are too lazy to take care of ourselves. We sit down and wait until this paunch comes on, and when we get bent over, then we try to correct it by heroic methods; and nine times out of ten, if you go along and do what you ought to, in the first place, you wouldn't have that situation."[17] Who says that promoting good health and taking responsibility for oneself are new ideas, as we find ourselves trying to cope with our newest epidemic, widespread and growing obesity? Harry Truman, a wise man, understood this half a century ago.

Now and in future years, whether our president is a Democrat or a Republican, a liberal or a conservative, a person who favors government health programs or a person who believes the principal responsibility for ensuring the nation's health should remain in the private sector—that president and all Americans have a solemn responsibility to answer the question Harry Truman put to us so many years ago: Shouldn't "the right to adequate medical care, the right to achieve and enjoy good health," and "the right to adequate protection from the economic fears of old age, sickness, accident, and unemployment"[18] be the birthright of every American? Until all Americans can answer that question with a resounding "Yes!" we will have failed President Truman. And we will have failed ourselves.

Notes

[1] Truman, Special Message to the Congress Presenting a 21-Point Program for the Reconversion Period, 6 September 1945, in *Public Papers of the Presidents, Truman, 1945*, 263–309.

[2] Truman, Special Message to the Congress Recommending a Comprehensive Health Program, 19 November 1945, in *Public Papers of the Presidents, Truman, 1945*, 475–91; and An Act to Authorize and to Provide for the Approval of Plans of Compensation for Injured Employees (5 May 1908), Chapter 489, *Acts and Resolves of Massachusetts, 1908*.

[3] Poen, *Harry S. Truman Verses the Medical Lobby*, 2–3.

[4] Brandeis, "The Road to Social Efficiency."

[5] Poen, *Harry S. Truman Verses the Medical Lobby*, 7–8, 12.

[6] Poen, *Harry S. Truman Verses the Medical Lobby*, 11–12, 19–20.

[7] Poen, *Harry S. Truman Verses the Medical Lobby*, 17.

[8] Truman, Remarks at the National Health Assembly Dinner, 1 May 1948, in *Public Papers of the Presidents, Truman, 1948*, 240.

[9] Truman, Remarks at the National Health Assembly Dinner, 240.

[10] Truman, Special Message to the Congress Recommending a Comprehensive Health Program, *Public Papers of the Presidents*, Truman, 1945, 478.

[11] Truman, Special Message to the Congress Recommending a Comprehensive Health Program, *Public Papers of the Presidents*, Truman, 1945, 479.

[12] Truman, Special Message to the Congress Recommending a Comprehensive Health Program, *Public Papers of the Presidents*, Truman, 1945, 481.

[13] Truman, Special Message to the Congress Recommending a Comprehensive Health Program, *Public Papers of the Presidents*, Truman, 1945, 487–88.

[14] Health Message [1 of 3], Samuel I. Rosenman Papers, Truman Library.

[15] Quoted in Greenburg, "Give 'em Health, Harry," 20–21.

[16] Poen, *Harry S. Truman Verses the Medical Lobby*, 87, 145, 162–64, 199–200, 229–30.

[17] Truman, Remarks at the National Health Assembly Dinner, *Public Papers of the Presidents*, Truman, 1948, 241.

[18] Truman, Special Message to the Congress Presenting a 21-Point Program for the Reconversion Period, *Public Papers of the Presidents*, Truman, 1945, 280.

HONORING TRUMAN'S CIVIL RIGHTS LEGACY

The Truman Library and Truman's Civil Rights Legacy

Raymond H. Geselbracht

President Harry S. Truman has left his country a strong legacy of accomplishment in the area of civil rights. This legacy is not a monument intended to commemorate or celebrate the man who created it. It is, rather, a living thing that changes day by day as people come in contact with it and are changed by it. This gift to the country lingers and continues to influence the lives of all those who consent to receive it.

The most important mission of the Harry S. Truman Library is to provide access to information and historical documentation about all of President Truman's many legacies, including his civil rights legacy. This information is available to the American people and, increasingly, to an electronically linked and global society comprised of people all over the world, through all of the Truman Library's program units: museum, archives, and educational and public programs.

It is generally not the Truman Library's role to interpret Truman's legacies, though inevitably the library must engage in some interpretation in its museum exhibits. Even the exhibits, though, present the story of Truman's life and career as a work in progress, a living legacy whose meaning for the country must be continually interpreted by the American people. The museum visitors, in their role as interpreters of the Truman legacy, are an essential part of the museum exhibits. They, together with all those who come in contact with Truman's legacy through whatever means, are the true and inevitable interpreters of that legacy, and they are the people who will determine what influence the legacy will have on the future.

In the library's museum, in a Presidential Gallery crowded with exhibits about Truman's very eventful presidency, one exhibit panel presents his major civil rights accomplishments. His creation of the President's Committee on Civil Rights is featured here, as are his speech to the annual meeting of the National Association for the Advancement of Colored People (NAACP) on 29 June 1947; his Executive Orders 9980 and 9981, which ordered the desegregation of, respectively, the federal civil service and the armed forces; the civil rights legislation he submitted to an unsympathetic Congress; his appointment of African Americans to important positions; and his appointment of justices to the Supreme Court who handed down decisions that advanced civil rights. The interpretation put forward in this panel is based on the work of Donald McCoy and Richard Reutten, Michael Gardner, William E. Leuchtenburg, Richard Dalfiume, Harvard Sitkoff, and William C. Wiecek, as well as on the three recent biographies of Truman by David McCullough, Robert H. Ferrell, and Alonzo Hamby.[1] The panel will eventually have to be revised to take into account the recent work of Carol Anderson and other scholars. These historians argue that the Truman administration was more interested in fighting the Cold War than in fighting for civil rights for African Americans and that it consequently pursued only a limited civil rights agenda and forcibly limited the human rights agenda of the United Nations.[2] Anderson's negative assessment of President Truman as a person will also have to be taken into account:

> Even after the president recognized that this nation had to do better [in the area of civil rights] Truman still could not rid himself of Missouri's Confederate-leaning, slaveholding roots. Truman, for all of his strengths, was simply not philosophically or psychologically equipped to accept true black equality. His penchant for referring to African Americans as "niggers" was well known. His disdain for social equality was a matter of public record. And his contempt for nonviolent protests against Jim Crow was clearly documented.[3]

Museum visitors are drawn into the interpretation of President Truman's civil rights record when they encounter, at the bottom right of the exhibit panel, a flip book containing several documents that present quite different insights into Truman as president and into the civil rights record he created. One document, a letter that Truman wrote to his wife, Bess, on 19 July 1946, reveals the race prejudice that Truman felt. "Everybody in town is going to the big fight today," he writes, referring to a championship boxing match between Joe Louis and Billy Conn that was to take place in New York later that day. "Of course I can't go. I can't even go to the television show here. To tell you the truth it is no disappointment to me. I wouldn't go if I could. I don't like that yellow nig and I wouldn't like to see him knock out a fool white Irishman."[4] Visitors can then turn the page and find something very different and, if they have Truman's letter to Bess about the Joe Louis fight in mind, intellectually challenging. On 12 January 1953, only a week before the end of the Truman administration, NAACP Assistant Director Roy Wilkins wrote to tell Truman how much he appreciated all he had done for African Americans. "As you leave the White House," Wilkins wrote, "you carry with you the gratitude and affectionate regard of millions of your Negro fellow citizens who in less than a decade of your leadership, inspiration and determination, have seen the old order change right before their eyes."[5]

Museum visitors are also challenged, in a "decision theater" (later Decision Center) located near the civil rights panel, to determine what motivated President Truman to issue the executive order that mandated the desegregation of the armed forces. A film narrates the story of Truman's decision, then asks visitors to decide whether the president acted to end segregation in the armed forces because of pressure from interest groups and public opinion, because of his personal values, because of the recommendations he received from his advisors, or because of his perception of the long-term national interest. A large majority of the visitors who have cast votes in the decision theater feel that Truman desegregated the armed services either because of his personal values (45 percent) or his perception of the long-term national interest (30 percent), rather than because of the other, less idealistic reasons.

The Truman Library also makes information and documentation about President Truman's civil rights legacy available through its archives program. The library's holdings of historical materials include tens of thousands of pages relating to civil rights—in President Truman's papers, in those of many of his assistants, including George Elsey, Clark Clifford, David Niles, and Philleo Nash, and in collections of the records of the commissions and committees Truman established to study and make recommendations regarding different aspects of civil rights policy. All of these materials are available to researchers in the library's research room, and copies may be ordered by email, mail, or telephone. Thousands of copies of the library's important documents relating to civil rights have been sent all over the world in the forty-five years that the research room has been open.

During the last few years, the Internet has brought revolutionary changes to the Truman Library's archival program. The library has put over one thousand pages of documents relating to civil rights on its website (www.trumanlibrary.org) and a significant collection of photographs and oral history interviews as well. In future years, this virtual collection of civil rights materials will grow substantially. The library may never be able to do more than estimate how many people worldwide access civil rights materials on its website. One can imagine how happy this would have made Harry Truman, who had an epigraph carved on the wall next to the entrance to his library that reads, "The papers of the presidents...ought to be preserved and they ought to be used." Truman would also have been very pleased that a great many—maybe most—of the people who access the library's civil rights materials online are young people doing research for school projects. Truman had a special devotion to young people and made it his life's work after he left the presidency to share with them his love of history and his faith in the goodness and greatness of the United States.

The archives staff has created collections of documents, comprised of five hundred to a thousand pages each, relating to important topics drawn from Truman's life and career. These collections are called the Student Research Files and include seven collections relating to civil rights topics. Two of the civil rights collections— those relating to the desegregation of the armed forces and to the incarceration of Japanese Americans during World War II—are currently accessible online and others will be made so in future years. In addition, four copies of the entire collection of Student Research Files, totaling about forty thousand pages, have been placed in three college and university libraries and one public library in the Kansas City area.[6]

All who access the materials relating to President Truman's civil rights legacy become—in some way, on some level—historians who interpret the legacy for themselves and others. One person, a university professor, might write a book or article that affects the way other historians think and write about Truman and civil rights; another person, a high school student, might make a presentation in class, or prepare an exhibit or video for History Day that is seen by other students and by parents and teachers; yet another person, someone simply pursuing an interest in Truman's presidency, might share the information he or she discovers, or argue some point based on it to friends or family or coworkers. These individuals are all interpreters of Truman's civil rights legacy. They are parts of that legacy's daily life, and participants in the changes that the legacy will influence or cause to occur.

The Truman Library, almost fifty years old now, is still receiving and opening historical materials. A few of the items that have been opened recently are very revealing, not of Truman's civil rights program considered as administration policy, but rather of the inner beliefs and attitudes of the man who ultimately bore responsibility for the program. Historians have often expressed surprise that the first president since the Reconstruction era to make civil rights for African Americans a priority for the federal government was a man whose grandparents owned slaves, whose family was Southern in background and sympathies, and who lived essentially all of his life in a border state that retained much of the race prejudice of pre–Civil War days. Perhaps President Truman did not pursue his civil rights agenda as forcefully and as passionately as some people would have liked, but he did take important actions both to state the responsibility of the federal government to assure the civil rights of all Americans, and to make those civil rights a reality. Truman arguably did not have to do much of anything about civil rights; the condition of the country was such that he probably could have avoided taking any serious actions. His predecessor, Franklin D. Roosevelt, had done very little for African Americans, and his successor, Dwight D. Eisenhower, who faced pressures for action that Truman never encountered, also did very little.

Truman's behavior does need explanation, and one looks for that explanation at least partly on a very intimate level. Who was this man, this president, who did these things? Or, as is usually asked nowadays, what was the character of this president? A discovery made by archivists in early 2003 sheds light on this question.

A book that had sat unused in a stack area for almost forty years, bearing the title *1947 Diary and Manual of the Real Estate Board of New York, Inc.* had been earmarked for removal from the collection. The archives staff who examined it prior to disposal discovered—in the back, past all the pages listing the officers and members of the Real Estate Board—diary entries written by President Truman. Among the forty-two entries, comprising about 5,500 words in all, was one that provides insight into Truman's attitude toward African

Americans. The entry tells of an encounter Truman had with an African American member of the service staff in the White House. The man approached Truman, who was probably working at his desk in his study on the second floor of the White House, to explain that he had made some mistake in the household accounts and was very worried he would get in trouble. Truman listened sympathetically and promised to help the man. Afterwards, Truman wrote this in his diary:

> I wonder why nearly everyone makes a father confessor out of me. I must look benevolent or else I'm a known easy mark. Well any way [sic] I like people and like to help 'em and keep 'em out of trouble when I can and help 'em out when they get into it.
>
> The rule around here is that no one may speak to the President. I break it every day and make 'em speak to me. So—you see what I get. But I still want 'em to tell me.[7]

Presumably not every president has behaved in this way toward the White House service staff, but this one did. One may speculate that this man who wanted to help someone out of his small trouble might react similarly to people who were facing much greater problems, even those he did not know personally. There was perhaps something in this president that made him, as he says, like just about everybody and want to help everyone he could, including those Americans who most needed their president's help.

Other important insights into Truman's attitudes toward race and toward his civil rights program as president have been provided by recently opened outtake materials. The outtakes were created during the production in the early 1960s of a series of documentary films about Truman's life and presidency called *Decision: The Conflicts of Harry S. Truman.* Truman was one of the partners in the enterprise, and he was as well the star of the series, which he viewed as a film version of his memoirs. He gave many interviews during the production, and when he was on the set during filming, he often spoke extemporaneously. After the films were broadcast in 1964, Truman had all the outtakes, which filled about 2,600 film cans, shipped to the Truman Library. Archivists have been reviewing this large and technically demanding material for years. In 2003, the library began opening the preserved outtakes, which are collectively called the Screen Gems Collection.

In one of the outtakes, a sound recording, Truman talks about the slaves his ancestors owned. The interviewer is Merle Miller, later the author of a well known book about Truman, *Plain Speaking*.

> MILLER: Did any of your ancestors have slaves?
> TRUMAN (*sounding amused and very engaged in the subject matter*):   Yes, they all had, they all had slaves. Brought 'em out here with 'em from Kentucky. Most of 'em were wedding presents. (*chuckles*)
> MILLER   You mean that was one of the gifts....
> TRUMAN   That's right.
> MILLER   How many slaves would a normal, a fairly normal family have? How many?
> TRUMAN   Oh, about five or six. They'd have a cook, all of 'em would have a cook, and a nurse for the children, and a maid of all work, and then they'd have maybe a couple of field hands to go along with 'em.[8]

This is what the former president, who fifteen years before had committed the federal government to the achievement of civil rights for African Americans, said about his family background.

In another outtake, also a sound recording, Truman gives a rambling account of the reasons why bigotry exists in the United States, and how he believes the American people are going to overcome it. The following statement was made on the Screen Gems production set in about 1963:

> A foreigner, when he comes to this country, is usually always puzzled to find that there is to some extent bigotry in regard to the treatment of the Negro. Usually, the matter is explained to him on this basis, which I expect to do now and I hope it'll explain a great many things to people. He'll understand the situation. The South in the War Between the States...eleven of those states left the Union, and about three and a half million Negroes were freed and turned loose. And Abraham Lincoln was assassinated before he had a chance to implement the situation that he had in mind. And the freed Negroes felt that due to their emancipation and the amendments to the Constitution that were passed in 1868 [they] had the same rights as the white people.
>
> Well, the Southerners, having been raised in the slave time, just couldn't see it. And if the men from the North would have patience and stay out of the situation down South—they're always sticking their noses in someplace where they're not wanted and stirrin' up trouble. The Southerners are not bigots. They understand the situation. They know that eventually the situation will have to develop so there is equality among the races, and when that equality comes you'll find those Southern Negroes who came

up here to New York—there's a million of 'em here—and who went to Chicago—there's a million and a half of 'em in Chicago—are now wishing they were back home, for the simple reason that they found that they don't get any better treatment from these so-called Northern friends of theirs, not half as good treatment as they get down South because a Southerner understands 'em, and if they'll approach this thing in a level-headed, easy manner, in the long run the whole thing will work out as it should.

The Southerners believe in equality of opportunity. They believe in equality of the political approach to the Government of the United States, and they understand that the Constitution provides for just that, and that the civil rights law which had been passed to implement that—and I got that law through the Congress after about four years fight—and it has now been, to some extent but not entirely, implemented. There is another civil rights law now in contemplation, and eventually the whole situation will be worked out. But it takes patience and understanding, and the people in New York, Chicago, and Boston, particularly, can't understand the attitude of the Southerners in this matter. If they'd stayed home and tended their own business and the niggers who'd been invited to go up there and have find [sic] out that they're not half as well treated as they are down South. And after a while, there won't be any difficulty with it because I *know*—I come from a state, as I told you, a Southern state....

And the situation in Missouri has developed so that there is no objection whatever, as I told you, about riding in a dining car, coming to New York, where a table full of nigger women and nigger men were eating just like the rest of us were and nobody paid any attention to it. And as soon as the people get used to it and the new generation grows up, we won't have any trouble with the subject. I'm not worried about it 'tall.[9]

Truman begins this statement in a formal tone, but toward the end he is clearly getting caught up in his subject matter, and he begins saying "as I told you" to the producer of the program, Ben Gradus, and he drops the correct (for the time) word "Negro" for the less acceptable form of that word that he typically used in casual conversation. Historians may have some difficulty hearing in this statement the voice of the president of the United States, who created the President's Committee on Civil Rights, ordered the desegregation of the armed forces, and took other important actions intended to achieve civil rights for African Americans. But that person is clearly audible here, although he is probably more unguarded and folksy in his safe old age than he ever could have been during his presidency. One hears Truman's keen sense of history, which informs him that the United States turned decisively away from slavery and toward civil rights for all Americans during the Civil War and the Reconstruction era. One also detects his empathy with the feelings of Southerners, who are probably more his people than are the Northerners, and his idealistic—some would say naïve—belief that Southerners are good in their hearts and will eventually accept racial equality. Finally, there is his deep faith that common sense and shared humanity will always in time prevail, that folks will in the long run be just folks, and that everything will work out, life will go on, and there's really nothing to worry about after all. These attitudes and beliefs, clearly evident in these words were undoubtedly part of the motivation that led to his civil rights program. They seem to add up to a strange passivity that suggests Truman, essentially a Southerner, could undertake a civil rights program without much pain because he believed he was just going to nudge good people along to do what they knew was right and inevitable but would not have done for a while yet on their own. Whatever the meaning of this small new piece of evidence, historians of Truman's civil rights program will at least have to consider it as they evaluate his civil rights legacy.

The Truman Library sponsors educational and public programs that are intended to engage people with President Truman's civil rights legacy. One of these programs is called the White House Decision Center, in which secondary school students take the roles of President Truman and several of his advisors in confronting important crises and problems that the Truman administration faced. One such problem is the racial segregation that existed in the armed forces when Truman became president. After studying the background to segregation in the military during several class periods at their schools, students come to the White House Decision Center to determine what should be done about this problem. First, they read documents from the library's holdings so they can understand the information that was available to Truman and his advisors in the summer of 1948. Then they come together in cabinet-like meetings to decide what the administration should do in response to the problem. The president listens to the points of view put forward by his or her advisers, and then makes a decision.

Following the presidential decision, all the students except the president change roles and become members of the press. A press conference is convened; the president steps up to a podium and delivers a

brief address. Should something be done to end or ameliorate segregation in the military? If so, what will that action be? Every young president who comes to the podium in the White House Decision Center
announces a decision that is in important respects his or her own, but
that also reflects the advice given by advisors earlier in the day. The
students involved in this program struggle through all the dilemmas
and options that faced the president, and they collectively make a
decision; as members of the press, they begin to question that decision
and perhaps even to doubt whether it was the best path to take. Truman's civil rights legacy comes to life every time students come to the
White House Decision Center and engage in this program.

Truman issued Executive Order 9981, ordering the desegregation of the armed forces, on 26 July 1948. On approximately this
date every year, the Truman Library, together with the American
Jazz Museum, sponsors an address by someone prominent in civil
rights advocacy. This series of commemorative but also forward-
looking events had a memorable beginning in 1998 when General
Colin Powell presented a moving address, a version of which is
included in this volume, about the effects Truman's desegregation
order had on his life and career, and the effects it has had as well on
the lives and careers of other young African Americans. Like all the
activities relating to civil rights the Truman Presidential Library
undertakes, this public program seeks to renew Truman's legacy,
keeping it vital and relevant to new generations who have the
responsibility of building the country's and the world's future.

The Truman Library's programs relating to President Truman's
civil rights legacy are founded on the belief that the American people
must do more than simply celebrate Truman's record. They must
become engaged with it, understanding the ways in which it was wor-
thy and admirable but also understanding the ways in which it was
limited; and they must try to determine why Truman's actions sometimes fell short of the promise implicit in his rhetoric. President Truman wanted his civil rights legacy to be a dynamic one, driven by the
ideals, commitment, and cognitive force of every new generation of
Americans. The result, he believed, would be a world better than the
one he himself had the ability or the will to create during the few
short, crowded years of his presidency. He knew what was right and
did what he could, and he left the rest to the young people whom he
loved and to whom he entrusted the responsibility of creating a better future for the country—a country that possessed, as he so many
times said, "the greatest government in the history of the world."[10]

Notes

[1] McCoy and Ruetten, *Quest and Response;* Gardner, *Harry Truman and Civil Rights;* Leuchtenburg, "Conversion of Harry Truman"; Dalfiume, *Desegregation of the U.S. Armed Forces;* Sitkoff, "Civil Rights," and Wiecek, "United States Supreme Court," in *Harry S. Truman Encyclopedia,* ed. Kirkendall, 57–59, 347–50; McCullough, *Truman;* Ferrell, *Harry S. Truman;* and Hamby, *Man of the People.*

[2] Anderson, *Eyes Off the Prize,* 5. See also Dudziak, *Cold War Civil Rights;* and Borstelmann, *Cold War and the Color Line.*

[3] Anderson, *Eyes Off the Prize,* 155.

[4] Harry S. Truman to Bess Wallace Truman, 19 June 1946. Truman Papers, Papers Pertaining to Family, Business, and Personal Affairs, Truman Library.

[5] Roy Wilkins to Harry S. Truman, 12 January 1953. Truman Papers, Official File: OF 596, Truman Library.

[6] Student Research Files, "Desegregation of the Armed Forces" and "The War Relocation Authority & the Incarceration of Japanese Americans During World War II." Available online at www.trumanlibrary.org.

[7] Entry for 16 January 1947, Harry S. Truman 1947 Diary. Truman Papers, President's Secretary's Files, Truman Library. Available online at www.trumanlibrary.org.

[8] MP2002–115, Screen Gems Collection, Truman Library.

[9] MP2002–78, Screen Gems Collection, Truman Library.

[10] Truman, *Mr. Citizen,* 27.

Appendix A
President Truman's Major Speeches Relating to Civil Rights

Address Before the National Association for the Advancement of Colored People

June 29, 1947

Mr. Chairman, Mrs. Roosevelt, Senator Morse, distinguished guests, ladies and gentlemen:

I am happy to be present at the closing session of the 38th Annual Conference of the National Association for the Advancement of Colored People. The occasion of meeting with you here at the Lincoln Memorial affords me the opportunity to congratulate the association upon its effective work for the improvement of our democratic processes.

I should like to talk to you briefly about civil rights and human freedom. It is my deep conviction that we have reached a turning point in the long history of our country's efforts to guarantee freedom and equality to all our citizens. Recent events in the United States and abroad have made us realize that it is more important today than ever before to insure that all Americans enjoy these rights.

When I say all Americans I mean all Americans.

The civil rights laws written in the early years of our Republic, and the traditions which have been built upon them, are precious to us. Those laws were drawn up with the memory still fresh in men's minds of the tyranny of an absentee government. They were written to protect the citizen against any possible tyrannical act by the new government in this country.

But we cannot be content with a civil liberties program which emphasizes only the need of protection against the possibility of tyranny by the Government. We cannot stop there.

We must keep moving forward, with new concept of civil rights to safeguard our heritage. The extension of civil rights today means, not protection of the people *against* the Government, but protection of the people *by* the Government.

We must make the Federal Government a friendly, vigilant defender of the rights and equalities of all Americans. And again I mean all Americans.

As Americans, we believe that every man should be free to live his life as he wishes. He should be limited only by his responsibility to his fellow countrymen. If this freedom is to be more than a dream, each man must be guaranteed equality of opportunity. The only limit to an American's achievement should be his ability, his industry, and his character. These rewards for his effort should be determined only by those truly relevant qualities.

Our immediate task is to remove the last remnants of the barriers which stand between millions of our citizens and their birthright. There is no justifiable reason for discrimination because of ancestry, or religion, or race, or color.

We must not tolerate such limitations on the freedom of any of our people and on their enjoyment of basic rights which every citizen in a truly democratic society must possess.

Every man should have the right to a decent home, the right to an education, the right to adequate medical care, the right to a worthwhile job, the right to an equal share in making the public decisions through the ballot, and the right to a fair trial in a fair court.

We must insure that these rights—on equal terms—are enjoyed by every citizen.

To these principles I pledge my full and continued support.

Many of our people still suffer the indignity of insult, the narrowing fear of intimidation, and, I regret to say, the threat of physical injury and mob violence. Prejudice and intolerance in which these evils are rooted still exist. The conscience of our Nation, and the legal machinery which enforces it, have not yet secured to each citizen full freedom from fear.

We cannot wait another decade or another generation to remedy these evils. We must work, as never before, to cure them now. The aftermath of war and the desire to keep faith with our Nation's historic principles make the need a pressing one.

The support of desperate populations of battle-ravaged countries must be won for the free way of life. We must have them as allies in our continuing struggle for the peaceful solution of the world's problems. Freedom is not an easy lesson to teach, nor an easy cause to sell, to peoples beset by every kind of privation. They may surrender to the false security offered so temptingly by totalitarian regimes unless we can prove the superiority of democracy.

Our case for democracy should be as strong as we can make it. It should rest on practical evidence that we have been able to put our own house in order.

For these compelling reasons, we can no longer afford the luxury of a leisurely attack upon prejudice and discrimination. There is much that State and local governments can do in providing positive safeguards for civil rights. But we cannot, any longer, await the growth of a will to action in the slowest State or the most backward community.

Our National Government must show the way.

This is a difficult and complex undertaking. Federal laws and administrative machineries must be improved and expanded. We must provide the Government with better tools to do the job. As a first step, I appointed an Advisory Committee on Civil Rights last December. Its members, fifteen distinguished private citizens, have been surveying our civil rights difficulties and needs for several months. I am confident that the product of their work will be a sensible and vigorous program for action by all of us.

We must strive to advance civil rights wherever it lies within our power. For example, I have asked the Congress to pass legislation extending basic civil rights to the people of Guam and American Samoa so that these people can share our ideals of freedom and self-government. This step, with others which will follow, is evidence to the rest of the world of our confidence in the ability of all men to build free institutions.

The way ahead is not easy. We shall need all the wisdom, imagination and courage we can muster. We must and shall guarantee the civil rights of all our citizens. Never before has the need been so urgent for skillful and vigorous action to bring us closer to our ideal.

We can reach the goal. When past difficulties faced our Nation we met the challenge with inspiring charters of human rights—the Declaration of Independence, the Constitution, the Bill of Rights, and the Emancipation Proclamation. Today our representatives, and those of other liberty-loving countries on the United Nations Commission on Human Rights, are preparing an International Bill of Rights. We can be confident that it will be a great landmark in man's long search for freedom since its members consist of such distinguished citizens of the world as Mrs. Franklin D. Roosevelt.

With these noble charters to guide us, and with faith in our hearts, we shall make our land a happier home for our people, a symbol of hope for all men, and a rock of security in a troubled world.

Abraham Lincoln understood so well the ideal which you and I seek today. As this conference closes we would do well to keep in mind his words, when he said,

> if it shall please the Divine Being who determines the destinies of nations, we shall remain a united people, and we will, humbly seeking the Divine Guidance, make their prolonged national existence a

source of new benefits to themselves and their successors, and to all classes and conditions of mankind.

NOTE: The President spoke at the Lincoln Memorial at 4:30 PM. In his opening words he referred to Walter F. White, Executive Secretary of the National Association for the Advancement of Colored People, who served as chairman of the conference, and to Mrs. Franklin D. Roosevelt and Senator Wayne Morse who also spoke. The address was carried on a nationwide radio broadcast.

Special Message to the Congress on Civil Rights
February 2, 1948

To the Congress of the United States:

In the State of the Union Message on January 7, 1948, I spoke of five great goals toward which we should strive in our constant effort to strengthen our democracy and improve the welfare of our people. The first of these is to secure fully our essential human rights. I am now presenting to the Congress my recommendations for legislation to carry us forward toward that goal.

This Nation was founded by men and women who sought these shores that they might enjoy greater freedom and greater opportunity than they had known before. The founders of the United States proclaimed to the world the American belief that all men are created equal, and that governments are instituted to secure the inalienable rights with which all men are endowed. In the Declaration of Independence and the Constitution of the United States, they eloquently expressed the aspirations of all mankind for equality and freedom.

These ideals inspired the peoples of other lands, and their practical fulfillment made the United States the hope of the oppressed everywhere. Throughout our history men and women of all colors and creeds, of all races and religions, have come to this country to escape tyranny and discrimination. Millions strong, they have helped build this democratic Nation and have constantly reinforced our devotion to the great ideals of liberty and equality. With those who preceded them, they have helped to fashion and strengthen our American faith—a faith that can be simply stated:

We believe that all men are created equal and that they have the right to equal justice under law.

We believe that all men have the right to freedom of thought and of expression and the right to worship as they please.

We believe that all men are entitled to equal opportunities for jobs, for homes, for good health and for education.

We believe that all men should have a voice in their government and that government should protect, not usurp, the rights of the people.

These are the basic civil rights which are the source and the support of our democracy.

Today, the American people enjoy more freedom and opportunity than ever before. Never in our history has there been better reason to hope for the complete realization of the ideals of liberty and equality.

We shall not, however, finally achieve the ideals for which this Nation was rounded so long as any American suffers discrimination as a result of his race, or religion, or color, or the land of origin of his forefathers.

Unfortunately, there still are examples—flagrant examples—of discrimination which are utterly contrary to our ideals. Not all groups of our population are free from the fear of violence. Not all groups are free to live and work where they please or to improve their conditions of life by their own efforts. Not all groups enjoy the full privileges of citizenship and participation in the government under which they live.

We cannot be satisfied until all our people have equal opportunities for jobs, for homes, for education, for health, and for political expression, and until all our people have equal protection under the law.

One year ago I appointed a committee of fifteen distinguished Americans and asked them to appraise the condition of our civil rights and to recommend appropriate action by Federal, state and local governments.

The committee's appraisal has resulted in a frank and revealing report. This report emphasizes that our basic human freedoms are better cared for and more vigilantly defended than ever before. But it also makes clear that there is a serious gap between our ideals and some of our practices. This gap must be closed.

This will take the strong efforts of each of us individually, and all of us acting together through voluntary organizations and our governments.

The protection of civil rights begins with the mutual respect for the rights of others which all of us should practice in our daily lives. Through organizations in every community—in all parts of the country—we must continue to develop practical, workable arrangements for achieving greater tolerance and brotherhood.

The protection of civil rights is the duty of every government which derives its powers from the consent of the people. This is equally true of local, state, and national governments. There is much that the states can and should do at this time to extend their protection of civil rights. Wherever the law enforcement measures of state and local governments are inadequate to discharge this primary function of government, these measures should be strengthened and improved.

The Federal Government has a clear duty to see that Constitutional guarantees of individual liberties and of equal protection under the laws are not denied or abridged anywhere in our Union. That duty is shared by all three branches of the Government, but it can be fulfilled only if the Congress enacts modern, comprehensive civil rights laws, adequate to the needs of the day, and demonstrating our continuing faith in the free way of life.

I recommend, therefore, that the Congress enact legislation at this session directed toward the following specific objectives:

1. Establishing a permanent Commission on Civil Rights, a Joint Congressional Committee on Civil Rights, and a Civil Rights Division in the Department of Justice.

2. Strengthening existing civil rights statutes.

3. Providing Federal protection against lynching.

4. Protecting more adequately the right to vote.

5. Establishing a Fair Employment Practice Commission to prevent unfair discrimination in employment.

6. Prohibiting discrimination in interstate transportation facilities.

7. Providing home-rule and suffrage in Presidential elections for the residents of the District of Columbia.

8. Providing Statehood for Hawaii and Alaska and a greater measure of self-government for our island possessions.

9. Equalizing the opportunities for residents of the United States to become naturalized citizens.

10. Settling the evacuation claims of Japanese-Americans.

Strengthening the Government Organization

As a first stop, we must strengthen the organization of the Federal Government in order to enforce civil rights legislation more adequately and to watch over the state of our traditional liberties.

I recommend that the Congress establish a permanent Commission on Civil Rights reporting to the President. The Commission should continuously review our civil rights policies and practices, study specific problems, and make recommendations to the President at frequent intervals. It should work with other agencies of the Federal Government, with state and local governments, and with private organizations.

I also suggest that the Congress establish a Joint Congressional Committee on Civil Rights. This Committee should make a continuing study of legislative matters relating to civil rights and should consider means of improving respect for and enforcement of those rights.

These two bodies together should keep all of us continuously aware of the condition of civil rights in the United States and keep us alert to opportunities to improve their protection.

To provide for better enforcement of Federal civil rights laws, there will be established a Division of Civil Rights in the Department of Justice. I recommend that the Congress provide for an additional Assistant Attorney General to supervise this Division.

Strengthening Existing Civil Rights Statutes

I recommend that the Congress amend and strengthen the existing provisions of Federal law which safeguard the right to vote and the right to safety and security of person and property. These provisions are the basis for our present civil rights enforcement program.

Section 51 of Title 18 of the United States Code, which now gives protection to citizens in the enjoyment of rights secured by the Constitution or Federal laws, needs to be strengthened in two respects. In its present form, this section protects persons only if they are citizens, and it affords protection only against conspiracies by two or more persons. This protection should be extended to all inhabitants of the United States, whether or not they are citizens, and should be afforded against infringement by persons acting individually as well as in conspiracy.

Section 52 of Title 18 of the United States Code, which now gives general protection to individuals against the deprivation of Federally secured rights by public officers, has proved to be inadequate in some cases because of the generality of its language. An enumeration of the principal rights protected under this section is needed to make more definite and certain the protection which the section affords.

Federal Protection Against Lynching

A specific Federal measure is needed to deal with the crime of lynching--against which I cannot speak too strongly. It is a principle of our democracy, written into our Constitution, that every person accused of an offense against the law shall have a fair, orderly trial in an impartial court. We have made great progress toward this end, but I regret to say that lynching has not yet finally disappeared from our land. So long as one person walks in fear of lynching, we shall not have achieved equal justice under law. I call upon the Congress to take decisive action against this crime.

Protecting the Right to Vote

Under the Constitution, the right of all properly qualified citizens to vote is beyond question. Yet the exercise of this right is still subject to interference. Some individuals are prevented from voting by isolated acts of intimidation. Some whole groups are prevented by outmoded policies prevailing in certain states or communities.

We need stronger statutory protection of the right to vote. I urge the Congress to enact legislation forbidding interference by public officers or private persons with the right of qualified citizens to participate in primary, special and general elections in which Federal officers are to be chosen. This legislation should extend to elections for state as well as Federal officers insofar as interference with the right to vote results from discriminatory action by public officers based on race, color, or other unreasonable classification.

Requirements for the payment of poll taxes also interfere with the right to vote. There are still seven states which, by their constitutions, place this barrier between their citizens and the ballot box. The American people would welcome voluntary action on the part of these states to remove this barrier. Nevertheless, I believe the Congress should enact measures insuring that the right to vote in elections for Federal officers shall not be contingent upon the payment of taxes.

I wish to make it clear that the enactment of the measures I have recommended will in no sense result in Federal conduct of elections. They are designed to give qualified citizens Federal protection of their right to vote. The actual conduct of elections, as always, will remain the responsibility of State governments.

Fair Employment Practice Commission

We in the United States believe that all men are entitled to equality of opportunity. Racial, religious and other invidious forms of discrimination deprive the individual of an equal chance to develop and utilize his talents and to enjoy the rewards of his efforts.

Once more I repeat my request that the Congress enact fair employment practice legislation prohibiting discrimination in employment based on race, color, religion or national origin. The legislation should create a Fair Employment Practice Commission with authority to prevent discrimination by employers and labor unions, trade and professional associations, and government agencies and employment bureaus. The degree of effectiveness which the wartime Fair Employment Practice Committee attained shows that it is possible to equalize job opportunity by government action and thus to eliminate the influence of prejudice in employment.

Interstate Transportation

The channels of interstate commerce should be open to all Americans on a basis of complete equality. The Supreme Court has recently declared unconstitutional state laws requiring segregation on public carriers in interstate travel. Company regulations must not be allowed to replace unconstitutional state laws. I urge the Congress to prohibit discrimination and segregation, in the use of interstate transportation facilities, by both public officers and the employees of private companies.

The District of Columbia

I am in full accord with the principle of local self-government for residents of the District of Columbia. In addition, I believe that the Constitution should be amended to extend suffrage in Presidential elections to the residents of the District.

The District of Columbia should be a true symbol of American freedom and democracy for our own people, and for the people of the world. It is my earnest hope that the Congress will promptly give the citizens of the District of Columbia their own local, elective government. They themselves can then deal with the inequalities arising from segregation in the schools and other public facilities, and from racial barriers to places of public accommodation which now exist for one-third of the District's population.

The present inequalities in essential services are primarily a problem for the District itself, but they are also of great concern to the whole Nation. Failing local corrective action in the near future, the Congress should enact a model civil rights law for the Nation's Capital.

Our Territories and Possessions

The present political status of our Territories and possessions impairs the enjoyment of civil rights by their residents. I have in the past recommended legislation granting statehood to Alaska and Hawaii, and organic acts for Guam and American Samoa including a grant of citizenship to the people of these Pacific Islands. I repeat these recommendations.

Furthermore, the residents of the Virgin Islands should be granted an increasing measure of self-government, and the people of Puerto Rico should be allowed to choose their form of government and their ultimate status with respect to the United States.

Equality in Naturalization

All properly qualified legal residents of the United States should be allowed to become citizens without regard to race, color, religion or national origin. The Congress has recently removed the bars which formerly prevented persons from China, India and the Philippines from becoming naturalized citizens. I urge the Congress to remove the remaining racial or nationality barriers which stand in the way of citizenship for some residents of our country.

Evacuation Claims of the Japanese-Americans

During the last war more than one hundred thousand Japanese-Americans were evacuated from their homes in the Pacific states solely because of their racial origin. Many of these people suffered property and business losses as a result of this forced evacuation and through no fault of their own. The Congress has before it legislation establishing a procedure by which claims based upon these losses can be promptly considered and settled. I trust that favorable action on this legislation will soon be taken.

The legislation I have recommended for enactment by the Congress at the present session is a minimum program if the Federal Government is to fulfill its obligation of insuring the Constitutional guarantees of individual liberties and of equal protection under the law.

Under the authority of existing law, the Executive branch is taking every possible action to improve the enforcement of the civil rights statutes and to eliminate discrimination in Federal employment, in providing Federal services and facilities, and in the armed forces.

I have already referred to the establishment of the Civil Rights Division of the Department of Justice. The Federal Bureau of Investigation will work closely with this new Division in the investigation of Federal civil rights cases. Specialized training is being given to the Bureau's agents so that they may render more effective service in this difficult field of law enforcement.

It is the settled policy of the United States Government that there shall be no discrimination in Federal employment or in providing Federal services and facilities. Steady progress has been made toward this objective in recent years. I shall shortly issue an Executive Order containing a comprehensive restatement of the Federal non-discrimination policy, together with appropriate measures to ensure compliance.

During the recent war and in the years since its close we have made much progress toward equality of opportunity in our armed services without regard to race, color, religion or national origin. I have instructed the Secretary of Defense to take steps to have the remaining instances of discrimination in the armed services eliminated as rapidly as possible. The personnel policies and practices of all the services in this regard will be made consistent.

I have instructed the Secretary of the Army to investigate the status of civil rights in the Panama Canal Zone with a view to eliminating such discrimination as may exist there. If legislation is necessary, I shall make appropriate recommendations to the Congress.

The position of the United States in the world today makes it especially urgent that we adopt these measures to secure for all our people their essential rights.

The peoples of the world are faced with the choice of freedom or enslavement, a choice between a form of government which harnesses the state in the service of the individual and a form of government which chains the individual to the needs of the state.

We in the United States are working in company with other nations who share our desire for enduring world peace and who believe with us that, above all else, men must be free. We are striving to build a world family of nations—a world where men may live under governments of their own choosing and under laws of their own making.

As a part of that endeavor, the Commission on Human Rights of the United Nations is now engaged in preparing an international bill of human rights by which the nations of the world may bind themselves. by international covenant to give effect to basic human rights and fundamental freedoms. We have played a leading role in this undertaking designed to create a world order of law and justice fully protective of the rights and the dignity of the individual.

To be effective in those efforts, we must protect our civil rights so that by providing all our people with the maximum enjoyment of personal freedom and personal opportunity we shall be a stronger nation—stronger in our leadership, stronger in our moral position, stronger in the deeper satisfactions of a united citizenry.

We know that our democracy is not perfect. But we do know that it offers freer, happier life to our people than any totalitarian nation has ever offered.

If we wish to inspire the peoples of the world whose freedom is in jeopardy, if we wish to restore hope to those who have already lost their civil liberties, if we wish to fulfill the promise that is ours, we must correct the remaining imperfections in our practice of democracy.

We know the way. We need only the will.

Harry S. Truman

NOTE: The President's Committee on Civil Rights was established on 5 December 1946, by Executive Order 9808 (3 CFR, 1943–1948 Comp., p. 590). The Committee's report, entitled *"To Secure These Rights,"* was made public 29 October 1947 (Government Printing Office, 178 pp.)

On 2 July 1948, the President signed a bill in. response to his request for legislation dealing with evacuation claims of Japanese-Americans (62 Stat. 1231). On 26 July he issued Executive Order 9980 relating to fair employment practices in the Federal service, and Executive Order 9981 establishing the President's Committee on Equality of Treatment and Opportunity in the Armed Services (3 CFR, 1943–1948 Comp., pp. 720, 722).

Address in Harlem, New York, Upon Receiving the Franklin Roosevelt Award

October 29, 1948

Dr. Johnson, and members of the Ministerial Alliance which has given me this award:

I am exceedingly grateful for it. I hope I shall always deserve it. This, in my mind, is a most solemn occasion. It's made a tremendous impression upon me.

Franklin Roosevelt was a great champion of human rights. When he led us out of the depression to the victory over the Axis, he enabled us to build a country in which prosperity and freedom must exist side by side. This is the only atmosphere in which human rights can thrive.

Eventually, we are going to have an America in which freedom and opportunity are the same for everyone. There is only one way to accomplish that great purpose, and that is to keep working for it and never take a backward step.

I am especially glad to receive the Franklin Roosevelt award on this day—October 29. This date means a great deal to me personally, and it is a significant date in the history of human freedom in this country.

One year ago today, on October 29, 1947, the President's Committee on Civil Rights submitted to me, and to the American people, its momentous report.

That report was drawn up by men and women who had the honesty to face the whole problem of civil rights squarely, and the courage to state their conclusions frankly.

I created the Civil Rights Committee because racial and religious intolerance began to appear after World War II. They threatened the very freedoms we had fought to save.

We Americans have a democratic way of acting when our freedoms are threatened.

We get the most thoughtful and representative men and women we can find, and we ask them to put down on paper the principles that represent freedom and a method of action that will preserve and extend that freedom. In that manner, we get a declaration of purpose and a guide for action that the whole country can consider.

That is the way in which the Declaration of Independence was drawn up.

That is the way in which the Constitution of the United States was written.

The report that the Civil Rights Committee prepared is in the tradition of these great documents.

It was the authors of the Declaration of Independence who stated the principle that all men are created equal in their rights, and that it is to secure these rights that governments are instituted among men.

It was the authors of the Constitution who made it clear that, under our form of government, all citizens are equal before the law, and that the Federal Government has a duty to guarantee to every citizen equal protection of the laws.

The Civil Rights Committee did more than repeat these great principles. It described a method to put these principles into action, and to make them a living reality for every American, regardless of his race, his religion, or his national origin.

When every American knows that his rights and his opportunities are fully protected and respected by the Federal, State, and local governments, then we will have the kind of unity that really means something.

It is easy to talk of unity. But it is the work that is done for unity that really counts.

The job that the Civil Rights Committee did was to tell the American people how to create the kind of freedom that we need in this country.

The Civil Rights Committee described the kind of freedom that comes when every man has an equal chance for a job—not just the hot and heavy job—but the best job he is qualified for.

The Committee described the kind of freedom that comes when every American boy and girl has an equal chance for an education.

The Committee described the kind of freedom that comes when every citizen has an equal opportunity to go to the ballot box and cast his vote and have it counted.

The Committee described the kind of freedom that comes when every man, woman, and child is free from the fear of mob violence and intimidation.

When we have that kind of freedom, we will face the evil forces that are abroad in the world—whatever or wherever they may be—with the strength that comes from complete confidence in one another and from complete faith in the working of our own democracy.

One of the great things that the Civil Rights Committee did for the country was to get every American to think seriously about the principles that make our country great.

More than 1 million copies of the full text of the civil rights report have been printed in books and newspapers.

More than 30 different pamphlets based on the report have been printed and distributed by private organizations.

Millions of Americans have heard the report discussed on the radio.

In making its recommendations, the Civil Rights Committee did not limit itself to action by the President or by the executive branch. The Committee's recommendations included actions by every branch of the Federal Government, by State and local governments, and by private organizations, and by individuals.

That is why it is so important that the Civil Rights Committee's report be studied widely. For in the last analysis, freedom resides in the actions of each individual. That is the reason I like to hear that scriptural reading from the Gospel according to St. Luke. That's just exactly what it means. It means you and I must act out what we say in our Constitution and our Bill of Rights. It is in his mind and heart—and to his mind and heart—that we must eventually speak to the individual.

After the Civil Rights Committee submitted its report, I asked Congress to do ten of the things recommended by the Committee.

You know what they did about that.

So I went ahead and did what the President can do, unaided by the Congress.

I issued two Executive Orders.

One of them established the President's Committee on Equality of Treatment and Opportunity in the Armed Services.

The other one covered regulations governing fair employment practices within the Federal establishment.

In addition to that, the Department of Justice went into the Supreme Court and aided in getting a decision outlawing restrictive covenants.

Several States and municipalities have taken action on the recommendations of the Civil Rights Committee, and I hope more will follow after them.

Today the democratic way of life is being challenged all over the world. Democracy's answer to the challenge of totalitarianism is its promise of equal rights and equal opportunity for all mankind.

The fulfillment of this promise is among the highest purposes of government.

Our determination to attain the goal of equal rights and equal opportunity must be resolute and unwavering.

For my part, I intend to keep moving toward this goal with every ounce of strength and determination that I have.

NOTE: The President spoke at 3:50 PM in Dorance Brooks Square. In his opening words he referred to Dr. C. Aspansa-Johnson, president of the Inter-denominational Ministers Alliance, who presented him with the Franklin D. Roosevelt Memorial Brotherhood Medal.

The report of the President's Committee on Civil Rights (PCCR) is entitled *To Secure These Rights* (Government Printing Office, 1947, 178 pp.). For the President's statement upon making the report public, see 1987 volume, this series, Item 215.

The President referred to Executive Order 9980. "Regulations Governing Fair Employment Practices Within the Federal Establishment" and Executive Order 9981 "Establishing the President's Committee on Equality of Treatment and Opportunity in the Armed Forces" (26 July 1948; 3 CFR 1943–1948 Comp., pp. 720, 722).

Commencement Address at Howard University
June 13, 1952

Mr. President of the University, Mr. Ewing, distinguished guests:

I am happy to be here today at this Howard University commencement.

Dr. Johnson has asked me to come to your commencement several times, and I am glad that I was able to do it before the end of my term of office.

You who are graduating here today can always be proud of this university. This institution was founded in 1867 to give meaning to the principles of freedom, and to make them work.

The founders of this university had a great vision. They knew that the slaves who had been set free needed a center of learning and higher education. They could foresee that many of the freedmen, if they were given a chance, would take their places among the most gifted and honored American citizens. And that is what has happened. The long list of distinguished Howard alumni proves that the wisdom of those who established this university was profoundly true.

This university has been a true institution of higher learning which has helped to enrich American life with the talents of a gifted people.

For example, every soldier and every civilian who received the lifesaving gift of a transfusion from a blood bank can be grateful to this university. For this was the work of a distinguished Howard University professor, the late Dr. Charles Drew, that made possible the very first blood bank in the whole world.

This is a practical illustration of the fact that talent and genius have no boundaries of race, or nationality, or creed. The United States needs the imagination, the energy, and the skills of every single one of its citizens.

Howard University has recognized this from the beginning. It has accepted among its students, faculty, and trustees, representatives of every race, every creed, and every nationality.

I wish I could say to you who are graduating today that no opportunity to use your skills and knowledge would ever be denied you. I can say this: I know what it means not to have opportunity. I wasn't able to go to college at all. I had to stay at home and work on the family farm. You have been able to get the college education that is so important to everyone in this country. Some of us are denied opportunity for economic reasons. Others are denied opportunity because of racial prejudice and discrimination. I want to see things worked out so that everyone who is capable of it receives a good education. I want to see everyone have a chance to put his education to good use, without unfair discrimination.

Our country is founded on the proposition that all men are created equal. This means that they should be equal before the law. They should enjoy equal political rights. And they should have equal opportunities for education, employment, and decent living conditions. This is our belief, and we know it is right. We know it is morally right. And we have proved, by experience, that the more we practice that belief, the stronger, more vigorous, and happier our Nation becomes.

That is why, 6 years ago, I created the President's Committee on Civil Rights. Nearly 5 years have passed since this Committee made its report to me and to the whole American people. Today, I want to talk about some of the progress that has been made in those 5 years.

Back in 1947, a good many people advised me not to raise this whole question of civil rights. They said it would only make things worse. But you can't cure a moral problem, or a social problem, by ignoring it.

It is no service to the country to turn away from the hard problems—to ignore injustice and human suffering. It is simply not the American way of doing things. Of course, there are always a lot of people whose motto is "Don't rock the boat." They are so afraid of rocking the boat, that they stop rowing. We can never get ahead that way. We can only drift with the current and finally go over the falls into oblivion with nothing accomplished.

If something is wrong, the thing to do is to dig it out, find why it is wrong, and take sensible steps to put it right. We are all Americans together, and we can solve our hard problems together, including the problem of race relations.

The experience of the last 5 years demonstrates clearly that this is true. Now, instead of making things worse, our efforts in the field of civil rights have made things better—better in all aspects of our national life, and in all parts of our country. One of my southern friends said to me the other day, "The last 5 years are the best years in race relations this country has ever had." And the record proves it.

Of course, the forward movement did not begin with the civil rights report. It was already in motion. It had been started in the 1930's, and had gained momentum during World War II.

It looked for a while in 1946 and 1947 as if this progress would come to an end. You remember that, after the First World War, a wave of hate and violence and Ku Kluxism swept over the country. The problem we faced after the Second World War was this: Would we have to go through another experience such as that, or could we hold fast to the gains that had been made?

We did neither. Instead, we went forward. In many lines we have made gains for human freedom and equal opportunity that go far beyond anything accomplished during the war. And most of these gains have been permanent. They have been written quietly, but firmly, into our basic laws and our institutions. They will never be undone.

These things have been accomplished without dividing our people. None of the talk about the country being torn apart has come to pass. These things were done because people wanted them to be done. There has been a great working of the American conscience. All over the land there has been a growing recognition that injustice must go, and that the way to equal opportunity is better for us all.

The civil rights report and the civil rights program give voice and expression to this great change of sentiment. They are the necessary instrument of progress. They are the trumpet blast outside the walls of Jericho—the crumbling walls of prejudice.

And their work is not yet done. We still have a long way to go.

I should like to turn to the record now, and speak of the progress that has been made, and the tasks that still await us.

First, in the field of political rights. In the last 5 years, two more States, Tennessee and South Carolina, have abolished the poll tax. Now there are only five poll tax States where there were eleven not so long ago.

Opportunities for all our citizens to participate in our political life have increased steadily and rapidly. Court decisions have given protection to the right of equal participation in primary elections.

These are notable advances. But there is a lot to do. The poll tax and other discriminatory restrictions on voting should be removed in all the States.

Second, let us take the field of education.

I am glad to say that the principle of not discrimination—the principle that has always been followed here at Howard University—is the law of this country today in institutions of higher learning supported by public funds. Since the court decisions outlawing discrimination, more than a thousand Negro graduate and professional students have been accepted by 10 State universities that were closed to Negroes before. In the last 5 years legislation has been passed in 10 other States to abolish segregation or discrimination in schools and colleges.

And the gloomy prophecies of the opponents of civil rights have not been fulfilled. The universities have not been deserted. On the contrary, the faculties and students of the universities which are now open to all have welcomed and accepted the new students on their merits as individuals.

This is only one instance of the way educational opportunities have been opening up to Negroes in recent years. Since 1930 the enrollment of Negro college students has gone up eight times. Just stop and think what that means. For every 100 Negro college students enrolled in 1930 there are 800 today.

In the field of housing we have also been making progress. The congested, segregated areas of our great cities are breeding grounds of poverty, delinquency, and poor health. We have been trying to improve conditions in these areas. A major step was taken in this direction when the Supreme Court outlawed the enforcement of restrictive covenants, which so often make bad housing conditions worse.

We have begun to make progress in public housing also. In 1950, 177 public housing projects were freely opened to families of all races and creeds. This is eight times as many as eight years ago. In the last few years nine States and eight cities have forbidden discrimination or segregation in public housing.

Another problem is that of protecting the right to safety and security of the person. There is no more important duty of the Government. We must protect our citizens from mob violence. And here again we have been moving forward.

In the last 5 years two States have enacted antilynching laws, and four States and six cities have passed laws against wearing masks in public. The Civil Rights Section of the Department of Justice and the Federal Bureau of Investigation have used their powers to reinforce the State and local law enforcement agencies. The latest instance was in Illinois, where the State Governor stopped an outbreak of mob violence and the Federal authorities brought to justice the local law enforcement officers who abetted the mob.

Now, this kind of action hasn't interfered with States rights or upset our system of government. Most of our citizens, wherever they live, have welcomed it. They want to be helped in suppressing lynching. And they would be helped by Federal legislation to safeguard the rights of the individuals when local law enforcement officers fail to do their duty. Such legislation ought to be on the books.

Now I want to speak of something that gives me considerable pride. That is the progress in fair employment in the Federal service.

If there is any place where fair employment practices ought to prevail, it is the Federal Government. But experience shows that the departments and agencies of the Federal Government, no less than other organizations, need to be helped and encouraged. Sometimes they need to be compelled. In 1948 I set up a Fair Employment board in the Civil Service Commission. This Board has gone about its task quietly and effectively, and has done a great deal to insure the success of our nondiscrimination policy.

The Federal Government makes billions of dollars worth of contracts every year to buy the things it needs. The money to pay for these contracts comes from all the people, without discrimination. It should be spent in the same way—without discrimination. For over 10 years we have had a policy that every Government contract must contain a clause binding the contractor and his sub-contractors to practice nondiscrimination. But it is not always easy to be sure that such a clause is being followed in practice. To meet that situation, I set up a Committee on Government Contract Compliance last year. It is the duty of that Committee to work with the contracting agencies and to help them get better compliance with the rule of nondiscrimination.

States and cities have also been going ahead to see that their fair employment practices are followed in their jurisdictions. In the last few years 11 States and 20 municipalities have adopted fair employment laws. Unions and employers in many places have voluntarily done away with the color bar. And the results have been peaceful and beneficial. None of the disorder that was so freely predicted has taken place.

Some of the greatest progress of all has been made in the armed services. Service in the Armed Forces of our country is both a duty and a right of citizenship. Every man or woman who enters one of our services is certainly entitled to equal treatment and equal opportunity.

There has been a lot of talk about the need for segregation in the armed services. Some of our greatest generals have said that our forces had to have segregated units. But experience has proved that this is just plain nonsense.

Quite some time ago, the Navy and the Air Force eliminated all racial distinctions, and the Army has been moving step by step toward this goal. For over 2 years every soldier coming into a training unit has been assigned on a basis of individual merit without racial discrimination. In the Far East, when General Ridgeway took command, he ordered the progressive integration of all the troops in his command, and you have seen the results in the wonderful performance of our troops in Korea. Only recently a similar order was issued by the European Command at the direction of the Secretary of the Army. From Tokyo to Heidelberg these orders have gone out that will make our fighting forces a more perfect instrument of democratic defense.

All these matters have been taken care of in a quiet and orderly way. The prophets of doom have been proved wrong. The civil rights program has not weakened our country—it has made our country stronger. It has not made us less united—it has made us more united.

The progress we have made so far is a source of deep satisfaction to us all. But that does not man we have reached the goal or that we can stop working. Much remains to be done.

Voluntary action can carry us a long way, and we must encourage it. State and local legislation is necessary, and we must have it. But let us remember this: The President's Committee on Civil Rights led the way. The debate over the civil rights program has stimulated much of the progress of the last 5 years. We still need the legislation I recommended to the Congress in 1948. Only two of the recommendations I made in my civil rights program have been adopted so far. I shall continue, in office and out, to urge the Congress to adopt the remainder.

I am not one of those who feel that we can leave these matters up to the States alone, or that we can rely solely on the efforts of men of good will. Our Federal Government must live up to the ideals professed in the Declaration of Independence and the duties imposed upon it by the Constitution. The full force and power of the Federal Government must stand behind the protection of rights guaranteed in the Federal Constitution.

In this country of ours that we all love so much, we have built a way of life that has brought more satisfaction to more people than any other that has ever been devised. Our American way of life is the envy and admiration of people everywhere in the world. But this fact should not make us proud and arrogant. It places a heavy—a critical—responsibility upon us.

The technical skills and knowledge that have been brought to such perfection in our country depend upon scientific discoveries that have come to us from all over the world. We have used this knowledge to build for ourselves a prosperous and a happy country, but we know that we hold these skills in trust for all mankind. It is not our way to use the power that has come to us to oppress or victimize others. Our way is to use the power that has come to us to lift up the weak and the downtrodden.

In many countries of the world, misery, poverty, and poor health are widespread. Some of these countries were formerly possessions or colonies. Their people are now determined to improve their welfare and to preserve national independence.

And we can help those new countries reach their goals.

One of the means to do this is our point 4 program, through which we are helping to bring better health, more education, more and better food to millions of people. Graduates of this university are working on point 4 teams in many countries throughout the world. Negro professional workers from this and other universities are helping to cure sickness in Burma and Lebanon, to increase the farm output in Liberia, to improve education in Ethiopia and Iran. They are working in India, and Thailand, and Indochina. In these and other countries, Americans are working together, regardless of race, creed, or ancestry, to help the progress of mankind.

This American Nation of ours is great because of its diversity—because it is a people drawn from many lands and many cultures, bound together by the ideals of human brotherhood. We must remember these things as we go forward in our efforts for world peace.

We should realize that much of the trouble in this world today is the result of false ideas of racial superiority. In the past the conduct of the democratic nations has too often been marred by racial pride that has left its scars on the relations between the East and the West.

Today, as we reach a fuller understanding of the brotherhood of man, we are laying these old prejudices. We are working with the new nations of Asia and Africa as equals. Anything less would be a betrayal of the democratic ideals we profess. Better than any other country, the United States can reach out, through our diversity of races and origins, and deal as man to man with the different peoples of the globe.

In this way—in this spirit—we can help other peoples to build better lives for themselves. And we can show that free peoples working together can change misery into happiness.

There are those who have said that this is American's century, but we want it to be more than that. We want it to be humanity's century. If all the people of the world, including the people of the Soviet Union, could know and appreciate this fact, lasting peace and universal justice would mot be a dream. It would be a reality. With courage, with vision, and with God's help, we will yet make these ideals a reality around the world.

NOTE: The President spoke at 5:30 PM. His opening words referred to Dr. Mordecai Johnson, President of Howard University, and Oscar R. Ewing, Administrator of the Federal Security Agency.

Appendix B
Executive Orders
Relating to Civil Rights

EXECUTIVE ORDER 9808

Establishing the President's Committee on Civil Rights

WHEREAS the preservation of civil rights guaranteed by the Constitution is essential to domestic tranquility, national security, the general welfare and the continued existence of our free institutions; and

WHEREAS the action of individuals who take the law into their own hands and inflict summary punishment and wreak personal vengeance is subversive of our democratic system of law enforcement and public criminal justice, and gravely threatens our form of government; and

WHEREAS it is essential that all possible steps be taken to safeguard our civil rights;

NOW THEREFORE, by virtue of the authority vested in me as President of the United States by the Constitution and the statutes of the United States it is hereby ordered as follows:

1. There is hereby created a committee to be known as the President's Committee on Civil Rights, which shall be composed of the following-named members; who shall serve without compensation:

    Mr. Charles E. Wilson, Chairman; Mrs. Sadie T. Alexander; Mr. James B. Carey; Mr. John S. Dickey; Mr. Morris L. Ernst; Rabbi Roland G. Gittelsohn; Dr. Frank P. Graham; The Most Reverend Francis J. Haas; Mr. Charles Luckman; Mr. Francis P. Matthews; Mr. Franklin D. Roosevelt, Jr.; The Right Reverend Henry Knox Sherrill; Mr. Boris Shishkin; Mrs. M.E. Tilley; Mr. Channing H. Tobias.

2. The Committee is authorized on behalf of the President to inquire into and to determine whether and in what respect current law-enforcement measures and the authority and means possessed by Federal, State, and local governments may be strengthened and improved to safeguard the civil rights of the people.

3. All executive departments and agencies of the Federal Government are authorized and directed to cooperate with the Committee in its work, and to furnish the

Committee such information or the services of such persons as the Committee may require in the performance of its duties.

4. When requested by the Committee to do so, persons employed in any of the executive departments and agencies of the Federal Government shall testify before the Committee and shall make available for the use of the Committee such documents and other information as the Committee may require.

5. The Committee shall make a report of its studies to the President in writing, and shall in particular make recommendations with respect to the adoption or establishment, by legislation or otherwise of more adequate and effective means and procedures for the protection of the civil rights of the people of the United States.

6. Upon rendition of its report to the President, the Committee shall cease to exist, unless otherwise determined by further Executive order.

Harry S. Truman

The White House
December 5, 1946

EXECUTIVE ORDER 9980

Regulations Governing Fair Employment Practices Within the Federal Establishment

WHEREAS the principles on which our Government is based require a policy of fair employment throughout the Federal establishment, without discrimination because of race, color, religion, or national origin; and

WHEREAS it is desirable and in the public interest that all steps be taken necessary to insure that this long-established policy shall be more effectively carried out:

NOW, THEREFORE, by virtue of the authority vested in me as President of the United States, by the Constitution and the laws of the United States, it is hereby ordered as follows:

1. All personnel actions taken by Federal appointing officers shall be based solely on merit and fitness; and such officers are authorized and directed to take appropriate steps to insure that in all such actions there shall be no discrimination because of race, color, religion, or national origin.

2. The head of each department in the executive branch of the Government shall be personally responsible for an effective program to insure that fair employment policies are fully observed in all personnel actions within his department.

3. The head of each department shall designate an official thereof as Fair Employment Officer. Such Officer shall be given full operating responsibility, under the immediate supervision of the department head, for carrying out the fair-employment policy herein stated. Notice of the appointment of such Officer shall be given to all officers and employees of the department. The Fair Employment Officer shall, among other things—

   a) Appraise the personnel actions of the department at regular intervals to determine their conformity to the fair-employment policy expressed in this order.

b) Receive complaints or appeals concerning personnel actions taken in the department on grounds of alleged discrimination because of race, color, religion, or national origin.

c) Appoint such central or regional deputies, committees, or hearing boards, from among the officers or employees of the department, as he may find necessary or desirable on a temporary or permanent basis to investigate, or to receive, complaints or discrimination.

d) Take necessary corrective or disciplinary action, in consultation with, or on the basis of delegated authority from, the head of the department.

4. The findings or action of the Fair Employment Officer shall be subject to direct appeal to the head of the department. The decision of the head of the department on such appeal shall be subject to appeal to the Fair Employment Board of the Civil Service Commission, hereinafter provided for.

5. There shall be established in the Civil Service Commission a Fair Employment Board (hereinafter referred to as the Board) of not less than seven persons, the members of which shall be officers or employees of the Commission. The Board shall—

a) Have authority to review decisions made by the head of any department which are appealed pursuant to the provisions of this order, or referred to the Board by the head of the department for advice, and to make recommendations to such head. In any instance in which the recommendation of the Board is not promptly and fully carried out the case shall be reported by the Board to the President, for such action as he finds necessary.

b) Make rules and regulations, in consultation with the Civil Service Commission, deemed necessary to carry out the Board's duties and responsibilities under this order.

c) Advise all departments on problems and policies relating to fair employment.

d) Disseminate information pertinent to fair-employment programs.

e) Coordinate the fair-employment policies and procedures of the several departments.

f) Make reports and submit recommendations to the Civil Service Commission for transmittal to the President from time to time, as may be necessary to the maintenance of the fair-employment program.

6. All departments are directed to furnish to the board all information needed for the review of personnel actions or for the compilation of reports.

7. The Term "department" as used herein shall refer to all departments and agencies of the executive branch of the Government, including the Civil Service Commission. The term "personnel action," as used herein, shall include failure to act. Persons failing of appointment who allege a grievance relating to discrimination shall be entitled to the remedies herein provided.

8. The means of relief provided by this order shall be supplemental to those provided by existing statutes, Executive orders, and regulations. The Civil Service Commission shall have authority, in consultation with the Board, to make such additional regulations, and to amend existing regulations, in such manner as may be found necessary or desirable to carry out the purposes of this order.

Harry S. Truman

The White House
July 26, 1948

EXECUTIVE ORDER 9981

Establishing the President's Committee on Equality of Treatment and Opportunity in the Armed Services

WHEREAS it is essential that there be maintained in the armed services of the United States the highest standards of democracy, with equality of treatment and opportunity for all those who serve in our country's defense:

NOW, THEREFORE, by virtue of the authority vested in me as President of the United States, by the Constitution and the statutes of the United States, and as Commander in Chief of the armed services, it is hereby ordered as follows:

1. It is hereby declared to be the policy of the President that there shall be quality of treatment and opportunity for all persons in the armed services without regard to race, color, religion or national origin. This policy shall be put into effect as rapidly as possible, having due regard to the time required to effectuate any necessary changes without impairing efficiency or morale.

2. There shall be created in the National Military Establishment an advisory committee to be known as the President's Committee on Equality of Treatment and Opportunity in the Armed Services, which shall be composed of seven members to be designated by the President.

3. The Committee is authorized on behalf of the President to examine into the rules, procedures and practices of the armed services in order to determine in what respect such rules, procedures and practices may be altered or improved with a view to carrying out the policy of this order. The Committee shall confer and advise with the Secretary of Defense, the Secretary of the Army, the Secretary of the Navy, and the Secretary of the Air Force, and shall make such recommendations to the President and to said Secretaries as in the judgment of the Committee will effectuate the policy hereof.

4. All executive departments and agencies of the Federal Government are authorized ad directed to cooperate

with the Committee in its work, and to furnish the Committee such information or the services of such persons as the Committee may require in the performance of its duties.

5. When requested by the Committee to do so, persons in the armed services or in any of the executive departments and agencies of the Federal Government shall testify before the Committee and shall make available for the use of the Committee such documents and other information as the Committee may require.

6. The Committee shall continue to exist until such time as the President shall terminate its existence by Executive order.

Harry S. Truman

The White House
July 26, 1948

EXECUTIVE ORDER 10210

Authorizing the Department of Defense and the Department of Commerce to Exercise the Functions and Powers Set Forth in Title II of the First War Powers Act, 1934, as Amended by the Act of January 12, 1951, and the Prescribing Regulations for the Exercise of Such Functions and Powers

[...]

7. There shall be no discrimination in any act performed hereunder against any person on the ground of race, creed, color or national origin, and all contracts hereunder shall contain a provision that the contractor and any subcontractors thereunder shall not so discriminate

[...]

Harry S. Truman

The White House
February 2, 1951

EXECUTIVE ORDER 10308

Improving the Means for Obtaining Compliance with the Non-discrimination Provisions of Federal Contracts

WHEREAS existing Executive orders require the contracting agencies of the United States Government to include in their contracts a provision obligating the contractor not to discriminate against any employee or applicant for employment because of race, color, creed, or national origin and obligating him to include a similar provision in all subcontracts; and

WHEREAS it is necessary and desirable to improve the means for obtaining compliance with such nondiscrimination provisions:

NOW THEREFORE, by virtue of the authority vested in me by the Constitution and statutes, and as President of the United States, including the authority conferred by the Defense Production Act of 1950, as amended, and pursuant to the authority conferred by and subject to the provisions of section 214 of the act of May 3, 1945, 59 Stat. 134 (31 U.S.C. 691), it is ordered as follows:

SECTION 1. The head of each contracting agency of the Government of the United States shall be primarily responsible for obtaining compliance by any contractor or subcontractor with the said nondiscrimination provisions of any contract entered into, amended or modified by his agency and of any subcontract thereunder and shall take appropriate measures to bring about the said compliance.

SEC. 2. There is hereby established the Committee on Government Contract Compliance, hereinafter referred to as the Committee. The Committee shall be composed of eleven members as follows:

a) One representative of each of the following-named agencies (hereinafter referred to as the participating agencies), who shall be designated by the respective heads of the participating agencies: the Department of Defense, the Department of Labor, the Atomic Energy Commission, the General Services Administration, and the Defense Materials Procurement Agency.

b) Six other members, who shall be designated by the President.

The Committee shall have a chairman and a vice-chairman, both of whom shall be designated by the President from among its members.

SEC. 3. The Committee is authorized on behalf of the President to examine and study the rules, procedures, and practices of the contracting agencies of the Government as they relate to obtaining compliance with Government contract provisions prohibiting the discrimination referred to above in order to determine in what respects such rules, procedures, and practices may be strengthened and improved. The Committee shall confer and advise with the appropriate officers of the various contracting agencies and with other persons concerned with a view toward the prevention and elimination of such discrimination, and may make to the said officers recommendations which in the judgment of the Committee will prevent or eliminate discrimination. When deemed necessary by the Committee it may submit any of these recommendations to the Director of Defense Mobilization, and the Director shall, when he deems it appropriate, forward such recommendations to the President, accompanied by a statement of his views as to the relationship thereof to the mobilization effort. The Committee shall establish such rules a may be necessary for the performance of its functions under this order.

SEC. 4. All contracting agencies of the Government are authorized and directed to cooperate with the Committee and, to the extent permitted by law, to furnish the Committee such information and assistance as it may require in the performance of its functions under this order. The participating agencies shall defray such necessary expenses of the Committee as may be authorized by law, including section 214 of the act of May 3, 1945, 59 Stat. 134 (31 U.S.C. 691).

Harry S. Truman

The White House
December 3, 1951

Truman and Civil Rights—A Chronology

Prior to Truman's Presidency

November 1932: A majority of African Americans who vote in the presidential election support Republican Herbert Hoover. Since the Civil War, African Americans who vote have regularly supported Republic candidates for president.

November 1936: African Americans desert the Republican Party en masse to support Franklin D. Roosevelt, who receives about three-quarters of the African American vote for president.

February 3, 1939: A Civil Rights Section is established within the U.S. Department of Justice.

June 15, 1940: In a speech in Sedalia, Missouri, Senator Truman says, "I believe in the brotherhood of man; not merely the brotherhood of white men; but the brotherhood of all men before the law. I believe in the Constitution and the Declaration of Independence. In giving to the Negroes the rights that are theirs, we are only acting in accord with ideas of a true democracy."

July 14, 1940: In a speech in Chicago, Senator Truman says, "I wish to make it clear that I am not appealing for social equality of the Negro...We all know the Negro is here to stay and in no way can be removed from our political and economic life and we should recognize his inalienable rights as specified in our Constitution."

June 25, 1941: President Roosevelt issues Executive Order 8802 establishing a temporary Fair Employment Practices Commission (FEPC) in response to a threat by A. Philip Randolph to bring 100,000 African Americans to Washington to agitate for an FEPC.

1941–44: Senator Truman supports all legislation to finance the FEPC; introduces a bill calling for a combat command for African American General Benjamin O. Davis; votes for cloture to end debate on a filibuster opposing legislation to end the poll tax; and supports a resolution to investigate the effects of segregation within the military on African Americans. On one occasion, Truman votes against an anti-poll tax measure.

1941–46: Over one million African Americans migrate from the South to cities in the North, Midwest, and West.

August 3, 1944: Following his nomination as Democratic Party candidate for vice president, Truman says in an interview: "I have always been for equality of opportunity in work, working conditions and political rights. I think the Negro in the armed forces ought to have the same treatment and opportunities as every other member of the armed forces.... I have a record of fair play toward my Negro fellow citizens that will stand examination."

During Truman's Presidency

1945

June 23: A Conference of Negro Leaders, including representatives of thirty-four African American organizations, meets to consider the perceived failure of the United Nations Conference in San Francisco to adequately address the human rights needs of African Americans and people living in colonial regions of the world. Conference convener Mary McLeod Bethune says the United Nations Conference demonstrated the common bond between African Americans and colonial peoples and had made clear that the "Negro in America" held "little more than colonial status in a democracy."

July 13: Truman signs a law providing funding at a very modest level for the FEPC only through 30 June 1946. He had favored a law establishing a permanent FEPC.

October 3: Truman nominates Irvin C. Mollison to be a judge on the United States Customs Court. Mollison is the first African American to be appointed to a federal judgeship.

December 20: Truman issues Executive Order 9964, which removes the authority of the FEPC to issue "cease and desist" proclamations. Instead, the FEPC is to report its findings and recommendations to the president.

1946

January 21: Truman calls for the establishment of a permanent FEPC in his State of the Union message.

February 13: Isaac Woodard is beaten and blinded by police officers in Batesburg, South Carolina.

February 24 and 25: An outbreak of mob violence against African Americans begins in Columbia, Tennessee. Seventy African Americans are arrested and two others are shot and killed while they are in jail.

April 6: Truman says poll tax legislation is a state responsibility. On 11 April, Truman modifies his position, saying both state and federal actions were needed to bring about the abolition of the poll tax and the establishment of an FEPC.

April: An internal army report, titled "Utilization of Negro Manpower in the Postwar Army Policy," concludes that the army's future policy should be to "eliminate, at the earliest practicable moment, any special consideration based on race." The report, however, does not recommend that segregation in the army be ended. The Secretary of the Army later characterizes this policy as "equality of opportunity on the basis of segregation."

June 6: The National Negro Congress, an organization with strong ties to the Communist party, submits a petition regarding the plight of African Americans to the United Nations. The petition says the United Nations, unlike any court in the United States, would understand that African Americans had been "bound to the soil in semi-feudal serfdom," "lynched," "terrorized," and "segregated like pariahs."

June 28: The members of the FEPC resign and submit their final report to the president.

July 25: Four African Americans are brutally murdered by a mob in Monroe, Georgia.

September 19: Truman meets with members of the National Emergency Committee against Mob Violence. The committee, headed by Walter White, delivers a petition requesting that Truman call a special session of Congress to pass legislation to mandate federal action against mob violence and lynching. The committee also tells Truman about acts of racial violence. Truman says, "My God! I had no idea that it was as terrible as that! We've got to do something!"

September 23: Truman meets with members of the American Crusade to End Lynching, headed by Paul Robeson. Truman disagrees with Robeson's arguments and declines to issue a presidential statement regarding lynching, saying the political situation makes such an action difficult.

September 24: Truman sends a message to be read to a convention of the National Urban League in which he says, "If the civil rights of even one citizen are abused, government has failed to discharge one of its primary responsibilities....We as a people must not, and I say to you we shall not, remain indifferent in the face of acts of intimidation and violence in our American communities."

December 5: Truman issues Executive Order 9808, establishing the President's Committee on Civil Rights.

1947

January 15: Truman, speaking to the first meeting of the President's Committee on Civil Rights, says "I want our Bill of

Rights implemented in fact. We have been trying to do this for 150 years. We are making progress, but we are not making progress fast enough.... I have been very much alarmed at certain happenings around the country that go to show there is a latent spirit in some of us that isn't what it ought to be.... I don't think the Federal Government ought to be in a position to exercise dictatorial powers locally; but there are certain rights under the Constitution of the United States which I think the Federal Government has a right to protect."

February 8: Truman asks Congress to pass legislation creating a permanent FEPC.

June 23: The Supreme Court accepts for review a case, *Shelley v. Kraemer,* questioning the constitutionality of racially restrictive housing covenants. The Truman administration receives many requests to submit an amicus curiae brief on behalf of the plaintiffs in the two cases. On 5 December 1947, the administration submits an amicus brief, and on 15 January 1948, Solicitor General Philip Perlman participates in oral argument before the Supreme Court.

June 29: Truman speaks to an NAACP gathering at the steps of the Lincoln Memorial in Washington DC. He says, "Every man should have the right to a decent home, the right to an education, the right to adequate medical care, the right to a worthwhile job, the right to an equal share in making public decisions through the ballot, and the right to a fair trail in a fair court. We must insure that these rights—on equal terms—are enjoyed by every citizen." After the speech, Truman tells Walter White, "I mean every word of it—and I am going to prove that I do mean it."

October 10: A. Philip Randolph and Grant Reynolds organize the Committee against Jim Crow in Military Service and Training.

October 23: The NAACP submits a petition to the United Nations titled *An Appeal to the World: A Statement on the Denial of Human Rights to Minorities in the Case of Citizens of Negro Descent in the United States of America and an Appeal to the United Nations for Redress.* On 4 December 1947, the United

Nations Commission on Human Rights rejects a proposal by the Soviet Union to investigate the NAACP's charges.

October 29: The President's Committee on Civil Rights submits to Truman its report, *To Secure These Rights.* The report documents the failure of the United States to accord fundamental civil rights to many of its citizens, argues that the federal government must be the guardian and protector of civil rights, and puts forward a detailed program for action.

November 19: Counsel to the president Clark Clifford forwards to Truman a lengthy memorandum outlining a strategy for winning election in 1948. The memorandum argues, among other things, that the South will support Truman, that a civil rights program can be pursued without fear of alienating the South, and that the African American vote will be important in the northern cities.

December 9: Truman asks his counsel, Clark Clifford, to work with the attorney general to draw up recommendations for a civil rights program.

1948

January 7: Truman announces in the State of the Union Message that he will send a special message on civil rights to Congress.

February 2: Truman sends his special message on civil rights to Congress, requesting that Congress pass legislation in ten areas to strengthen the ability of the president to protect civil rights, and he reports he has instructed the secretary of defense to eliminate discrimination in the armed services.

February 5: A. Philip Randolph meets with Democratic Party officials and asks them to issue a strong statement denouncing segregation in the military.

February 6 to 8: A majority of governors attending the Southern Governors' Conference refuse to sanction secession from the national Democratic Party.

February 12: Governor Fielding Wright of Mississippi calls a mass meeting of state politicos in Jackson, Mississippi. Four thousand gather in the city auditorium and excoriate President Truman and his civil rights proposals, and condemn the national Democratic Party.

March 11: Truman indicates at a press conference that he will not formally present to Congress the legislative measures proposed in his civil rights message of February 2.

March 12: Truman attends a lunch with cabinet members and representatives of the Democratic National Committee, including from the South, at which he says of his civil rights proposals, "I stand on what I said [in his 2 February 1948 message to Congress]; I have no changes to make."

March 13: Seven of the fifteen southern governors publicly repudiate Truman's civil rights program and urge Southerners to cast their electoral college votes for candidates who do not support civil rights legislation.

March 22: A. Philip Randolph and others concerned with civil rights request Truman's support for anti-discrimination amendments to the proposed draft bill. Randolph says that unless the government changes the segregationist policies in the armed forces, a civil disobedience campaign will begin.

March 30: A. Philip Randolph testifies before the Senate Armed Services Committee, saying, "I personally pledge myself to openly counsel, aid, and abet youth, both white and colored, to quarantine any Jim Crow conscription system, whether it bears the label Universal Military Training or Selective Service."

May 3: The Supreme Court rules unanimously in *Shelley v. Kraemer* that restrictive housing covenants designed to achieve segregation are unconstitutional.

May 13: Truman denies at a press conference that his administration is preparing an executive order to end discriminatory practices in the federal government.

June 4 to 18: Truman makes a coast to coast "non-political" tour by train during which he visits eighteen states and makes seventy-three speeches. He does not mention civil rights in any of the speeches.

June 22: Congressman John Rankin, after meeting with Truman, says to the press, "I am not without hope that the Democratic convention will reach a satisfactory agreement on the civil rights issue. If that convention adopts the same plank that was inserted in the platform of 1944, I am assured that it will be adhered to."

June 26: A. Philip Randolph announces the formation of the League for Non-Violent Civil Disobedience against Military Segregation.

July 14: The Democratic Party's platform committee presents to the Democratic national convention assembled in Philadelphia a civil rights plank regarded as weak by many liberals and African American leaders. This plank, which is essentially the same as that in the 1944 Democratic platform, is supported by President Truman.

July 17: Delegates at the Democratic National Convention approve, against Truman's wishes, a strong civil rights plank that demands Congress take action to end mob violence against African Americans and ensure fair employment practices, equality in political participation, and nondiscrimination in military service. Following adoption of this plank, delegates from Mississippi and half of those from Alabama walk out of the convention hall. Two hundred and sixty-three other Southern delegates refuse to support Truman's nomination, voting instead for Georgia senator Richard B. Russell.

July 17: A conference of rebellious States' Rights Democrats (as they called their faction) meets in Birmingham, Alabama. Six thousand delegates listen to speeches against Truman and his civil rights proposals and nominate South Carolina governor Strom Thurmond as their candidate for president.

July 20: The Progressive party convenes in Philadelphia and nominates Henry Wallace as its candidate for president.

July 26: President Truman signs Executive Orders 9980 and 9981. The first of these prohibits discrimination because of race, color, religion, or national origin in the federal government's personnel actions and establishes the Fair Employment Board within the Civil Service Commission. The second order states the president's policy "that there shall be equality of treatment and opportunity for all persons in the armed services without regard to race, color, religion, or national origin." The order also establishes the President's Committee on Equality of Treatment and Opportunity in the Armed Services (called the Fahy Committee, after its chairman, Charles H. Fahy) to oversee desegregation of the armed services.

July 26: Army staff officers state anonymously to the press that Executive Order 9981 does not specifically forbid segregation in the army. On 27 July, Army Chief of Staff General Omar N. Bradley states that desegregation will come to the army only when it becomes a fact in the rest of American society.

July 27: Truman asks Congress (assembled in the "Turnip Day" special session) to pass the civil rights legislation he requested in his 2 February 1948 speech: "I believe that it is necessary to enact the laws I have recommended to make the guarantees of the Constitution real and vital." Congress did not pass any of this legislation during the special session.

September 9: Truman receives a memorandum from a staff assistant that says there is no longer any serious opposition to the draft because of the army's race policies, and that A. Philip Randolph and Grant Reynolds have withdrawn from the Committee Against Jim Crow in Military Service and Training.

October 29: Truman is the first president ever to deliver a speech in Harlem. Sixty-five thousand people hear him say, "Our determination to attain the goal of equal rights and equal opportunity must be resolute and unwavering. For my part, I intend to keep moving toward this goal with every ounce of strength and determination I have."

November 2: Truman wins a surprise victory and both houses of Congress become Democratic by large margins. Truman receives about 66 percent of the African American vote, which totals about 750,000 and is about three times larger than in the 1940 election.

1949

January 5: In his State of the Union address, Truman says "The civil rights proposals I made to the 80th Congress, I now repeat to the 81st. They should be enacted in order that the Federal Government may assume the leadership and discharge the obligations placed upon it by the Constitution."

January 12: The Fahy Committee holds its first meeting with Truman and secretaries of the army, navy, air force, and Defense Department. "I want the job done," Truman says, "and I want it done in a way so that everyone will be happy to cooperate to get it done."

January 12: Truman tells members of the National Citizens Council on Civil Rights that his administration is drafting bills to implement the recommendations made in his 2 February 1948 civil rights speech.

January 13: The Fahy Committee holds its first hearings. Representatives of the army defend segregation of African Americans. The marine corps also defends its segregation policy and admits that only one of its 8,200 officers is African American. The navy and air force both indicate they will integrate their units. The navy admits that only five of its 45,000 officers are African American.

January 20: Truman is inaugurated president. His inaugural ceremonies are almost completely integrated.

February 28: Truman tells Senate Democratic leaders to fight to change Senate rules so civil rights legislation can be brought to a vote, even if the fight necessary to bring such legislation to a vote will mean other legislation must be delayed.

March 3: Truman endorses a change in Senate rules that would make it easier to end filibusters intended to prevent his civil rights measures from being brought to a vote.

March 17: The Senate votes to change its rules to make it extremely difficult to end filibusters designed to prevent civil rights legislation from coming to a vote. This action effectively blocks any of Truman's proposed civil rights measures from becoming law through congressional action.

April 6: The secretary of defense issues a directive to the service secretaries proclaiming that equality of treatment and opportunity in the armed forces is the policy of the government, and that enlistments, assignments, promotions, and training opportunities will be based on individual merit and ability.

April 28 to May 16: Most of Truman's civil rights measures are introduced into Congress, despite the near certainty that the Senate will not pass any of them.

May 11: The secretary of defense approves the air force integration plan, but rejects the plans of the army and navy. On about 7 June, he approves a revised navy integration plan.

May 26: The National Association for the Advancement of Colored People (NAACP) publicly urges Truman to call a special session of Congress that would focus on civil rights matters.

July 5: The army presents a revised integration plan to the Fahy Committee. The new plan would retain segregated units and continue an existing 10 percent African American recruitment quota. On 25 and 27 July, the Fahy Committee advises the secretary of defense, the secretary of the army, and Truman that the revised army plan should be rejected.

September 30: The secretary of defense approves the army's integration plan, despite its inclusion of segregated units and a 10 percent African American enlistment quota. Truman, during a 6 October press conference, calls the army's plan "a progress report" and says his goal is integration of the army.

October 3: Senate majority leader Scott Lucas announces to the press that "it seems doubtful that a prolonged discussion of any civil rights bill at this session would be helpful."

October 5: The Truman administration submits an amicus curiae brief on behalf of the plaintiff in *Henderson v. United States,* a case involving racial discrimination in interstate transportation. The attorney general and solicitor general appear before the Supreme Court to argue on behalf of the plaintiff on 3 and 4 April 1950.

October 15: Truman appoints African American William H. Hastie to be a judge on the Third Circuit Court of Appeals.

November 11: Speaking to the National Conference of Christians and Jews, Truman says "I have called for legislation to protect the rights of all [American] citizens, to assure their equal participation in national life, and to reduce discrimination based upon prejudice. In view of the fundamental faith of this country and the clear language of our Constitution, I do not see how we can do otherwise than adopt such legislation."

December 2: The FHA changes its rules to refuse federal financing assistance to any property whose occupancy or use will be restricted on the basis of race, creed, or color. On 12 December, the FHA announces that after 15 February 1950, it will not insure mortgages on homes whose deeds contain restrictive covenants. In neither case does the rule change affect existing racially restrictive arrangements.

1950

January 4: Truman submits a budget message to Congress that calls for the establishment of a permanent Fair Employment Practices Commission, saying, "To keep minority groups economically submerged is not only unjust and discriminatory, but also prevents the best use of available manpower."

February 23: The House of Representatives passes a bill providing for the establishment of a Fair Employment Practices Commission that has no enforcement powers.

May 5: Senate majority leader Scott Lucas presents to the Senate a motion calling for the introduction of the Truman administration's FEPC bill. Southern Democrats immediately begin a filibuster. On 19 May, the Senate defeats an attempt to end the filibuster.

May 22: The Fahy Committee submits to Truman its report, "Freedom to Serve," which affirms that segregation has formally been abolished in the armed forces. Truman says he is confident the committee's recommendations will be fully carried out and "within the reasonably near future, equality of treatment and opportunity for all persons within the armed services would be accomplished."

May 22: A conference of representatives of civil rights organizations, called by the NAACP, convenes in Washington DC. Attendance is poor in comparison with the similar conference convened in January 1950.

June 5: The Supreme Court rules in favor of plaintiffs in three cases involving civil rights: *Henderson v. United States, McLaurin v. Oklahoma State Regents,* and *Sweatt v. Painter.* The first case involves discrimination in interstate transportation, the other two cases, discrimination in higher education. In all three cases, the unanimous court rules that the civil rights of African Americans have been violated. The court does not decide the cases in a broad constitutional context and its rulings do not clearly overturn the separate but equal doctrine of *Plessy v. Ferguson.*

June 25 and following: Segregation in army units serving in Korea gradually breaks down as white combat units suffer combat casualties and the number of African American recruits becomes too large for absorption into segregated black units.

July 12: The Senate for a second time fails to end a filibuster preventing the Truman administration's FEPC bill from being introduced into the Senate.

July 16: A. Philip Randolph asks Truman to establish an emergency wartime FEPC by executive order. He makes the same request publicly on 10 September. Truman does not respond to these requests.

November 7: The Democratic majorities in both houses of Congress are significantly reduced in the midterm elections.

December: The Fair Employment Board, established by Executive Order 9980 to oversee the desegregation of the federal civil service, sends a report to Truman claiming that "considerable progress has been made and...continuing progress may be expected." Truman's minority affairs assistants advise him the report lacks substance and should not be made public.

1951

January 3: On the opening day of the 82nd Congress, two opponents of civil rights legislation become majority leader and whip in the Senate, and a coalition of Republicans and Southern Democrats in the House of Representatives augments the ability of the Rules Committee to prevent civil rights legislation from being considered by the full House.

January 8: In his State of the Union speech, Truman does not emphasize civil rights and does not specifically urge the passage of civil rights legislation.

January 12: Truman delivers his annual budget message to Congress. Again, as in the prior year's budget message, Truman calls for the creation of a FEPC, but his proposed budget does not include any specified appropriation for it.

January 17: Truman issues a National Manpower Mobilization Policy that urges government agencies to provide assistance to private industry in "promoting maximum utilization of the labor force including women, physically handicapped, older workers, and minority groups." The program is largely voluntary and allows agencies to decide to what extent they will encourage employment of minorities.

February 2: Truman issues Executive Order 10210, which declares there shall be no discrimination in work performed by contractors and subcontractors working for the Departments of Defense and Commerce, and requires that all federal contracts involving these agencies contain a nondiscrimination provision. Six subsequent executive orders extend this requirement to contracts involving an additional nine executive departments and agencies.

February 28: African American leaders meet with Truman and argue for stronger executive action to prevent employment discrimination than is provided by Executive Order 10210. They advocate creation of a permanent FEPC with enforcement powers. On 20 March, one of the leaders sends Truman a telegram that reads in part, "Let us know when Executive Order for FEPC will be signed by you." On 4 April, two of the leaders write Truman asking him when he will act to establish an FEPC; Truman does not respond.

May 22–23: Representatives of thirty-one national African American organizations meet in Washington DC to formulate a wartime civil rights program. In a speech, Walter White, head of the NAACP, says, "Truman, we all know, is hogtied by his opposition among his own party and Republicans. But sympathy for his plight must not blind us to the fact that his cessation of active support for civil rights legislation...can be interpreted only as surrender on this issue."

June 25: On the tenth anniversary of President Roosevelt's issuance of the executive order that established a wartime FEPC, sixteen national civil rights, labor, and other organizations send a telegram to Truman urging him to establish a permanent FEPC "to assure to every American, regardless of race, religion, or national origin, an equal opportunity to contribute his utmost skills and talents to the production of the tools and weapons so urgently needed by our armed forces, and to demonstrate to the peoples of the world that the United States is the exemplar as well as the exponent of democracy."

November 2: Truman vetoes a bill that contains a provision requiring integrated schools situated on federal property, on military bases for example, to conform to the laws, including laws requiring segregated facilities, of the states in which the schools were located. "This proposal, if enacted into law," Truman says in his veto message, "would constitute a backward step in the efforts of the Federal Government to extend equal rights and opportunities to all our people."

November: The Civil Rights Congress, an African American organization with ties to the Communist party, submits a petition, titled "We Charge Genocide," to the United Nations. The petition argues that the U.S. government, by failing to act against the lynching of African Americans, was guilty of genocide under the terms of the United Nations genocide convention.

December 3: Truman issues Executive Order 10308, establishing a Government Contract Compliance Committee, charged with ensuring compliance with provisions in government contracts prohibiting discrimination. The committee is given the power to hold hearings, but it cannot issue subpoenas or cease-and-desist orders.

1952

January 8: The second session of the 82nd Congress convenes, but passes no significant civil rights legislation.

January 9: In his State of the Union message, Truman again calls on Congress to permit civil rights legislation to come to a vote.

February 18: The NAACP convenes a two day "civil rights mobilization" at which representatives of fifty-two national organizations call on Congress to pass civil rights legislation and vow to carry the fight for civil rights to the local level.

March 8: Twenty-one African American leaders publicly urge Truman to run for reelection. On 29 March, Truman announces that he will not seek reelection.

May 17: In a speech to the Americans for Democratic Action in Washington DC, Truman says the Democratic Party must stand by the civil rights pledges it made in its 1948 platform.

June 13: In a speech at Howard University in Washington DC, Truman says, "There has been a great working of the American conscience. All over the land there has been a growing recognition that injustice must go, and that the way of equal opportunity is better for all of us." He also speaks of "the crumbling walls of prejudice."

June 23: Truman sends a telegram to the NAACP, which is meeting in Oklahoma City, which says that "the ten-point program I sent to Congress in 1948 is still my civil rights program for the American people."

July: The two major political parties adopt platforms at their national conventions. The Republican Party's platform includes a weak civil rights plank that in large measure defers to the right of states "to order and control [their] own domestic institutions." The Democratic Party adopts a platform that the delegates intend to state a real commitment to civil rights in language mild enough to keep the South in the party. Truman praises the Democratic Party's civil rights plank in a speech to the convention.

October: Truman makes several campaign speeches in which he attacks Republican candidate Dwight D. Eisenhower's position on civil rights. In one of these speeches, he described the Democratic civil rights plank as "the strongest civil rights stand ever taken by a major political party in this country."

November 4: Democratic presidential candidate Adlai Stevenson receives 73 percent of the African American vote, compared with the 66 percent received by Truman in 1948.

December 2: The attorney general submits to the Supreme Court an amicus curiae brief in support of five African American plaintiffs in *Brown v. Board of Education.* The case concerns discrimination in elementary education. The brief states that if the court decides to address the separate but equal doctrine of *Plessy v. Ferguson,* that doctrine should be found unconstitutional. The case was decided in favor of the plaintiffs and the separate but equal doctrine was overturned by the court's ruling on 17 May 1954.

1953

January 7: In his last State of the Union message, Truman says, "There has been a great awakening of the American conscience on the issues of civil rights. And all this progress—still far from complete but still continuing—has been our answer, up to now, to those who questioned our intention to live up to the promises of equal freedom for us all."

January 15: Truman gives his farewell address. "We have made progress in spreading the blessings of American life to all of our people," he says. "There has been a tremendous awakening of the American conscience on the great issue of civil rights—equal economic opportunities, equal rights of citizenship and equal educational opportunities for all our people, whatever their race, religion, or status of birth."

---

[1]Compiled by Raymond H. Geselbracht from Dalfiume, *Desegregation of the U.S. Armed Forces*; Berman, *Politics of Civil Rights in the Truman Administration*; McCoy and Ruetten, *Quest and Response*; Frederickson, *Dixiecrat Revolt*; and Anderson, *United Nations and the African American Struggle for Human Rights*.

BIBLIOGRAPHY

Ambrose, Stephen. *Eisenhower: The President.* New York: Simon & Schuster, 1984.

Anderson, Carol. *Eyes Off the Prize: The United Nations and the African American Struggle for Human Rights, 1944–1955.* Cambridge: Cambridge University Press, 2003.

Benedict, Michael Les. *The Blessings of Liberty: A Concise History of the Constitution of the United States.* Lexington: Houghton Mifflin, 1996.

Berman, William. *The Politics of Civil Rights in the Truman Administration.* Columbus: Ohio State University Press, 1970.

Bernstein, Barton J. "America in War and Peace: The Test of Liberalism." In *Towards a New Past: Dissenting Essays in American History*, edited by Barton J. Bernstein. New York: Random House, 1968.

———. "The Ambiguous Legacy: The Truman Administration and Civil Rights." In *Politics and Policies of the Truman Administration*, edited by Barton J. Bernstein, 269–314. Chicago: Quadrangle Books, 1970.

Billington, Monroe. "Freedom to Serve: The President's Committee on Equality of Treatment and Opportunity in the Armed Forces, 1949-1950." *Journal of Negro History* 51, no. 4 (October 1966): 268.

Borstelmann, Thomas. *The Cold War and the Color Line: American Race Relations in the Global Arena.* Cambridge, MA: Harvard University Press, 2001.

Brandeis, Louis. "The Road to Social Efficiency: An Address before the National Congress of Charities and Correction at Boston on June 8, 1911." *The Outlook,* 10 June 1911. Later published in Louis D. Brandeis, *Business: A Profession.* Boston: Small, Maynard, 1914.

Brown v. Board of Education, 347 U.S. 483 (1954).

Brown, William H., Jr., "Access to Housing: The Role of the Real Estate Industry," *Economic Geography* 48, no. 41 (Jan. 1972): 68.

Clifford, Clark, with Richard Holbrooke. *Counsel to the President: A Memoir.* New York: Random House, 1991.

Conley, Dalton. *Being Black, Living in the Red: Race, Wealth, and Social Policy in America.* Berkeley: University of California Press, 1999.

Cox, Oliver C. "The Programs of Negro Civil Rights Organizations," *Journal of Negro Education* 20, no. 3 (Summer 1951): 354.

Dalfiume, Richard. *Desegregation of the U.S. Armed Forces: Fighting on Two Fronts, 1939–1953.* Columbia: University of Missouri Press, 1969.

Daniels, Jonathan. *The Man of Independence.* Philadelphia: Lippincott, 1950.

Dray, Philip. *Hands of Persons Unknown: The Lynching of Black America.* New York: Random House, 2002.

Dudziak, Mary L. "Desegregation as a Cold War Imperatative." *Stanford Law Review* 41, no. 1 (Nov. 1988): 61–120.

———. *Cold War Civil Rights: Race and the Image of American Democracy.* Princeton: Princeton University Press, 2000.

Edgerton, Robert D. *Hidden Heroism: Black Soldiers in America's Wars.* Boulder, CO: Westview Press, 2001.

Emmons, Caroline. " 'Somebody Has Got to Do That Work': Harry T. Moore and the Struggle for African-American Voting Rights in Florida." *Journal of Negro History* 82, no. 2 (Spring 1997): 232–43.

Executive Order 9981, "Establishing the President's Committee on Equality of Treatment and Opportunity in the Armed Services." In *Code of Federal Regulations, Title 3: The President, 1943–1948 Compilation.* Washington DC: Government Printing Office, 1957.

Feldman, Glenn. "Soft Opposition: Elite Acquiescence and Klan-Sponsored Terrorism in Alabama, 1946–1950." *Historical Journal* 47, no. 3 (Sept. 1997): 753–77.

Ferrell, Robert H. *Harry S. Truman: A Life.* Columbia: University of Missouri Press, 1994.

———, ed. *Dear Bess: The Letters from Harry to Bess Truman, 1910–1959.* New York: W. W. Norton, 1983.

———, ed. *Off the Record: The Private Papers of Harry S. Truman.* New York: Harper & Row, 1980.

Frederickson, Kari. *The Dixiecrat Revolt and the End of the Solid South, 1932–1968.* Chapel Hill: University of North Carolina Press, 2001.

Gallup Organization. "How do you feel about Truman's civil rights program? Do you think Congress should or should not pass the program as a whole?" 5 April, 1948. Princeton, New Jersey.

Gardner, Michael R. *Harry Truman and Civil Rights: Moral Courage and Political Risks.* Carbondale: Southern Illinois University Press, 2002.

Ginzberg, Eli. *The Negro Potential.* New York: Columbia University Press, 1956.

Greenberg, Jonathan. "Give 'em Health, Harry: Harry S. Truman's Failed Health Reforms." *New Republic* 209 (Oct. 1993): 20–21.

Grill, Johnpeer Horst, and Robert L. Jenkins. "The Nazis and the American South in the 1930s: A Mirror Image?" *Journal of Southern History* 58, no. 4 (Nov. 1992): 667–94.

Gropman, Alan L. *The Air Force Integrates: 1945–1964.* Washington DC: Office of Air Force History, U.S. Air Force, 1978.

Gross, Gerald G. "Truman Holds Civil Rights a Key to Peace." *Washington Post,* 30 June 1947.

Hale, Grace Elizabeth. *Making Whiteness: The Cultures of Segregation in the South, 1980–1940.* New York: Pantheon Books, 1998.

Hamby Alonzo. *Man of the People: A Life of Harry S. Truman.* New York: Oxford University Press, 1995.

———. *Beyond the New Deal: Harry S. Truman and American Liberalism.* New York: Columbia University Press, 1973.

———. "The Clash of Perspectives and the Need for New Synthesis." In *The Truman Period as a Research Field, A Reappraisal, 1972*, edited by Richard S. Kirkendall, 137–39. Columbia: University of Missouri Press, 1974.

Hastie, William. Oral history interview, 1972. Truman Library.

Heller, Francis H., ed., *The Truman White House: The Administration of the Presidency, 1945–1953*. Lawrence: Regents Press of Kansas, 1980.

Horton, David S., ed. *Freedom and Equality: Addresses by Harry S. Truman*. Columbia: University of Missouri Press, 1960.

Johnson, Whittington B. "The Vinson Court and Racial Segregation, 1946–1953." *Journal of Negro History*, Vol. 63, no. 3 (July 1978): 220–30.

Karabell, Zachary. *The Last Campaign: The Election of 1948*. New York: Knopf, 2000.

Kerber, Linda K. "The Meanings of Citizenship." *Journal of American History* 84, no. 3 (Dec. 1997): 833–54.

King, Martin Luther, Jr. *Where Do We Go From Here: Chaos or Community*. New York: Harper & Row, 1967.

Kirkendall, Richard S., ed. *The Truman Period as a Research Field*. Columbia: University of Missouri Press, 1967.

"Klan at Convention Hall." *Jackson* (MO) *Examiner*, 13 October 1922.

"Klan Puts Out Ticket," *Independence* (MO) *Examiner*, 6 November 1922.

Kluger, Richard. *Simple Justice: The History of Brown v. Board of Education and Black America's Struggle for Equality*. New York: Vintage Books, 1977.

Lauren, Paul Gordon. *The Evolution of International Human Rights: Visions Seen*. Philadelphia: University of Pennsylvania Press, 1998.

Lawson, Steven F. ed. *To Secure These Rights*. Boston: Bedford St. Martin's, 2004.

Leuchtenburg, William E. "The Conversion of Harry Truman." *American Heritage* (Nov. 1991): 55–68.

Lewis, Earl M. "The Negro Voter in Mississippi." *Journal of Negro Education*, Vol. 26, no. 3 (Summer 1957): 329–50.

Lichtman, Allan. "The Federal Assault Against Voting Discrimination in the Deep South, 1957–1967." *Journal of Negro History*, Vol. 54, no. 4 (October 1969): 346–67.

Lipsitz, George. *The Possessive Investment in Whiteness: How White People Profit from Identity Politics*. Philadelphia: Temple University Press, 1998.

MacGregor, Morris J., Jr., *Integration of the Armed Forces, 1940-1965*. Defense Studies Series. Washington DC: Center of Military History, U.S. Army, 1981.

"Made Illegal By 3 Rulings." *Baltimore Afro-American*, 17 June 1950.

Massey, Douglas S., and Nancy A. Denton. *American Apartheid: Segregation and the Making of the Underclass*. Cambridge, MA: Harvard University Press, 1993.

McCoy, Donald R., and Richard T. Ruetten. *Quest and Response: Minority Rights and the Truman Administration*. Lawrence: University Press of Kansas, 1973.

———, Richard Reutten, and J. R. Fuchs, eds. *Conference of Scholars on the Truman Administration and Civil Rights,* April 5–6, 1968, at the Truman Presidential Library. Independence: Harry S. Truman Library Institute for National and International Affairs, 1996.

McCullough, David "Harry S. Truman." In *Character Above All: Ten Presidents from FDR to George Bush.* Edited by Robert A. Wilson. New York: Simon & Schuster, 1996.

———. *Truman.* New York: Simon & Schuster, 1992.

McFadden, Robert D. "Bishop Spottswood of N.A.A.C.P. Dies." *New York Times,* 3 December 1974.

McMillen, Neil R. "Black Enfranchisement in Mississippi: Federal Enforcement and Black Protest in the 1960s." *Journal of Southern History* 43, no. 3 (Aug. 1977): 351–72.

Miller, Merle. *Plain Speaking: An Oral Biography of Harry S. Truman.* New York: Berkeley Publishing, 1974. Distributed by Putnam.

Nash, Phileo. Oral history interviews conducted in 1966, 1967, 1969. Truman Library.

National Committee on Segregation in the Nation's Capital. *Segregation in Washington.* Washington DC: Government Printing Office, 1948.

Nelson, Dennis D. *The Integration of the Negro into the U.S. Navy.* New York: Farrar, Straus and Young, 1951.

Nichols, Lee. *Breakthrough on the Color Front.* New York: Random House, 1954.

"Not What, But How," *Christian Science Monitor,* 1 July 1947.

O'Reilly, Kenneth. *Racial Matters: The FBI's Secret File on Black America, 1960–1972.* New York: Free Press, 1989.

Orfield, Gary. "Federal Policy, Local Power, and Metropolitan Segregation," *Political Science Quarterly* 89, no. 4 (Winter 1974–75): 785.

Ottley, Roi. *New World A-Coming.* 1943. Reprint, New York: Arno Press, 1968.

Pauly, Garth E. *The Modern Presidency and Civil Rights: Rhetoric on Race From Roosevelt to Nixon.* College Station: Texas A & M University Press, 2001.

Pika, Joseph A. "Interest Groups Under Roosevelt and Truman." *Political Science Quarterly* 102, no. 4 (Winter 1987–88): 665–66.

Poen, Monte M. *Harry S. Truman Versus the Medical Lobby: The Genesis of Medicare.* Columbia: University of Missouri Press, 1979.

"Police Chief Freed in Negro Beating," *New York Times,* 6 November 1946.

President's Committee on Civil Rights. *To Secure These Rights.* Washington DC: Government Printing Office, 1947.

Public Papers of the Presidents of the United States, Harry S. Truman. Washington DC: Government Printing Office, 1961–66.

"Racial Wall U.S. Peril, Truman Says." *Los Angeles Times,* 30 June 1947.

Reddick, L. D. "The Negro Policy of the American Army Since World War II." *Journal of Negro History* 38, no. 2 (April 1953): 194–215.

Shull, Steven A. *American Civil Rights Policy From Truman to Clinton: The Role of Presidential Leadership.* Armonk, NY: M. E. Sharpe, 1999.

Sitkoff, Harvard. "Civil Rights." In *The Harry S. Truman Encyclopedia*, edited by Richard S. Kirkendall, 57–59. Boston: G. K. Hall, 1989.

———. "Harry Truman and the Election of 1948: The Coming of Age of Civil Rights in American Politics." *Journal of Southern History* 37, no. 4 (Nov. 1971): 598–616.

Streator, George. "Truman Demands We Fight Harder to Spur Equality." *New York Times*, 30 June 1947.

Sugrue, Thomas J. "Crabgrass-Roots Politics: Race, Rights, and the Reaction against Liberalism in the Urban North, 1940–1964." *Journal of American History* 82, no. 2 (Sept. 1995): 551–78.

To Secure These Rights: The Report of the President's Committee on Civil Rights. Washington DC: Government Printing Office, 1947.

Truman, Harry S. *Memoirs*. Vol. 1, *Year of Decisions, 1945*. Garden City, NY: Doubleday, 1955; reprinted New York: Signet Books, 1965.

———. *Memoirs*. Vol. 2, *Years of Trial and Hope*. Garden City, NY: Doubleday, 1956.

———. *Mr. Citizen*. New York: Bernard Geis Associates, 1953.

Truman, Margaret M. *Harry S. Truman*. New York: William Morrow, 1973.

"Truman Sees Rights Report as 'Human Freedom Charter.'" *Washington Post,* 30 October 1947.

Vaughan, Philip H. "The City and the American Creed: A Liberal Awakening During the Early Truman Period, 1946–1948," *Phylon* 34, no. 1 (1973): 57.

———. "The Truman Administration's Fair Deal for Black America." *Missouri Historical Review* 70 (March 1976): 291–305.

Verney, Kevern. *Black Civil Rights in America*. New York: Routledge, 2000.

Washington, James A. "The Program of the Civil Rights Section of the Department of Justice." *Journal of Negro Education* 20, no. 3 (Summer 1951): 343–44.

Wexler, Laura. *Fire in a Canebrake: The Last Mass Lynching in America.* New York: Scribner, 2003.

White, Walter. *A Man Called White: The Autobiography of Walter White.* Bloomington: University of Indiana Press, 1970.

Wiecek, William C. "United States Supreme Court." In *The Harry S. Truman Encyclopedia*. Edited by Richard S. Kirkendall, 347–50. Boston: G. K. Hall, 1989.

Wilson, Charles E. *To Secure These Rights: The Report of the President's Committee on Civil Rights.* New York: Simon & Schuster, 1947.

Wynn, Neil A. "The Impact of the Second World War on the American Negro." *Journal of Contemporary History* 6, no. 2 (1971): 42–53.

CONTRIBUTORS

Carol Anderson is an associate professor of history at the University of Missouri and has recently completed a fellowship at Harvard University's Charles Warren Center for Studies in American History. She is the author of *Eyes off the Prize: The United Nations and the African American Struggle for Human Rights, 1944–1955,* which won both the Gustavus Myers and Myrna Bernath Book Awards. She is on the board of directors of the Truman Library Institute for National and International Affairs and has taken a prominent part in Truman Library programs relating to Truman's civil rights legacy.

Michael Dukakis is a professor of political science and public policy at Northeastern University and the University of California, Los Angeles. He served four terms in the Massachusetts legislature, and three terms as governor of Massachusetts. In 1988, Dukakis was nominated by the Democratic Party as its candidate for president. After his defeat in the presidential election, he completed his term as governor of Massachusetts, then entered academic life. His articles on health care and public policy have appeared in professional journals. He has recently been active as an advocate within the Democratic Party of grassroots campaigning and the appointment of precinct level coordinators of local campaign activities.

Raymond Frey is a professor of history at Centenary College in Hackettstown, New Jersey. He is recipient of the Evening Division Teaching Award from Pace University, the Lindback Foundation Award for Distinguished Teaching from Centenary, and the Award for Teaching New Jersey History, and was the 2005–2006 Gates-Ferry Foundation Distinguished Lecturer. He has contributed to several books on the Truman administration and first ladies, and is the author of *William James Durant. An Intellectual Biography* (1991). He was keynote speaker at the Truman Library's 2002 commemoration of the birthday of Bess Truman and is on the editorial board of the journal *White House Studies*.

Michael R. Gardner is a communications policy lawyer in Washington DC. He has taught a course on the modern American presidency at Georgetown University for eight years. His book, *Harry Truman and Civil Rights: Moral Courage and Political Risks,* won the Henry Adams Prize for 2003. Gardner has served on presidential commissions under Nixon, Ford, Reagan and George H. W. Bush.

Raymond H. Geselbracht is special assistant to the director at the Harry S. Truman Library. He previously served as an archivist at the Franklin D. Roosevelt Library and the Richard M. Nixon Presidential Materials Project. He has published many articles on historical and archival subjects, including a recent series of articles on personal aspects of Truman's life and career. He has also published a descriptive map of places in the Kansas City area that were especially important to Truman, and a history of the Truman Library.

Ken Hechler was a special assistant to President Truman from 1949 to 1953. He served nine terms in Congress (1959–1977) as a representative from West Virginia where he helped organize support for the Civil Rights Act of 1964 and the Voting Rights Act of 1965. He was the only sitting member of Congress to march with Martin Luther King Jr. at Selma, Alabama in 1965. He served as West Virginia's secretary of state from 1985 to 2001. Hechler received a doctorate in political science from Columbia University and taught at Columbia University, Barnard College, Princeton University, and Marshall University. He worked with Samuel I. Rosenman and President Franklin D. Roosevelt to edit the thirteen volume *Public Papers and Address of Franklin D. Roosevelt*. He also served as a combat historian in the European theater during World War II. He has written six books, including *The Bridge at Remagen*.

Tom Lansford is assistant dean of the College of Arts and Letters and associate professor of political science at the University of Southern Mississippi. He is author or coauthor of a number of books, including *A Bitter Harvest: US Foreign Policy and Afghanistan* (2003) and *Strategic Preemption: US Foreign Policy and the Second War in Iraq* (2004). He is also coeditor of several collections including *America's War on Terror* (2003), *George W. Bush: A Political and Ethical Assessment at Midterm* (2004), and *Transatlantic Security Dilemmas: Old Europe, New Europe and the US* (2005).

John Lewis has been a member of Congress from Georgia since 1987. He first became active in the civil rights movement while a college student in Nashville, Tennessee and became nationally recognized as a civil rights leader after his prominent role during the Selma to Montgomery marches. He became chairman of the Student Nonviolent Coordinating Committee and spoke at the March on Washington in 1963. He has been jailed more than forty times as a result of his activism on behalf of civil rights. He was elected to the Atlanta City Council in 1982 and to Congress in 1986. In 1998, he published *Walking with the Wind: A Memoir to the Movement,* chronicling his service in the civil rights movement.

Carrie Meek is president of the Carrie Meek Foundation, whose goal is the economic and community empowerment of the people of south Florida. She served in the Florida House of Representatives and the Florida Senate before being elected as U.S. Representative in 1992. During her tenure in the Florida Senate, she developed much of Florida's current housing finance policy. She holds a master's degree from the University of Michigan and has been awarded Doctor of Laws degrees by the University of Miami, Florida A&M University, and Rollins College. The *Congressional Quarterly* has recognized Meek as one of the "50 Most Effective Members of Congress," and she was awarded the LeRoy Collins Lifetime Achievement Award by business and community leaders in Florida.

Colin Powell has served as Assistant to the President for National Security Affairs (1987–1989), Chairman of the Joint Chiefs of Staff (1989–1993), and Secretary of State (2001–2005). He was the first African American to serve in each of these three positions. He served in the Office of Management and Budget under President Nixon, as an assistant to the Secretary of Energy and assistant to the Deputy Secretary of Defense under President Carter, and as senior military assistant to the Secretary of Defense under President Reagan. He was the first chairman of America's Promise—The Alliance for Youth, which he founded in 1997. In 1995, he published his autobiography, *My American Journey.*

Richard M. Yon completed his master's degree in political science at Florida Atlantic University in 2004 and is currently a doctoral student at the University of Florida. Yon has written or co-authored several book chapters, journal articles, and book reviews relating to the presidency. He recently co-edited an encyclopedia on the presidency.

INDEX